RIPPLES OF TIME
A harrowing read!

Who better than a former Black Panther and Adjunct Professor to navigate the history of White Domestic Terrorism and Policing in America from 1619 to the present.

Readers will be taken on a surreal journey thru Ripples of Time as the Dehumanization. Demonization and Desecration of Black Bodies unfold.

- Hotep Book Publishing

RIPPLES OF TIME:

MEMOIR OF A FORMER
BLACK PANTHER

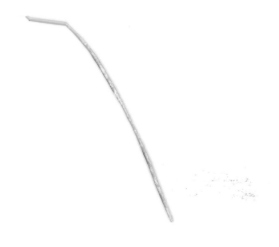

RIPPLES OF TIME:

MEMOIR OF A FORMER
BLACK PANTHER

**How Domestic White Terrorism and Policing
Has**

**Demonized
Dehumanized
&
Desecrated
BLACK BODIES:**

**Domestic White Terrorism & Policing
from Slavery to the
Rise of Trumpism & Fascism in America**

Jon-Jamal Turner

**HOTEP BOOK PUBLISHING
Charlotte, North Carolina**

RIPPLES OF TIME

Published by:
Hotep Book Publishing
Charlotte, North Carolina
hotepbkpg@gmail.com

Jamal Turner, Publisher
Quality Press.info, Book Packager

Paperback ISBN: 978-1-0878-9295-5
Hardcover ISBN: 978-1-0878-9303-7
Ebook ISBN: 978-1-0878-9296-2
Library of Congress Control Number: 2021914107

DEDICATION

This book is dedicated to the Mothers of the Movement:

To the original Mothers of the Movement:

Georgia Bea Jackson and Mamie Till

And to all the countless millions of Mothers whose sons and daughters were snatched from them by the brutal hand of slavey, systemic racism, and police violence. Never should you had to bury your sons and daughter under such cruelty and inhumanity. You have and always will be our rock, our strength, our salvation as a people.

Ripples of Time

ACKNOWLEDGEMENTS

My gratitude and never-ending love to my parents, John and Bertha Turner who gave me life and steered me thru the horrifying experiences of a young black child in a hostile white world. Gratitude to my two loving sisters, Marlonna Mobley and Rochelle Turner-Gorin who have always been at my side and showered me with the love that of a sister has for their brother. To my brother-in law Fred Gorin, truly my brother and loving husband to my sister. To my nieces Faiza, Mecca and Sanaila, and my nephews Yameen Thomas, Naheem Turner and Damien Williams, what joy you guys have gifted me in this journey called life. To my special cousins Elliot Mayes, Bonita Sutton, Angela Gee and Jesse Barnes, your recognition of my true character when others rebuked me during my journey of recovery from the traumas of revolutionary activism and captivity meant the world to me and I will always hold a special place in my heart for your support. Much gratitude to my loving Son, Anthony and Brandon Turner, especially Brandon who has always remained at my side, and Daughter Jamaila Turner who has grown into a Quintessential Nubian Queen. Lastly to my Grands, Krystin, Tony and Fedayeen, much joy you have brought into my life.

Thanks also to David Hilliard, former Chief of Staff of the Black Panther Party who believed in me and allowed me the honor and privilege to found the Berkeley California Chapter of the Black Panther Party. And a special acknowledgement to Dr. Chimalum Nwankwo, the esteemed writer and Nigerian poet who gave me the opportunity to teach at North Carolina A&T University, and who later became a travel partner while exploring the wonders of Nigeria in all its splendor.

Finally, I wanted to give a special acknowledgement to my editor and esteemed Nigerian writer Noo Saro -WiWa whose encouragement and stellar expertise was a beacon of light on this journey into the world of literary writing. She taught me how to exorcise the emotional baggage wedded to our experience as a captured people and to with clarity convey the pain and suffering with a clear and concise message.

TRIBUTE

AN ODE TO OUR NUBIAN QUEENS
And – KAMALA HARRIS, MADAME VICE- PRESIDENT
OF THESE UNITED STATES OF AMERICA

On this day in time, we pay homage and honor to our beautiful Nubian Sisters in general and to Madame Vice President Kamala Harris. Perhaps it is because I have always recognized their intrinsic value to humanity from its beginnings, but I think primarily, because of the role they have played in some of our darkest hours as a race of captured and enslaved people during our black holocaust experience on these shores called America.

Throughout the Ripples of Time, they were always there, strong, beautiful, emboldened by the moment no matter the challenges to insure our survival as a family, as a community, as a village, as a race. Burning deep in their DNA, searing throughout the ages, the Black Mitochondrial Mother: it was you who gave birth to humanity, to Hatshepsut, the only female to become Pharaoh of Egypt. The world bowed and paid reverence to you as the Black Madonna, as the Queen of Sheba, and the Europeans tasted your wrath as Queen Nzinga, the noble African General who fought for the freedom of her people.

Your legends are countless, your accomplishments are incalculable and can never be measured in human terms. Even during our darkest hour, we heard your pain echoing through the ages as the slave master ravaged your body while ripping your most precious babies from your arms. Our beloved enslaved-sister, Harriet Jacobs ask:

"Where could a slave girl turn for protection, for her there is no shadow of law to protect her from the insults, or prevent the violation of her precious body from fiends baring the shape of white men? The Mistress who should protect the helpless victims, has no other feeling but jealously and rage. There is no joy in our house, in our hearts as we watch our men savagely beaten and our children screaming as they are snatched from our trembling arms. WE are always subject to their will. In slavery, the dawn of each morning bears witnesses to the

darkened shadow of slavery hovering over our lives every day of our wretched existence".

Yet, my Nubian Queens, our Mothers and Grandmothers still rose, yet our ancestors keep replenishing our cupboard when we thought it was bare; we give thanks to you Harriet Tubman and Harriet Jacobs. Thank you, Ida B. Wells, Zora Neale Hurston, Maya Angelou, Cicely Tyson, Viola Desmond, Beulah McDonald and Grand Nanny, the fierce Jamaican Maroon warrior, and Mitochondrial Mother to Donald Harris, the Jamaican born father of Madame Vice President. Moreover, we thank all the faceless Nubian Queens who ensured the darkness would turn into light, who lifted the race, who gave voice to our freedom's quest who nurtured our children, who gave solace to and mended the scars of our men, and who now are in the forefront to right the wrongs of systemic racism and social injustice, as we continue the fight for all that is due to our beleaguered souls in the Social Common.

Fifty-five years have passed since the passing of the Voting Rights bill ensuring a true democracy where all have an equal opportunity in a free and democratic society. Battles are still being waged and our Nubian Queens are instrumental in the fight. What beautiful examples have been set for present and future generations! Many thanks to our Majestic and Beautiful First Lady, Michelle Obama, the sister Congressional Warriors Maxine Waters and Karen Bass and our young Congressional Warriors Ayanna Pressley, Ilhan Omar and Cori Bush, and certainly let us pay homage to the rising star of cable news Joy Reid.

Lastly to the most powerful and beautiful grassroots sisters on the planet, to you Stacey Abrams and to Mayor Keisha Lance Bottoms, what sweet revenge; you were robbed of the governorship and you did what a quintessential Nubian Queen would do. You did not sulk, you regrouped, you organized, and you continued to carry the torch of freedom. Your efforts were astounding, and the beauty of your smile let us know that you just pulled off the greatest victory in the bastion of the Old Confederacy, in Georgia. You gave Black America a resounding victory. You gave the state of Georgia as well as two Democratic Senators to the Biden/Harris Presidency. Even though the Senate becomes a 50/50 split, it is only fitting that the tie breaker will be cast by the first Black Woman/Nubian Queen, Madame Vice President of These United States of America. I think it is called 'Poetic Justice'!

Certainly, with pride and adoration, we honor the first woman of color and the first woman elected as the Vice President of the United States, Kamala Harris.

Born in Oakland, CA on October 20,1964 to Shyamala Gopalan and Donald Harris both of whom were immigrant parents. Her Mother arrived in this country from India in 1958 as a graduate student in endocrinology at the UC, Berkeley where she received her PhD in 1964. Her father Donald Harris is a Stanford University Professor of Economics and arrived from Jamaica in 1961 for graduate study at UC, Berkeley receiving his PhD in Economics in 1964.

Armed with the intelligence and the will to succeed Madame Vice President graduated from the prestigious HBCU, Howard University and adorned with the pink and green colors of the AKA Sorority, she graduated from another prestigious institute, the University of California, Hastings College of Law. Her journey into the criminal justice system started in the Alameda County District Attorney's Office and later in the San Francisco City Attorney's Office. She later was elected District Attorney of San Francisco in 2003 and then elected Attorney General of California in 2010 and reelected in 2014.

The arc of her life kept ascending as if destiny was calling, her path already etched out for greatness. In 2017, she was elected as the 2nd black woman and the first Asian woman to serve in the United States Senate. There, she was a strong advocate for criminal justice reform, health care re-forms, deregulation of cannabis, ban on assault weapons and immigration reform. However, her flash point in history occurred during the Brett Kavanaugh Supreme Court confirmation hearing. Bill Barr, the former Attorney General, and Trumps personal water boy, was tied up in a sea of lies as Madame Vice President exposed them in a masterful piece of cross examination that had Barr stuttering, head bowed, and his tail tucked between his legs. The world knew then her star had become a super nova. She was ready for the task at hand, and on January 20, 2021, she had arrived. Alongside President Joe Biden, Vice President Kamala Harris became the most powerful woman to ever hold public office in America!

We honor and salute you, our Madame Vice President, our Ruby Rose who when the morning dew gently kisses the rose petals, they open and shower us with your elegance and grace.! You are our Nubian Queen.

Ripples of Time

CONTENTS

Contents

PREFACE

At the beginning of 2021 Donald Trump, refusing to concede defeat in the presidential election, called on his supporters to storm the Capitol building and "Stop the steal." On January 6th, they followed his command. Stoked up by years of Trump's white nationalist race-baiting, his followers gathered outside and overpowered the police. The sight of them breaching Washington's security shocked the world.

The scenes were surprising yet unsurprising. I have seen this all before. As a former member of the Black Panthers, I dealt with the same racial divisiveness of government back in the 1960s and '70s. I will never forget the tandem President Richard Nixon and FBI Director Edgar Hoover as they unleashed the COINTELPRO which destroyed the Panther Party. The Panthers fought against racial and economic injustice, working tirelessly for our communities, setting up medical care programs and free breakfasts for children. We also successfully campaigned to introduce the African Studies Departments in American universities for the first time. In my fight for social justice, I went to jail and lost contact with my first-born son for many years.

Ripples of Time is my story about life as a Panther activist. It is also an unflinching examination of America's history, including how black bodies have been brutalized and policed tracing an unbroken line between the slave era and the present-day conditions. This book will expose the disinformation campaign waged by the 16th century European Enlightenment Thinkers against African people in order to justify slavery. This book will show how yesterday's injustices and racist tropes are still with us, albeit in a new form: slaves were economically exploited on plantations that were controlled by slave patrollers. Now we have neo-slavery, in which urban ghettos have replaced the plantations and police officers replaced the slave patrollers. The police still restrict (contain and control) the movements of African Americans and mete out physical abuse (e.g. George Floyd) to prop up an economic system that has white supremacy at its heart.

Little has changed; yesterday is today in Ripples of Time. While Trump's largely white supporters were able to enter the Capitol building with minimal resistance, lawful Black Lives Matter activists were met with the force of National Guard soldiers during protests over the death of George Floyd. Police brutalizing African Americans while white supremacists undermine democracy is nothing new. It's as American as apple pie. It is simply history repeating itself. The current generation of Black Lives Matter activists are facing the same issues we Panthers faced decades earlier, albeit to a lesser degree.

The third part of the book demonstrates how slavery hasn't gone away but instead manifests itself in the form of corporate fascism, which maintains the same old wealth inequalities and is promoted by right-wing conservatives like the Koch brothers.

Drawing on the works of Naomi Klein. Ida B. Wells and Black Panther leader George Jackson, *Ripples of Time* gives advice to today's BLM activists about what they can do to fight racial injustice. It is a timely reminder that fascism in all its forms must be fought by all of us. If not the fascist arrangement will consume us all. We need a return to community-based values, the same ones promoted by the Black Panthers. This book will appeal to anti-fascist, pro-equality, BLM supporters of all ethnic backgrounds. I hope you enjoy it.

INTRODUCTION

This book is a surreal journey of real-life experiences and historical travels backward through the ripples of time. It was written this way because I wanted to do something different, to take a different approach while highlighting the pain and suffering we have endured as a people of African descent. Take this journey with me whether dream walking with our Native American brothers/sisters or reaching back and summoning our African Ancestors for clarity and guidance, or whether embracing the theory of multi-verse, where time is a multiple time stream existing simultaneously in earth/cosmic time past and present. Doing so will allow you to grasp my personal journey from 1619 to the present: 146,730 days and 3,521,520 hours of days and nights of horror and pain inflicted on our Black bodies.

Captured, enslaved Africans held in the dungeons of Elmina Castle, in the bowel of slave ships, chained to the cotton, sugar and tobacco fields of plantations; bodies dangling like bitter fruit from the limbs of the popular tree; burned and desecrated in Elaine, Arkansas; massacred during the Wilmington, NC coup d'état, while experiencing genocide in Opelousas, La; massacres and murders committed in Tulsa, Oklahoma, and East St Louis by white domestic terror attacks; remembering the mangled and disfigured body of Emmett Till; four precious babies blown to bits in Birmingham, known then as (Bombingham). The time stream brings to the surface the assassinations of Malcolm x and Dr. King, and the total annihilation of the Black Panther Party, Fred Hampton's body riddled with 83 bullets. Alas we arrive in the dungeon of San Quentin where I languished as a political prisoner. As we are hurled into the present, we mourn all the Breonna Taylors and George Floyds as we continue to watch this travesty unfold before our very eyes. Yet we still stand.

This book tells that story about a person and a people who were captured, disarmed, enslaved, demonized, dehumanized; bodies desecrated and despised simply because of the darker hue of the skin. Bodies imposed upon, robbed of our own space and time. Spoon-fed a cacophony of foreign referents, symbols and names alien while dehumanizing to our soul. A body with two warring souls – the African spirit and that of the invaders vying for control of our black bodies. It is my wish that through these eyes you will understand the journey, the flow

1

of time as a captured people, the history of policing the captured and enslaved from the beginning to the present.

Hopefully, this book will shed light on how the terms whiteness and blackness are manufactured symbols to demonize one race at the expense of the other. How blackness became demonized as the negative color and whiteness, the positive and the light. Throughout the book I refer to white-infested demons, I am not inferring all whites are demons, only those who throughout the ripples of time have been contaminated with the virus of racism and how it has morphed, mutated and manifested its demonic spirit in many forms or different strands in certain white bodies and its institutions. There have been many whites who embrace the mantle of humanity and do not embrace such nonsense, they are immune to this virus called racism, immune to its demonic spirits and therefore embrace their humanity.

This book makes that distinction. History has clearly differentiated between the Redeemers, the Klu Klux Klan and the Abolitionist: both white, but the abolitionist was not infected. Today's Redeemers, the white supremacist, the Republican Tea Party who morphed into the MAGA Trumpists, these are the persons who are infected with the demons of the virus called racism and white supremacy. Those humans encased with white skin who weaponize their whiteness to terrorize people of color; they are the ones I am calling out in my journey to unearth truth exposing the rise of Trumpism for what it really represents. Be mindful America Fascism is peeling away the layers of democracy.

The vaccine or the remedy is to reconstruct our terminology. Redefine, educate and place into proper perspective the history unfolding before our very eyes. Mass movements must always organize around a common purpose and fight for structural change to revamp and reform the system to ferret out these demons no matter where they may nest.

PART ONE

Ripples of Time

CHAPTER 1

WHEN TRUMP CALLED-AMERICAS DEMONS ANSWERED

Illustration-by Brian Stauffer

I have had the unique experience of being an agent of history and its advocate. An active participant in the Black Liberation Freedom Struggle in America in the 1960s and '70s, while working with and in the presence of Bobby Seale, Huey Newton, Dr. King, George Jackson and others. It has left an indelible imprint on my life and shaped my world view. This world view motivated me to implement Free Medical Clinics while founding the Black Panther Party in Berkeley, California in order to fight racial injustice and defend our lives and our community against police brutality. It also placed me on the front lines in the fight to implement Africana Studies Departments throughout the country in general and the University of California Berkeley in particular.

I have witnessed the ebb and flow of history. My heartfelt pain is a testimony to those who fell victim to a racialized form of state violence: George Floyd, Breonna Taylor and Mike Brown are examples of the ongoing police state violence inflicted on black bodies. Today there are few Black Panthers still living, a forgotten treasure in the story of enslaved people of African descent on American soil. We have been shunned by history and rendered as footnotes in the ongoing struggle for freedom. Hopefully, this book will shed light on my experience in the Black Panther Party and how state-sponsored violence was responsible for its demise. Indeed, the book will explore the origins and history of such racialized and police state-sponsored violence perpetrated on the bodies of those of African descent.

Growing up as the child of former sharecroppers in the tobacco fields of Kentucky, I was acutely aware of discrimination based on race and class. This early childhood experience further enlightened me, and led me to become a student at the University of California, Berkeley and launched me into a decade of leftist activism that ranged from anti-Vietnam War protests and the Third World Liberation Front strike on the Berkeley campus, which was instrumental in establishing the Africana Studies Department. There are certain elements in history that are similar, the original BLM movement in the 1960s and the BLM movement of today, both fighting for and protesting racial injustice and police brutality. Today's Donald Trump was our Richard Nixon, both corrupt and both supporting police state violence against its black citizenry. However, Trump's racism has been taken to an altogether different level.

When I first embarked on this project, I asked myself, *how did someone like Donald Trump, who is so vile, so putrid, so petulant, so obscene and so insensitive to the plight towards people of color, become President of the United States?* Impeached for abuse of power, he is an avid supporter of white supremacism and presided over an administration that literally caged asylum-seeking brown children. He told countless lies and ran campaigns of dis-information while engaging, along with his relatives, in blatant self-enrichment. Trump mismanaged a pandemic that claimed more than 500,000 American lives under his leadership in 2020, before inciting an attempted insurrection in 2021, following his presidential election defeat. After much thought, I concluded everything Trump represented is a malignant disease called racism, an affliction that is firmly embedded in the American psyche, its spirit, its culture, and institutions. It is a system which from its inception did not include or benefit people of color.

The present-day exclusion of African Americans is rooted in America's past and its unwillingness to admit to and take responsibility for its crimes committed against people of color. America's soil is drenched with the blood of Native Americans and people of African descent. Its revisionist history does not recognize the slaughter of these people in their millions. Nor does it recognize the countless number of African bodies who were thrown to their watery graves during the Transatlantic Middle Passage as the victims of slavery and white domestic terrorism. America's unwillingness to accept full responsibility for the atrocities, committed in the name of white supremacy, must be addressed before there is reconciliation and or absolution for these crimes, against humanity.

To be clear, although Trump represents this very sickness he did not invent it. It is as American as apple pie. It is a history replete with such demonic acts of barbarity, and a psyche that has justified atrocities by fabricating aspects of its history and creating illusions of African American inferiority that are woven into the fabric of society. The original white slavers needed a moral justification for their criminality. They did so by categorizing African American souls outside of humanity. They created an illusionary world of concepts, symbols, and myths of African inferiority in their attempts to cover-up their terrorism and criminal activities while seeking an absolution that would never come.

Moreover, slavery as an institution never ended. Like a chameleon, it has morphed and evolved into an extended form of 'neo-slavery'.

In fact, this brutal, material and referential world created by Europeans cut Africans from their language and culture through a process called 'seasoning'. Kidnapped, Africans were forcibly removed from their physical, conceptual, and referential world, a world, which described their relationship to themselves, their people, their culture, their land, and their God. More importantly, it cut them off from their ancestors. In its place, they were spoon-fed a foreign language and concepts that were negative about themselves. It stripped them of their humanity, wrote them out of human history, and placed them outside the grace of God.

Western institutes of higher learning from the 16th to the 20th century have promoted the same company line, the inferiority of the African race; it was the White Man's Burden to civilize the lowly beastly black race. From Shakespeare's *The Tempest* to, David Hume, and Immanuel Kant's *On the Nature of the Human Race* to Thomas Jefferson's *Notes on Virginia,* they all created the illusion that

Africans are on the bottom rung of the ladder of humanity. They justify their sins by denigrating the 'other'.

David Walker, our esteemed brother who self-published his Appeal to The Coloured Citizens of Theses United States in 1829 and 1830, addressed their sins as enlightened Christians. He said, *we will take a view of them as Christians in which capacity we see them as cruel, if not more so than ever. In fact, take them as a body, they are ten times more cruel, more avaricious and unmerciful than ever before. Before they became Christians they were bad enough, but it is positively a fact that they were not quite so audacious as to go and take vessel loads of men, women and children, and in cold blood, and through devilishness, throw them into the sea, and murder them in all kinds of ways. While they were heathen they were too ignorant for such barbarity. But being Christians, enlightened and sensible, they are completely prepared for such hellish cruelty.*

Finally, Walker makes the point succinctly. Suppose God were to give them more sense, what would they do? *If it were possible, would they not dethrone Jehovah and seat themselves upon his throne.* Did our esteemed Brother visualize a Donald Trump? As would be the case, Donald Trump's actions have proven him to be a heathen, but in his mind's eye, a God sitting on his throne. He violated all principles of Democracy, Christianity and human decency while summoning the demons of the past into the present: yesterday's transgressions were summoned into the present. Yesterday is today in ripples of time. Racism is a continuum of the past; it does not die; it mutates into our today.

America's history of cover-ups and transgressions mirrors former President Donald Trump, who, according to CNN News, has lied more than thirty-two thousand times and still counting as he left office. Trump taps into these centuries-old perversions of truth on racism in America. We need only look to his infamous Charlottesville statement after a white supremacist killed a peaceful protester with his car. On August 12, 2017, a rally organized by the white supremacist group, Unite the Right, protested the proposed removal of the statue of the Confederate General Robert E. Lee. Thousands of white supremacists descended on the University of Virginia campus, carrying tiki torches and confederate flags, vowing to take back their country from Jews and Blacks. Trump, in response to the whole episode, said "There are good people on both sides." Trump's racist diatribes only exacerbate the burden of being of African descent as he carries the banner of white supremacy.

Moreover, Trump described the George Floyd protesters, who had witnessed a brutal execution by police officers of another black man on American soil, as criminals and thugs. Where and how did white supremacy morph into an institution of white supremacy and state sponsored violence? Moreover, we must understand who answered when Trump called. Who answers? It is the 72 million who voted for his failed re-election. Some are the children of the old South, the old Confederacy, the backbone of white supremacy. In effect, they are the Kyle Rittenhouse's, Dylan Roofs, and the Derrick Chauvin's, the modern-day neo-Nazis, the white militias like the Proud Boys and others, and every racist police officer in America, especially those who condoned the siege of Congress on January 6, 2021. Assuredly, they are politicians like Steve Hawley, Ted Cruz, Tom Cotton, Steven King, Lindsey Graham and Mitch McConnell.

According to Col. Lawrence Wilkerson, the former Chief of Staff for General Colin Powell, they are a small part of the regular members of the armed forces who would take to the streets when Trump calls. He was correct, as the investigation into the storming of the capitol continues members of the armed forces have been identified. Need we only look at the crowd who stormed the halls of Congress. They are the white militias who own roughly 30 percent of all guns in this country. They are the great-grandchildren and the great-great-grandchildren of those responsible for over 4,000 black bodies that hanged from the poplar trees on American soil after Reconstruction

A blending of white supremacist ideology and African inferiority was the mantra created by Europeans from the 17th century to the present. White supremacist historians, philosophers, psychologists, geneticists, and religious leaders were the purveyors of such nonsense. A blending of ideologies and spiritual dysfunction, starting with one person, then spreading through the family, then entire towns, cities, states, countries and across several generations, this infestation spreading inter-generationally through their familial DNA.

We must challenge the acceptable canons of knowledge, which have given cover for such negative imagery of African people. We must acknowledge that the European Enlightenment period provided intellectual cover for the rationalization of slavery. We must continue to give voice to slavery and show its evolution into modern-day society. Through these ripples of time, we must continue to recognize and give voice to the truths that have been buried alive. It will be those voices of truth, past, present and future, generations of African American people assessing and absorbing their true history and vowing never to be victims again. Indeed, it must be white America acknowledging its sinful past while taking responsibility for acts of barbarity. Only then will we understand the underlying psychosocial, material, institutional, and political bases of our oppression.

America did not hear our voices of protest in the 1960s. We warned you then, we marched and shut down college campuses while demanding and implementing African American Studies programs. We knew then that in order to challenge institutionalized racism we had to attack the core of Eurocentric thought. We had to challenge the old racist canons of the period of Enlightenment that abounded in those cloistered halls of learning.

To the young African American warriors of today, our voices were heard in the '60s, but only through direct action, and the result was the implementation of Africana Studies Departments throughout the country. To understand the underlying disease of institutionalized racism in America, we must continue to put this psychosocial dynamic into a historical perspective. When Europeans began to colonize two-thirds of the planet for financial gain, there was a need to justify their exploits. Their rallying cry became the White Man's Burden. Their God ordained them to 'civilize' the darker 'heathens' of the world. In the process, they committed atrocious and heinous crimes against humanity.

A turning point in the history of the world had occurred. People of color in general, and Africans, in particular, were the victims. Land was expropriated, and black bodies were enslaved. Subsequently, Europeans colonized information and disseminated illusions of African inferiority. They created complimentary imagery of themselves. They were God-sent; whites became the image of goodness, while they created the derogatory images of Africans. Blackness became evil and connected with the Biblical Ham sham. According to some interpretations, when Noah's son Ham saw the nakedness of his father, Noah cursed Canaan, his brother, even though it was Ham who saw the nakedness. The story's original purpose may have been to justify the enslavement of the

Canaanite people to the Israelites, but the later narrative morphed into Ham being cursed with black skin.

In addition, of course, Hume and Kant deemed Africans uncivilized and beastly creatures incapable of reasoning. Remember Trump's comment that *all African countries are shit hole countries?*

For those in the academic community, it is your responsibility, and it is in America's interest to unravel these falsehoods, these manufactured illusions of African inferiority. If we are to address the mistakes of yesterday, we must do it so that we may continue with the excavation of truth. We must attack the seeds, the demons of racism no matter where they are, even if it means insisting that white America began to recant the lies, the untruths. I challenge everyone to question the canon and show how the non-truths were developed. If we are to truly put the history of slavery in its proper perspective, we must go back to the Enlightenment period and hold all the Enlightenment thinkers accountable, as well as King James and Queen Elizabeth who wanted to rid their realm of all Negards or Blackmores while financing the Virginia Company and laying the foundation for England's involvement with the Trans-Atlantic slave trade.

CHAPTER 2
THE COLONIZATION OF TRUTH

The images below appeared in the *The Evolution of Man* (1874 edition) as part of an argument that blacks are evolutionarily close to apes.

Along with the zoo exhibits, visitors could purchase an information guides depicting the African bodies in the exhibits in animalistic terms, e.g. their heights, body types and colorings. The writer of the pamphlet describes our African Ancestors in animalistic terms, describing their bodies, and their 'colorings' from 'red brown to dark black,' as well likened some to apes in cages nearby'. It also describes them as a 'race' that is continuously fighting, stealing, looting, murdering with no remorse. They are also referred to as a 'primitive' people, who are resistant to progress, living as 'hunter gatherers. These exhibitions flourished during World's Fairs in London, Paris and Berlin during the late 1870s well into the early 20th century.

As we continue traversing the ripples of time, let us not forget Emperor Constantine's edicts in 325AD, at the Council of Nicaea. The emperor began the process of whitening African images in all biblical figures. Europeans claimed to the world that Africans lived in darkness, waiting for the Europeans to bring light and civilization. As the Catholic Church consolidated its power, most libraries of the known world, Alexandria included, were burned, and religious doctrines seized. In history's greatest forgery, white Europeans embarked on a destructive and censorship drive that silenced millions of black and brown voices. The murder and book burning, the destruction of temples, statues, inscriptions, and other traces of earlier Egyptian, Nubian and Coptic cultures, eventually led to the virtual ignorance of the Western world about the accomplishments of Kemetic Egypt, and the Kushite empires. All traces of

Egyptian religion and Kemetic contributions to civilization were sacrificed at the altar of deceit.

This misrepresentation of African humanity and its cognitive abilities were promoted by the Catholic church in Spanish and Portuguese societies. These misrepresentations were facilitated by King Ferdinand and Queen Isabella who in 1452 passed the *Purity of Blood law*, concluding that anyone in Iberian society who could not trace the origins of their four grandparents were not pure breeds and therefore not part of a white civil society. This would complete the cycle of ideas referencing informed 15-century Iberian society about race and slavery with their English counterparts in the Atlantic world. From these ripples of time the European model of race and slavery was taking place. Ultimately creating broadly conceived "European "white" supremacist identities. More specifically, one may ask whether racism was a function of more deeply entrenched ideas that were at the core of Western society and culture. The answer is yes!

Though rarely said overtly, the contemporary implications are clear enough: if racism is essentially a tool of the ruling elites, it can be assailed through class struggle. If, however, racism is somehow at the core of Western culture, the only way to remove it is through some fundamental restructuring of racialized institutions. We only need to examine the wealth gap between blacks and whites today knowing that this disparity was a direct result of slavery. Race and class are the Siamese twins of American racialized society. They are certainly joined at the hip.

The fact that the Catholic Church and its surrogates, Portugal and Spain, entered the slave trade earlier than England is a moot point. All evidence suggests that by the second half of the 16th century, England was more than a bit-player in the developing Atlantic world. While we certainly must acknowledge the differences in slave systems and racial hierarchies among various nations in the Atlantic world, we must also recognize that these systems were overlapping and interconnected and inseparable. When the first enslaved Africans arrived in Chesapeake around 1619, what followed was far less a historical "beginning" than a predictable continuation of a process that began as early as the 15th century on the Iberian Peninsula. What unquestionably ties the systems together is the overview that Africans were demonized as barbaric and incapable of reason.

Africans were in fact considered so "barbaric" that their human capacities were often called into question. Describing the first African slaves taken by the Portuguese via the Atlantic, royal chronicler Gomes Eames de Zurara noted that they were "bestial" and "barbaric." The demonization of the African Body had begun and would come to fruition during the Enlightenment Period throughout Europe. Similarly, during this early period, the cultural gulf that relegated Africans to barely human status meant that spiritual and cultural "redemption" was a virtual impossibility. Most Africans were thought to be sub-human and therefore subject to enslavement. The policies and ideas that flowed from these understandings of African inferiority only served to crystallize racial hierarchies, not only in Iberia, but across Europe, thus laying the framework for the moral justification of the massive slave trade which would follow.

By the second half of the fifteenth century, the term "*Negro*" was essentially synonymous with "*slave*" across the Iberian Peninsula. In Spain, the King's slaves were known simply as "*His Majesty's Negros.*" In Portugal, slave occupations were defined with "negro" as the operant noun, as in "negra do pote" [water carrier] or "negra canastra" [waste remover]. Lest we remember Shakespeare's play *'The Tempes*t, the enslaved native Caliban only value was the hewer of wood and the carrier of water. Unauthorized social gatherings of blacks were known as festas dos negros. Portuguese scholars have noted that in the popular language of the 16th century, the word "Preto" emerged as the term of choice to describe dark skin color, while "Negro" literally represented a race of people. This "race" of people was most often associated with black Africans, and certainly all black Africans were considered members of this inferior race of slaves and were therefore sub-human.

How European Enlightenment Thinkers Fabricated the Big Lie

The intersection between the edicts from the Catholic Church and the Enlightenment thinking on white superiority and black bestiality finds its growing roots in William Shakespeare's The Tempest, written in 1607, and Sir Francis Bacon and his treatise, The New Organon, in 1620. Both writings display the imagery and the assumptions that blacks are sub-human and therefore subject to white domination and instruction. In the Tempest, Prospero expropriates Caliban's Island while making him a slave. Prospero eventually releases him from his spell of ignorance and barbarity and exposes him to the glaring light of civility. And once released from his ignorance he begins the cycle of the black man's lust for the body of the fair, blonde maiden, Prospero's daughter, Miranda.

Bacon's, *The New Organon* depicts Africans as monsters that must be subdued and will lay the groundwork for racial classification and taxonomy. Peter Heylen will follow in 1689 in his *Little Description of The Great World*, using Bacon's formula to surmise that blacks were sub-human because they lacked wit, reason and therefore the ability to create culture, science, art and the humanities. Such soulless creatures must be placed on the lower rungs of humanity. We place them on the level just above apes and chimpanzees. Consequently, European Enlightenment thinkers further enhanced the process of demonizing blackness, while denying their humanity and relegating peoples of African descent to the lowest levels or subhuman levels of life on planet earth. The Enlightenment thinkers gave intellectual cover for the colonization of Africa and the enslavement of its people. During the late- and post-Enlightenment period, which is equivalent to America's colonial history, and, the beginning of slavery, the educational and religious institutions became the vehicle for spreading racist doctrines.

The conversion process had begun. Not only were black bodies subjugated, but so was the mind. European scholars, writers, and poets, such as Shakespeare, David Hume, Immanuel Kant, John Locke, and others of that period, must be called out and scrutinized for the racism unleashed into the ripples of time.

Kant was another European philosopher to equate color with intelligence. Writing in 1764 in his *Observations on The Feeling of the Beautiful and the Sublime*, he refers to blackness and stupidity as a given. Hume's essay titled Of *The Natural Character* in 1748, asserts with all certainty, *"I am apt to suspect the Negroes, and in general all other dark species to be naturally inferior to whites. There was never a civilization of any other complexion than white"*. Did not one of America's founding fathers, Thomas Jefferson reflect this worldview in his *Notes on Virginia*? Jefferson likened Africans to the level of sub-human because their blackness was caused by black bile running through their veins; proof positive of their inferiority because real humans had red blood running through their veins. Jefferson also noted in his writings, *"I have never heard a black utter a thought above the level of plain narration."* Such hypocrisy; it certainly did not stop him from lusting after Sally Hemings, his favorite slave.

Indeed, these Enlightenment Thinkers laid the groundwork for a methodology we would come to know as racial taxonomy, using pseudo-scientific means to catalogue racial differences. Racial dominance was dictated from this catalogue, with the Caucasian at the top and the African somewhere between Europeans and apes. This taxonomy was by the Europeans, and by their logic, blacks had a smaller brain and therefore did not have the capacity for reason, much like monkeys and apes. A prime example of Enlightenment thought can be seen in Johann Friedrich *Blumenbach's*, 1776 Volume, *On the Natural Varieties of*

Mankind. He also alleges biological differences between the races in which universal freedoms and individual liberties are based on the power of reasoning. Race seen by the Enlightenment thinkers was a socio-political order based on a permanent hierarchy of race, which turns physical differences into relationships of dominance, therefore white supremacy.

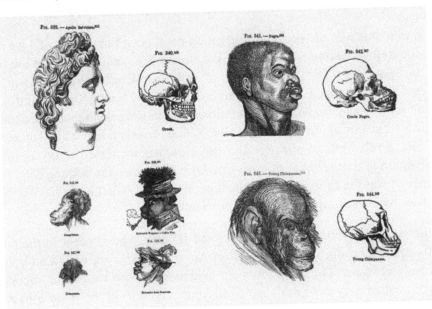

Furthermore, we can later look to Hegel, an eminent European philosopher who sealed the deal. In his publication in 1813 called *The Philosophy of History*, he says, "*Civilized people are judged by the reason and cognitive abilities to have in place written history and evidence of arts and science.*" Since there is no evidence of a written history, nor any evidence of art or culture, we must assume Africans lack memory and the cognitive ability to transfer those memories to writing. It is from this reasoning that Hegel, assumed that Africans had no collective cultural memory, were childlike and therefore incapable of reason. Even more reason for them to relegate Africans to the basement of sub-human existence while assuaging their consciousness as they enslaved millions of African bodies.

Certainly, we conclude this attractively packaged justification of African barbarity and inferiority is the product of the Enlightenment. This false instrument of measurement called taxonomy was the tool used by the Europeans to resolve the fundamental question/contradiction between professing liberalism, liberty, and freedoms while upholding slavery. The contradiction is at the heart of Enlightenment thinking. The paradox of human freedoms and the fundamental rights of human beings in nations that held other human beings in bondage, while exterminating native populations, was incompatible with human decency. Colonial dominance and expropriation of lands marched hand in hand with slavery. From this paradox arose white supremacy and some of the most atrocious and barbaric acts perpetrated on the bodies of human beings.

In addition, this was the period of Enlightenment. As it turned out, and we must continue to give testimony to history; the Europeans turned out to be the beast and savages, not their counterparts of color. Institutionalized racism had successfully demonized and dehumanized the black body. Slavers and white supremacy now had in their minds a rational and moral argument to unleash hell on earth while enslaving people of color. White terrorism and white supremacy had now given birth to slavery, and the violence witnessed today is only a continuation of those ripples of time. The knee on the neck is nothing new. If not the knee, it was the rope, and if not the rope, it was the bullet in the head or back, or it was the nauseating smell of burning black flesh.

For those of you who wish to move beyond slavery, who say it is in the past, I simply ask, especially if you are African American; who are you? Can you tell me your real name? Do you know your genealogy? Who were your ancestors? Do you realize they cut your seed from your past during the middle passage, forever cut off from your ancestors? America's racist history has totally reshaped and redefined who you were and currently are. We must return to the time stream, continuously searching the backwaters, the eddies, the ripples of time.

Unmasking Truth While Exposing the Carnival Barker

To be sure, institutionalized racism is still very much a part of America's history. We cannot understand white supremacy and racial violence perpetrated on African American bodies unless we understand the origins of white supremacist thought. How and where the demonization and dehumanization process began. Only then can we attack such evil thoughts projected into this world, this is how we attack the root of this evil.

A strategy employed by those of us who were involved in the revolutionary movements of the sixties, or the *struggle* as we called it then, was not only to confront police brutality but also to wage an assault on the educational institutions that promoted white supremacist ideology. We formed a coalition of Third World students and successfully implemented a Third World Department and what we know today as Africana Studies Departments throughout the country.

These newly formed departments became the focal point, which attacked racial referents and racist stereotypes. Major institutions, like the University of California, Berkeley, where I attended and graduated, were in many respects still teaching Eurocentric history. The canons of thought still preached Eurocentricity at the expense of ignoring Africa-centered history, slavery, and the effects of colonial domination of the Third World. Our strategy was to create curricula, which addressed the void left in African history and slavery, along with the transition of the world seen by our historical experience. We knew, in order to root out racism, there must continue to be a focus on redefining who we are in a historical context.

We must today, in this time and place, continue to deconstruct falsehoods, create new referents and definitions, create new curricula throughout the educational system, starting in middle schools, until white supremacist, Euro-Centric thought is eradicated. More emphasis must be placed on re-examining the enlightenment period the horrors of slavery to expose and root out the seeds of institutionalized racism sown in the 16th to 21st centuries. We must continue to resurrect, redefine, and reshape ourselves and our story, constantly using new referents and symbols redefining our experience.

Our history must be told within the context of our historical experience as a kidnapped, captured, demonized, dehumanized, disarmed and enslaved people. People who, over time, have evolved through this particular time stream in American history while enduring the most heinous attacks perpetrated on the black human body. The Emmett Tills, the Fred Hamptons, the George Floyds, the Breonna Taylors, Sandra Bland, and now, Jacob Blake, can only be understood within that context. White supremacist violence is symptomatic of the demons of racial hatred. Those racist demons are still infested in America's DNA.

As an illustration, Trump can tap into this collective stream of racism, rendering his base completely at his will. Trump became the embodiment of the demon, the trickster, and the misleader of gullible human types. He is an expert in using racist troupes, which are full of twisted logic and lies. As a result, Patrick Crusius answered Trump's call, and on August 3, 2019, in El Paso, Texas, he murdered 23 people of color. Kyle Rittenhouse, the Kenosha assassin, killed two BLM protestors in Wisconsin. Or the Michigan militia who were arrested and charged with plotting to kidnap and assassinate the governor of Michigan. Trump can tap into the dark side and awaken the demons in his base. That makes Trump an enemy of humanity, a threat to the living. This threat was never more evident than on January 6, 2021 as a horrified America watched insurrectionists lay siege on the bastion of democracy, the nation's Capital. Trump's projection of racist imagery as a negative force, all driven by the desire to dominate and control the actions of others is characteristic of a demagogue. Indeed, this is Trump's mantra; he makes raids on human consciousness.

At the same time, it is from these masses that arise the demons, answering his call to vilify the other, people of color. Just because he was not re-elected does not mean he is no longer a threat. Seventy-two million people voted for him and still pose a threat and will be waiting for additional marching orders even when he leaves office. Before his twitter account was deactivated it had 80 million followers, so racism and fascism will still be a threat to democratic principles and the sanctity of the rights and bodies of people of color. Undoubtedly, Trump nourishes his base's need for the old order. Bring back the Confederacy, protect their monuments; make America great again – *white* again! Keep the playing field tilted in favor of white people. Trump enslaves their minds with ideas that reinforce white populism. Trump crucifies truth on the cross of deception and terror, and as always, innocent human beings pay with their lives. Such was the case during Trump's call to action during the insurrection at the Capital on January 6th when an ardent Trump supporter, Ashli Babbitt, was shot and killed when she tried to storm the halls of Congress, a casualty of Trump's madness. Moreover, Trump supporters fatally assaulted a Capitol Police officer, Brian Sicknick as he attempted to prevent the rabid Trump supporters from breaching the Capital.

The person or persons infested with this perversion can be seen throughout the pages of history past and present throughout the ripples of time. The racial animosity directed toward black bodies manifests itself in horrific violence. Remember the disfigured body of Emmett Till, lying-in his casket, his mother's decision to show the world how an innocent boy was beaten to death by two white men in Mississippi in 1955. Remember the white supremacist, Dylann Roof's attack on Mother Emmanuel Church, killing nine African American human beings while they prayed? What about the 1963 Birmingham Church bombing, killing four precious black babies? Or the self-appointed slave catchers who gunned down Ahmaud Aubrey and Trayvon Martin who were both going about their lives innocently? What about the 9 minutes and 29 seconds of sheer evil as the modern-day slave patroller, Derek Chauvin, pressed his knee against the neck of George Floyd? Also, the horrific sight of the white police officer tugging at the shirt of Jacob Blake while shooting him seven times in the back. How sick is this disease?

As they spew their venom in the world, we must remain vigilant never to succumb to such evildoers. We must never forget that we were captive people, disarmed, by people who have no regard for human life. We were their enslaved who never owned our own space and time. They denied our humanity and mutilated our black human bodies throughout the ripples of time and still do so today. And yet we continue to rise!

For this reason, the higher voices of protest, the righteous voices amongst us must crown the world with clarity and purpose. We must continue to drown out the voices of hate. We must confront the purveyors of evil, and we must continue to organize and subdue the Trumpist ideology. We must call to task all that is detrimental to the human family. Our task is daunting. Keep preaching, sisters Joy Reid, Nicole Hannah-Jones and Angela Rye. Keep directing and producing, Oprah and Ava Duvernay. May your voices ring truth form the heavens and expose these demons for who they are.

The demonization of people of color and slave trade has infested the minds of humans for in excess of 600 years. How can America be cleansed of such wickedness done in her name? The bad things are done for good reasons; I think not. According to your thinking, you gave the world democracy, but for whom? In the name of democracy came slavery, torture, kidnapping, rape, flogging, murder, and genocide perpetrated against bodies of color. Moreover, you dare to claim it was for the common good. For instance, in 2020, Tom Cotton, a US senator from the state of Arkansas said, "*Slavery was a necessary evil to build America.*" This public servant claims, for the common good of white America, it was justifiable to enslave and terrorize millions of black bodies for their selfish aggrandizement and the building of America's institutions.

How dare Tom Cotton be so arrogant, so insensitive to the tens of millions who have suffered. The threads of slavery are too entangled in the fabric of America's institutions, as is the pain and suffering, inflicted on its victims. Nevertheless, make no mistake – slavery viewed in cosmic time was only yesterday. Freedom will remain elusive until slavery is **finally eradicated from** America's institutions, and it may be a few centuries to come.

With this in mind, as a product of the 1960s I was intimately involved in mass socio-political movements to unchain our freedom. We called it the Struggle.

Unlike today's mass movement, ours was a cornucopia of political persuasions. From the Black Nationalist Black Muslims to the Civil Rights Movement, from the Revolutionary Nationalism of the Black Panther Party to the Republic of New Africa, and the World Socialist Movement to end the war in Vietnam and American Imperialism abroad. We were not only interested in social justice, but a complete reorganization of the institutions of capitalism and its white supremacy. The police departments during that period were filled with members of the KKK. They traded in their sheets and ropes for badges and guns. They now had a legal license to carry on their century's old tradition of taking black life at their whim, much like their counterparts today. So, I ask, why were you surprised when you learned that some of Trump's supporters and insurrectionists were police officers? That is who they are, that is who they have always been: terrorists under cover. Remember, yesterday is today and a continuum into tomorrow.

The Black Panther Party (BPP), founded in 1966 in Oakland California by Huey P. Newton and Bobby Seale, was initially called the Black Panther Party for Self-Defense. Its sole purpose was to monitor the behavior of the Oakland, California Police Department. Armed self-defense groups were formed to combat white racist police, while the party eventually organized viable social programs to serve the material needs of our communities. The Sixties were one of the most transformative periods in our history. We were the first BLM, Black Liberation Movement. You heard our call, BLM, Black Lives Matter. What a welcome sight! Now you must take it to the next level, marching is not enough. Viable infrastructure servicing the needs of the people in their communities is the blueprint for success.

For these reasons, we remember George Floyd, Breonna Taylor, and say their names, for it is they who are present-day victims of white supremacy violence. Let us also remember and say, the names of BPP chairman Fred Hampton, shot 86 times as he lay sleeping in his bed. Panthers are the forgotten stories in state-sponsored violence. When you live through and survive as a participant in revolutionary moments in history, you appreciate the value of commitment. When you are caught up in the whirlwinds of change, you become an agent of history. You step into its process of changing dynamics. It transforms your mind, your stream of consciousness, and your values. Life is lived in the moment; you value the sanctity of life and the human condition. You grow rapidly, and the love forged out of a common struggle develops an unbreakable bond, unlike anything experienced under normal circumstances. Such were our experiences in the '60s.

Decidedly, we borrowed strategies of survival and rekindled that unbreakable bond from our storied past, from our ripples of time. Panthers called on our ancestors, always remembering we were a captive people, disarmed, enslaved and placed in bondage. We became the modern-day Maroons who established liberated zones in the modern-day black community. We fed, housed, clothed, educated, and provided health care to people while defending the integrity of the space in our community. We remembered Martin Delaney and his threshold theory of drawing a line in the sand. No one crossed that threshold without our permission or without a fight. We had to protect ourselves and our community with armed self-defense groups.

White militias did this, as did the Jewish Defense League. But when we did, it was an abomination against American values. Such hypocrisy. They painted a picture of 'crazy niggas' with guns who had to be destroyed. Yet today we watched a white terrorist, with an AR-15 kill two protestors in Kenosha and the police give him a bottle of water. Yet today we watched armed white militia storm the Michigan state capitol building with assault rifles. They were greeted with respect by white police officers, and these same militias later threatened the Michigan governor with kidnap and murder. When armed Panthers stormed the state capitol building in Sacramento, California, in 1967, we were arrested. Nothing has changed in the ripples of time! Same old hypocrisy, same double standard.

This innate fear of the black man, especially with a gun, has historical significance. Remember, we were a captured and disarmed people. The black male slave was beaten into submission, for the most part broken. The white overseer and slave master always carried this innate fear of retribution during their day-to-day activities. Would you not carry the same fear? Under those circumstances, they knew the brutality they had inflicted on their victims, the floggings, the rape of their wives, watching the selling of their children to another man. This innate fear of retribution, from the runaway, of the beastly, burly black man always was in the back of their minds. Consequently, this fear today is generational. It is in their DNA.

As a result, this fear from slavery has passed through the ripples of time. When a black man is seen walking down a street or driving a car, chances are he will be stopped by the police, and then the 'stop and frisk' syndrome may kick in. They are the modern version of the slave patroller. Instead of having to produce papers, one must produce a driver's license or ID. Likewise, remember during slavery, the 2nd amendment movement was accelerated by the creation of isolated farmers taking up arms to protect themselves and their property from runaways and slave insurrections. Conversely, the formation of slave patrollers were created to keep the slave population in check within a defined space. Stop and frisk. Let me see your papers, boy! The black runaway, the black man, became their worst nightmare; their worst fear, and still exists during this place in time.

Unity of Purpose is Your Greatest Strength

Clearly, young brothers and sisters and all members of the new rainbow coalition, you must continue to learn the history and root causes of racial hatred and violence and institutionalized racism. You must learn how it permeates throughout America's institutions. Thereupon the more you challenge institutional and racial injustice, the more violent the reaction. There is truth, and there is the brutal truth. Black suffering in America is a brutal truth. America has never wanted to hear the brutal truth. Such old, tired clichés like "slavery is in the past," or "it's time to move on," or, "we are making progress," all camouflage the naked truth of institutionalized racism and state sponsored violence, and social injustice.

Conversely, those of us who have cried out before you, who had enough, or who also cried "I can't breathe" were met with extreme violence. Our history is replete with those voices that had enough; Nate Turner, America heard and killed him. Voices throughout the ripples of time, Malcolm Medgar Evers, Dr. King, you heard them and silenced them with a bullet. You annihilated the Black Panther Party. You burned Down Tulsa while massacring over 2,000 black bodies in 13 cities during the infamous white terror attacks during the Red Summer of 1921. The Cheyenne and Apache in 1864 cried out at Sand Creek and you massacred old men, women and children while dismembering body parts for trophies.

Assuredly, my beautiful young children of the Black Lives Matter Movement and others, you have heard Brother Floyd's cry: I can't breathe. You heard it, and you will never forget it. History is a bloody reminder of how daunting the task may be, and it took his brutal death to draw the final line in the sand. Never forget his cry, for his cry represents the countless unnamed voices who too cried for their lives, cried out for their mothers' caressing arms, especially those taken from their mother's bosom during slavery. At the same time, remember those wretched souls in the bowels of the slave ships, packed like sardines, chained, and gagging on their own feces, lying in their own urine, crying out, "I can't breathe." In similar fashion, remember the countless souls that were locked away in the slave dungeons in Elmina Castle and Cape Castle on the Gold Coast of Ghana, awaiting a fate that would cast them into centuries of slavery and lives of unfathomable violence inflicted on black bodies. This is your moment. You are the children and grandchildren of the civil rights and black liberation movement of the 1960s. Much as we were, you are now caught up in the whirlwind of history. Beautiful, bold, fearless children, red, brown, black, and white, all marching in a unity of purpose. You are now cast into the ripples of time!

But be mindful – they will come for you as they did us. They will look to destroy you, divide you, and infiltrate your groups, to undermine your righteous cause. Be aware of the armed white militia who will use you as popup-targets in a shooting gallery. They have already done so in Charlotte, North Carolina; Seattle, Washington; Portland, Oregon; Oakland, California; and now Kenosha, Wisconsin. Keep your leadership out of the public eye, remain de-centralized, or once they identify you, they will neutralize you by any means necessary. Such are the demons called to action by Donald Trump. Welcome to the club. You now understand our fears, those of us who have gone before you. The fear you never knew; the bullet in the back, the tear-gas canister burning the nostrils and the eyes, the baton cracking your skull (remember John Lewis?) the boot or knee on your neck, the possibility of imprisonment. Remember those who suffered the pain from the rope or the smell of burnt bodies. Welcome to our world, the ripples of time.

Consequently, we must never allow you to forget our songs of sorrows, songs of chains that bound our flesh, the flesh songs of the overseer's whip, with thorns from the cotton ripping the flesh from our numb and overworked fingers while making the white supremacy slave-owner rich. Yes, we must always remind you of the sweetness of our sorrow songs, for they echo such pain, the horrors, and the terror of our past. Such are the threads that bind through the ripples of time. *It seems like the suffering the Gods visited only on the greatest beings because they are the only ones to endure it, bear the evils of humanity and still let the light of their sublimity shine through.* It seems like *a* suffering we bore as a sacrifice and purification of the continued racist history in America. For the injustice of it all, and the noble suffering we have endured is so heartbreaking, oh so painful, and yet we still stand. Power to the people!

The suffering hands that built America

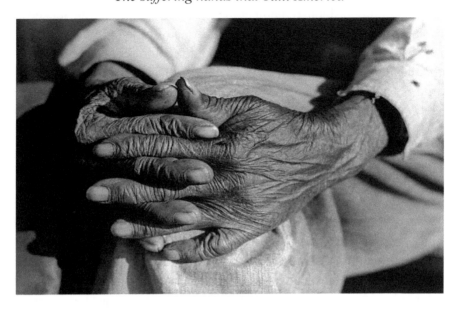

CHAPTER 3
THE CHAMELEON OF SLAVERY TAKES PLACE

The Virginia Colony and Slaves Sold at Auction

The Chameleon of Slavery Takes Shape

The disease of institutionalized racism, criminal justice and policing is rooted in America's violent slave history. Slavery's purpose was to contain, criminalize and brutalize black bodies solely for economic exploitation. What must not get lost in the historical time-stream is that African Americans are descendants of African people who were captured, disarmed, and enslaved for the sole purpose of providing forced and free labor to build a racialized capitalist system of class and economic exploitation.

Slavery in its proper context must be understood within the depth and vastness of cosmic time. Slavery is in its infancy, and only ended its first phase yesterday. Slavery is like a chameleon, a shift shaker morphing into new forms and colors of neo-slavery with the passing of time. The one common denominator is the systemic racism, which shows a complete devaluation of black life. Black bodies that were sold as objects of value, were then reduced to tools, as codified by law, to be used by whites who govern the movement and actions of black bodies, and criminalize them, even though the body demanded its inherent right of freedom. We became the criminal because of our resistance to the real criminal who kidnapped and assaulted our black bodies.

George Floyd was just the latest example of this system. For nine minutes and twenty-nine seconds, we watched the life drain from his body, much like those who came before him in the ripples of time as they swung helplessly from the limb of a tree, as life slowly drained from their helpless bodies.

Who are the mindless, soulless creatures who commit such atrocities, with hands in pocket while life slips out of another human's body? First, we need to understand their history. I will take you back into the ripples of time during slavery to allow a glimpse of their beginnings. These forerunners, who would eventually become modern-day police. These white farmers, whose descendants were the poor and indentured slaves brought from Europe, who were the inheritors of the second amendment rights to bear arms.

Once the American Revolution had ended and the militias were disbanded, only white citizens had the right to bear arms to better regulate and control the slave population. As the slave economy grew and slaves became a focal point of rebellion, white farmers were fearful of rebellion. These poor whites became the buffer between slaves and slave owners. Clearly, class and racial distinctions were being formed between poor whites and black slaves. The seeds of white privilege were being formed. It is from this lower class of whites that the 'Patty rollers' or Slave Patrollers would emerge.

More appropriately, the slave patrollers or slave catchers would morph into a loosely organized police force. Their major responsibility was to hold the line, to control the geographic proximity of black slaves, never allowing them to violate slave codes during those moments in time and space. The legal and policing components, and economic institutions of slavery created codes of conduct that controlled the movement of black bodies, out of which codified laws emerged to ensure the survival and dominance of one race over another. The way black bodies were to be treated, and the extent of violence inflicted upon them was shaped by the slowly emerging police force during those ripples of time.

The Many Shades of the Chameleon Policing Black Bodies: The Beginning

As I awoke from my dream state, I was fatigued by the length of the journey. I had encountered the Council of the Ancestors, and their wisdom, as always, was informative and overwhelming. They spoke of a time when our bodies were taken from us in the light of day, enchained and shipped to a place, far from our families in the bowels of a ship where there was suffering beyond endurance. Black bodies strewn all over a foreign land. Their black bodies taken from themselves to work the fields and the mines for white fiends who had no regard for the sanctity of life. Black bodies taken to a land that was stolen from the Native inhabitants.

Who were these people I ask? The elders answered. They are the original bandits, the original thieves; the body snatchers who feast on the flesh of humanity for their own selfish gain. But most of all they are the original con artists, the tricksters. Hear me well, my son. They come to our land, place us in chains and remove us from our own space and time. Once we were removed from our lands we were taken to a place where they have stolen the lands from the original inhabitants. Their egregious acts were just the beginning. They pillaged, they murdered, they brutalized and raped their black and red victims. They created codified or man-made laws to prevent us from taking back what was rightfully ours, our bodies, our humanity our freedom. When we attempted to reclaim those rights, the freedom to determine our own space, we were called criminals. In a state of confusion. The question was asked, "How could this be so?" The Elder answered, "Because they are wicked and delusional. Their hands can never be clean with such wickedness done in their name". Such hypocrites they are – they commit the original crime and then label the victims the criminals.

Who Were the Slave Patrollers?

Stuck in a strange land we tried to take our bodies back, reclaim that which was rightfully ours, but they created laws that governed our bodies, our time and space. They brought in people called 'patrollers'. These were second- and third-generation poor whites whose relatives were refugees from the earlier transatlantic institution of indentured servants. They were merchants and workers who had left England, Scotland and Ireland for America in the 17th century; they were a part of that white wind that blew across the planet and contaminated everything in its path. Some had been convicted of crimes and sentenced to penal servitude, while others were kidnapped. Moreover, some came by choice with hopes of doing several years of work in exchange for their freedom and a parcel of land expropriated from Native American tribes. This labor pool was extracted from the poor who occupied the port cities like London, Dublin, Liverpool, and Bristol. It was this lot, later joined by the Dutch and German immigrants, who would become slave patrollers. They would become the eyes and ears, the enforcers who carried out the dirty work and enforced the necessary pain on bodies with a darker hue than they. They would become the buffer between our black bodies and that of this monstrosity called slavery.

Slave patrols first began in South Carolina in 1704 and spread throughout the 13 colonies, lasting well into the late 19th century. The slaves called them *"pate rollers," "patrollers," "patter-roses," "patter-rolls", "paddy rollers," or "paddle rollers (because of their use of paddles to whip slaves); or "night riders," "night-watchers," and "Night Doctors.*

As the population of enslaved black bodies dramatically increased, especially with the invention of the cotton gin, so did the fear of resistance and revolution by the enslaved. The white slave owners' primary concern was the ability to control the body of the captured slaves. Plantations were patrolled since that is where captured slave populations were highly concentrated.

In the 19th century (1801 to 1899), patty rollers already existed, but with a growing slave population, they morphed into a mechanism to contain, police, watch, intimidate and brutalize the slave population and plantation community for the purpose of protecting the economic interests of the planter aristocracy. The patrollers kept the roads free of runaways or slaves — that is, those who were walking freely without a pass. 'Patty roller,' 'patroller,' or 'slave patrol' were the names given to teams of men who, usually located in the South, worked to maintain the wealth of the Southern elite. Commonly made up of three to six men on horses, they scoured the county or parish looking for unbound black bodies of slaves. They policed the area, containing all black bodies that were out of bounds and not operating within their confined space and time.

It became necessary to put newly emerging codified laws into place to regulate the activities of black bodies and their white slave patrollers. Without written permission from the master, boundaries could not be crossed. Black bodies were a fixed commodity, assigned to a particular place in time. As punishment for a runaway or violation of these boundaries, slaves' bodies were subjected to mental and physical terror, searches, whippings, beatings and other forms of harassment. If caught by patrols and returned to their masters, slaves may be placed on the auction block if masters no longer wanted to deal with their rebelliousness.

As rebellions and insurrections increased there became a need for more sophisticated and systematic mechanism of control. South Carolina and Virginia began selecting patrollers from organized state militias. State militia groups were also organized from among the cadets of the Southern military academies. The Citadel and the Virginia Military Institute, were founded to provide a military command structure and discipline within the slave patrols, and to detect, encounter, and crush any organized slave meetings that might lead to revolt or rebellion.

Slave patrols consisted mostly of white citizens. Most were poor farmers and the underserved class. They typically rode on horseback in groups of four or five, sometimes even family clans. They often worked sun-up to sundown, varying their times and locations of patrol in order to reduce the chances of slaves escaping. Slave patrollers had their own characteristics, duties, and benefits. They were often equipped with guns and whips. The physical control of black bodies was now becoming a part of the American landscape, the degree of violence was now being shaped by policing- to manage and control.

The power patrollers had limitations. For example, although whippings and beatings were allowed, a deterrent also existed. If whipped or beaten too severely, the slave would be of no use to their masters as laborers the next day. Moreover, the slave's body had value; they were a commodity which could not be completely devalued by excessive violence. For this reason, physical violence against the body of the slave had to be measured. With the continued rise and fear of slave rebellions and the eventual passing of The Fugitive Slave Laws, patrollers became patty rollers or slave catchers and it then became necessary for slave patrols to abide by new laws or rules of engagement. We now had codified laws which marked the beginning of the criminalization of the black body.

The Civil War, which lasted four years, directly threatened the existence of slavery. In turn, slave patrols had to transform their structure. The first year after the Civil War began, Whites were expecting slave revolts and so slave patrols increased and began to transform. As the war dragged on, white men were increasingly called to serve in the Confederate army. Some of those who were turned away by the army, mostly for medical reasons, found work within the slave patrolling community. As slave owners entered the Confederate army, some slaves lost the shield they once had to protect them from brutal beatings.

As the outcome of the war became more apparent, slaves lost their commercial value in the rapidly deteriorating infrastructure of the 'slaveocracy' and became targets for extreme violence and death. During these ripples of time, the former slaves would now become fair game and experience an acceleration of white terrorism never witnessed before during slavery.

When the Civil War ended in 1865, the use and physical formation of slave patrols changed. These groups and the concept of control, intimidation and physical violence would morph during the post-Reconstruction era into white supremacist terror groups such as the Redeemers and then the Ku Klux Klan, which continued to terrorize, threaten and determine the boundaries of the black community. In South Carolina, colonists began to write laws that restrained slaves long before slave patrols were established. Laws were created that set curfews for slaves and prevented slaves from bartering goods. The militias were strengthened, and nightrider patrols created. These are examples of some of the codified laws and ideas that would become part of a growing movement to transform the old form of slavery into a more refined and systematic policing mechanism to control black bodies. More codified laws were added, and criminalization of the Black Body was in full motion.

Walter Scott shot in the Back by modern day Patroller

Slave Patroller

At times, the enslaved developed many methods of challenging slave patrolling, occasionally fighting back violently. The American Civil War developed more opportunities for resistance against slave patrols and made it easier for enslaved people to escape. Slave patrol duties intensified as more rebellion became apparent. Eventually, slave patrols expanded and operated year-round. Gradually, the patrollers were given new duties and rights, including: "apprehending runaways, monitoring the rigid pass requirements for blacks traversing the countryside, breaking up large gatherings and assemblies of blacks, visiting and searching slave quarters randomly, inflicting impromptu punishments, and as the occasion arose, suppressing insurrections. Harriet Jacob's Incidents in the Life of a Slave Girl gives voice to *"these unfeeling wretches,who went around at night at will, like a troop of demons terrorizing helpless slaves while exorcising their brutal will."*

With the war lost, Southern whites' fears of African Americans increased in 1865 due to Reconstruction governments that were perceived as oppressive to the South. Even though slavery and patrols were now illegal, the patrol system still survived. White privilege had to be protected, now that former slaves were ascending to public office, voting in elections and gaining rudimentary self-sufficiency economically. In the aftermath of the war, informal patrols sprang into action. Later, city and **rural police squads**, along with the help of **Ex-Confederate army officers**, revived patrolling practices among free men. During the post-Civil War Reconstruction period of 1865–1877, old-style patrol methods resurfaced and were merged with postwar Southern police officers and organizations such as the KKK. Indeed, a rudimentary police force replete with white supremacy infrastructure was changing its color.

Today we have State Highway patrols. Police departments assign their officers to patrol certain containment areas. The terminology "patrol" was derived from the compound word "pattyroller. "In the 1800s there were few standards or methodical way of containment. In many areas, patty rollers had the authority to beat the bodies of slaves that they found out of bounds, much like today's assault on black bodies by police. In addition, the death of a slave was not necessarily a crime. Need we forget our beloved sister Breonna Taylor, Timer Rice or Eric Garner. In each case the officers were exonerated of committing any crime. As is to be expected, where there are no boundaries, rules or limitations ruthless pattyrollers committed abuses such as rape, violence, and murder. They carried guns and whips to control the body of slaves (compliant or non-compliant). Today the police carry guns and batons or billy clubs. They act on their license to carry out brutality in today's system of neo-slavery, maintaining a rule of law designed to maintain control over the black body.

What is not known to the masses is that the origins of modern police tactics in the United States have evolved from the slave patrol era. In fact, the institution of slavery and the control of the slave's black body were two of the most formidable aspects of the history of slavery, and how it shaped early policing. Slave patrols and Night Watches, which later became your modern-day police departments, were both created to control the behavior of slaves while confined to a particular geographical location.

These paddy rollers traveled in groups and what became known today as a "paddy wagon. Instead of horses we now have vehicles. Remember Freddie Grey a 25-year-old African American killed by Baltimore, Maryland police? He was murdered inside a paddy wagon. Slave laws were first established in Virginia in 1648 and were first established in South Carolina in 1704, then spread throughout the colonies.

Before slave patrols existed, the colonists wrote laws that constricted slave's behavior, thereby laying the groundwork for the legal and justice system controlling Black bodies. These laws set curfews for slaves, strengthened the Southern militia, prevented slaves from engaging in commerce, and established the "neighborhood watch". These are examples of some of the laws and ideas that molded what we know today as slave codes, hence a criminal 'injustice' system for enslaved. Codified laws were being written and the criminalization standards were being set for the black bodies of the captured slave. The original criminals, white kidnappers, thieves, rapists and murderers were now creating laws to criminalize their black victims.

Slave codes differed from state to state. 1705: The Virginia General Assembly declared: "*All servants brought into the Country...who were not Christians in their native Country...shall be accounted and be slaves. All Negro, mulatto and Indian slaves within this dominion...shall be held to be real estate. If any slave resists his master...correcting such slave and shall happen to be killed in such correction...the master shall be free of all punishment...as if such accident never happened.*" The black body was now by law property of the owner of that body and could do with it as he willed without fear of resistance by the slave. The law has rendered him totally submissive to the will of the white slave master.

The 1705 code, which would also serve as a model for other colonies, went even further. The passage of these codes now set the legal boundaries of a framework which would bring into play everyday policing policies within given boundaries and throughout the South. It stated that slaves needed written permission to leave their plantation. The laws of containment had been established and the slave was now legally restricted in time and space. Slaves found guilty of murder or rape of a white person would be hanged. For robbing or any other major offence, the slave would receive 60 lashes and be placed in stocks, where his or her ears would be cut off. And for minor offences, such as associating with whites, slaves would be whipped, branded, or maimed. The black body was now an object of legal torture when there were any acts of defiance, or when the slave reached a tipping point and engaged in acts of defiance to claim his/her rights taken by the original slaver and thief.

Furthermore, in 1723 Virginia's Anti-Assembly Law impeded slaves from meeting or having a sense of community. That same year, Virginia's Weapons Law forbade free blacks from keeping weapons. The Virginia colony also enacted laws to limit the number of free blacks to those who were born into that class or manumitted by special acts of the legislature. Free blacks were denied the right to vote and forbidden to carry weapons of any sort.

Clearly, the black body was now totally encased in an institution of slavery with codified laws giving white supremacist ownership of the black body and the freedom to work it, beat it, rape it, confine it and kill it without fear of legal retribution. The Chameleon's original shape and color had been formed. Because of the harsh implementation of these slave codes during these ripples of time, slaves resisted their bondage in various ways, including murdering their owners, sabotaging crops, animals, and tools; committing suicide, or escaping and forming liberated zones in Florida called maroon societies.

Some of the runaways in Georgia and South Carolina formed maroon societies, which often raided nearby plantations for food and slaves. Consequently, it would be these Black Seminoles, called Maroons, who waged a 100-year war against the institution of Slavery to retain their freedom. As for the government, the concept of black self-determination and freedom was a direct challenge to the concept that whites should rule in order to protect the institution of slavery. Slave patrols and plantation police, along with state militia, were organized by whites as legal and extra-legal means to stop this from occurring. The racialized system of policing, and the newly emerging codified laws laid the groundwork for a criminal justice system that was detrimental to black bodies in captivity. The legal injustice was slowly taking shape as the chameleon began its transformation through the ripples of time.

It was during those times of insurrections and times leading up to the Civil War, that the theory of Contraband prevented the return of Southern slaves who reached Union-held territory. This helped limit the role of slave patrols/catchers and changed the war. Another form of help for the enslaved was the Underground Railroad, which aided the enslaved in their escape to Northern states. Outside of the Underground Railroad, enslaved black people went further south to ensure their freedom. Black people also formed their own organized networks and means of escaping from slavery to Florida, where they would form alliances with Native Americans.

Captured slaves wanted to take back their bodies. They wanted to determine their own time and space, and they wanted to determine their own destinies. Men and women chained, gagged with metal, flesh torn by the whip, realized their lives were being sacrificed for the wealth of others and the building of a nation that did not recognize their humanity. Insurrection was their way of rejecting this barbarity committed against their bodies. The shores of eternity echo the voices from the Stono Rebellion, the voices of Demark Vesey and Nat Turner, of Harriet Tubman, David Walker, and the countless, faceless millions that lit a million candles for those to see light in the darkness of terror and fear. Yet we rise.

Uprisings constituted an additional form of protest. The slave population in the South made the fear of insurrection greater with their courageous acts of resistance. In fact, the largest slave rebellion of the colonial period, involving over one hundred slaves, occurred in Stono, South Carolina, in 1739: approximately 25 whites and 50 slaves were killed during the uprising and its suppression. After the Nat Turner uprising in 1831, more stringent slave codes were introduced. Slaves were forbidden to travel without the written permission of their owner and barred from congregating in large numbers without the presence of whites. Slaves found guilty of murder or rape were hanged; for petty offenses they were whipped, maimed, or branded. The Slave Law passed by Congress in 1850 federalized the police state apparatus, widening the containment field of black bodies. Policing was taken to another level as slaves who had escaped to the North now became fair game.

Interconnectednss of Policing Black Bodies Local, State and Federal 19th -21st Century

The development of the racialized American police force had now given birth to a many-headed hydra, a multitude of historical, legal and political-economic conditions born out of slavery which necessitated the control and containment of black bodies. The institution of slavery and the control of its captured African slaves were two of the more formidable historic features of American society that shaped early white supremacy policing. Slave patrols and Night Watches, which later became modern police departments, both were designed to control the behaviors, movements and attitudes of its intended black victims, especially after dark. In 1704, the colony of Carolina developed the nation's first slave patrol. Slave patrols helped to maintain the economic order and to assist the wealthy landowners in recovering and punishing the body of slaves who essentially were considered an object of value (property).

The slave codes had now established legally the enslaved as the property of their masters, the plantations boundaries as their wall of containment, they were forbidden to possess firearms. Laying hands on a white person was punishable by death. Policing and the legal system now became fully integrated into the system of slavery as an instrument of controlling black bodies. Slavery was now fully institutionalized in the American economic and legal order with laws being enacted at both the state and national divisions of government.

Virginia, for example, enacted more than 130 slave statutes between 1689 and 1865. Slavery and the abuse of people of color, however, was not merely a Southern affair as many have been taught to believe. Connecticut, New York and other colonies enacted laws to criminalize and control the bodies of black people.

Congress also passed fugitive Slave Laws in 1793 and 1850, allowing the detention and return of escaped slaves, in 1793 and 1850. Before the Civil War a legally sanctioned law enforcement system existed in America for the express purpose of controlling the slave population (or Black Bodies) and protecting the interests of the white supremacist slave owners. Remember, the enslaved were a captured and disarmed people, stripped of any human rights including the most fundamental right of self-determination and self-defense. They had absolutely no control over their bodies or its movement. They were prisoners in someone else's time and space.

The similarities between the slave patrols and modern American policing are too salient to dismiss or ignore. Hence, the slave patrol should be considered a forerunner of modern American law enforcement. The captors were constantly aware that their safety depended upon a constant surveillance of slave activities.

An enslaved could not leave the plantation without a written paper giving his name, identifying marks, and a specific route. Lack of such papers was presumptive evidence that the slave was running away and reclaiming his black body. In many places these patrollers were overworked, and this left the illiterate overseers as the backbone of patrolling. Elsewhere, the county of a given state hired a regular patrol from among the poor Whites or small farmers, thus giving those young men a special taste for abusing Black people, which remained lively in Southern lynch mobs until well into the 20th century. Those who swore to protect what white privilege they may have had. These ill-disciplined parties of young men — steeped in an inferiority complex and low self-esteem — may well have been the nucleus for the rise of the Ku Klux Klan in the post bellum South which would spawn the rise of white terrorism. They are who our esteemed sister Harriet Jacobs, wrote *"They were to us the low whites who were the lowest of whites and were the mean and cruel bloodhounds."*

Patty-Rollers

The pattyrollers of yesterday represent not only many of Trump's MAGA followers of today but also those police officers and the white supremacists of today. They are the mindless followers who must have someone to denigrate to cover up their shortcomings, protecting white privilege while vilifying the other. Much like the poor pattyrollers during those ripples of time, they need to place themselves above the lowly slave, the Other. Just as in the past, they show loyalty to an institution that lets them exercise authority, without understanding that the power which tramples people of color also keeps them impoverished and in a state of moral degeneracy. Indeed, some police officers of today patrol black communities with that same impunity, with that same bloodhound mentality so eloquently stated by our sister Harriet Jacobs.

Be it George Floyd with a knee on his neck, or Walter Scott gunned down, needlessly, or a faceless slave hanging from the limb of a tree, or Breonna Taylor murdered in her sleep – all were guilty of having a tinge of color in their face. They all became the meal for a hungry pack of wolves, demons in human form brutalizing the innocent blacks' souls whose only sin was being born black in America.

In communities of color the police's patterns of movement are predictable. Down every main artery their patrol cars cruise, just a few minutes apart. Each one of the cruisers are assigned to residential streets in the black community, which are patterned in square blocks. Let us look at it as a military style reconnaissance mission. Let's label P Street running north and south, two cars are assigned one going north on P Street, the other south. They converge, with one turning right onto 59th, and the other turning left. In that patterned surveillance package, each square block is always cut off, under siege, surrounded, sub-divided. We are always under surveillance in the black community. Yesterday is today and yesterday is now in the ripples of time. Slave, neo-slave, the chameleon is still the same it has only changed colors, as Michael Brown gunned down in cold blood lay dying in the streets of the slave colony in (Ferguson, Missouri).

INCIDENTS IN THE
LIFE OF A
SLAVE GIRL

HARRIET ANN JACOBS

Harriet Jacobs Slave Narration/George Jackson's Prison letters — an intersection in Ripples of time Policing Black Bodies

Today is only yesterday and can only help us understand the dynamics of the moment. The socio-economic conditions which breed police brutality have not changed It has never been portrayed more eloquently than in *The Soledad Brothers* the prison letters of George Jackson. Slavery is an economic condition. *Today's neo slavery must be defined in terms of economics. The chattel is a property, one man exercising the property rights of his established economic order, the other man as that property. The owners can move that property or hold it in one square yard of the earth's surface: he can let it breed other slaves ,he can sell it ,beat it ,work, maim it, fuck it ,kill it. But if he wants to keep and enjoy and enjoy all of the benefits that property of its kind can render, he must feed it sometimes,"* food stamps sound familiar, *"or he must cloth it against the elements, and he must provide a modicum of shelter."* It sounds like today's housing projects.

Chattel slavery was an economic condition, which manifested itself in the total loss or absence of self-determination and freedom of movement. The new slaver, the modern variety of chattel slavery, upgraded to disguise itself. It places the neo-slave in a factory or in support roles inside and around the factory systems (service trades), as well as all service industries, i.e., hospitals restaurants and any services fulfilling the need of the neo-slave master; all working for meager wages, not a living wage. The Chameleon keeps changing colors but is still a Chameleon. Slavery never ended; it has only changed its color.

Anyone who traverses the time space continuum can do so by reading slave narratives and finding the unique elements in its story – the bitterness of mental suffering, physical brutality, forced confinement and forced degradation he or she had to endure. There are amazing similarities in the experiences of Harriet Jacobs_and George even though their respective experiences as slave and neo-slave traversed the time-space continuum and the ripples of time by 120 years. Jacobs's journey spanned the early 1830s to 1860s, a time that saw the great abolitionist movement and slave uprisings, including Nat Turner's rebellion, which escalated the anti-slavery movement and the strengthening of the slave codes, the passing of the Fugitive Slave law and the fortification of the pattyrollers, federal and local policing. Jackson's journey, however, was shaped by the social and political upheavals of the 1960s, which lead to the second frontal assault on the system of slavery (neo-slavery) and the rise of repressive police tactics by modern-day slave patrollers.

According to Jacobs, whenever there was a runaway or any whispers of rebellion, slave patrollers would conduct a reign of terror and unleash unfathomable violence. She describes how everywhere men, women and children would be whipped until *"blood stood in puddles at their feet. They would be tortured with bucking paddles, which blisters the skin terribly. All day long these unfeeling wretches would go around all day long like a pack of demons tormenting and terrifying these helpless colored souls. At night, they went wherever they chose among the colored people, searching their huts, destroying their clothes, what little belongings they had, while acting out their brutal will."*

Conversely, if we travel forward in the time space continuum these brutal acts described by Jacobs are similar to those described in Jackson's *Soledad Brothers.* Jackson echoes that *we are going to have to draw a line in the sand. Remember* Delaney's threshold ultimatum? The threshold will no longer be allowed to cross by whites in their attempts to enforce their brutal will. Gun slinging policemen (modern day slave patrollers) gunned down innocent neo-slaves in the black community, the neo-plantation and black colonies. Mothers and babies were attacked by police dogs.

Need we be reminded of Bull Connor in Montgomery, Alabama, unleashing dogs on black babies or the babies bombed to death in the church in Birmingham? Mothers and their babies starving for lack of proper nutrition while their men are constantly under attack inside and outside prisons. A dozen or more slave patrollers can be expected to invade our cells at any moment. *They handcuff us from wrist to waist to ankles, then they attempt to beat us while searching and destroying what little personal effects we might have. Soledad 19*. Remember the voice of Harriet Jacobs who saw these unfeeling fiends, these slave patrollers scatter about and destroy what few belongings a poor slave might have.

The 1960s and 70s were a battlefield for blacks in their fight for emancipation from neo-slavery and the right to reclaim their black bodies. Insurrections, marches, protest, and much of the music and discussions, urged blacks to exercise their rights and rage against the discrimination and physical attacks by white supremacists. Both Jackson's and Jacobs' voices expose the brutality of slave patrollers, both past and present. Slaves identified the slave patrollers as white poor folk. They remember their relationship with them as perpetual race and class warfare. Jacobs recalls how the low-ranking whites *"show their subservience to the slaveholders, not reflecting that the power, which trampled on the poor slaves, also keeps them in poverty, ignorance and moral degradation."* (57).

Jacobs had a powerful sense of how rich white slave masters manipulated poor whites and slave patrollers, making them the whipping boys of the thoroughly abused slaves. Jackson echoes the same sentiment in *Soledad Brothers.* The great majority of pigs, overseers and slave patrollers inside and outside prison, are historical products of the South. *"They are the poor lower class that could not sell a car or insurance, who could not pass the civil service examination and are used by the slave masters to keep the niggers in their place"*. He continues, *"Some cannot even read or write. You might as well give a baboon a gun and set him loose on us. It is the same here as it is in the black colony. Who has loosed these things, these monsters on an already suffering people? (25)*. The answer was clear, in '60s and '70s America: it was the Nixons, the Reagans, Hoovers, the Bull Conners and such like who were representative of these white supremacist, state-sponsored white domestic terrorist attacks upon its black citizenry.

According to Jacobs the system of slavery had many poisonous fangs. One of these poisonous fangs was the physical brutality on the black body. In Incidents Jacobs describes the sheer brutality perpetrated against one of her fellow slaves. For being disobedient, this particular slave was placed between the screws of a cotton gin and pressed down so tightly, *"he could not move and when the press was unscrewed; the dead body was partially eaten by rats.*" Furthermore, when caught out of bounds, slaves were beaten by slave patrollers.

Jacobs's voice pains the heart as she describes how overseers would tie a rope around a man's body and suspend him from the ground. She describes how a fire would be kindled over him, from which was suspended a piece *of pork. As this cooked, the scalding drops of fat continually fell on the bare flesh. Those that were repeat offenders would be placed in the plantation's jail where cruelties were perpetrated unseen and without limits"(48).* Indeed, the slave environment was a brutal and fixed environment with absolutely no mobility nor protection of the black body.

Similarly, according to Jackson's Soledad narrative, the neo-slave of the '60s and '70s had no mobility because the meager wage would not allow him or her the financial freedom to leave the modern-day plantation/ghetto. Those who dared drive to another side of town, a white neighborhood or downtown, were often stopped by 'pigs' (slave patrollers) and were questioned, harassed and oftentimes beaten, shot or thrown in jail. Jackson contends that it is impossible for blacks to get used to the idea of some petty police officer, asking questions, demanding your papers ("Boy'), asking questions and calling on us to explain ourselves, our movements, demanding to know where we are going. Jackson makes the point succinctly; *"Imagine the colonizer, the usurer, the original thief murderer for personal gain a kidnapper/slaver, the slave patroller, the modern-day police having the right to limit our mobility under the threat of death, with the right to, at any given moment take our lives.*" Remember the voices of Jackson and Jacobs then you will understand those voices in the ripples of time singing in cadence, about oppression, (regardless of the century), fiends controlling the mobility of the oppressed black body; possessing the ultimate authority of ending a life at a moment's notice. This is our perpetual struggle, our perpetual grief, being locked in a cycle of never-ending violence.

Today's neo-slavery is the new color of the Chameleon, some call it minimum wage which does not allow enough wages for a modicum of food and shelter. One only must watch the long lines of cars and bodies waiting at food banks during these troubled times in order to retrieve their next meal to understand. You are free, but free to starve and die a slow death. If you do not make any more in wages than you need to live, you are a neo-slave living off a meager wage. Some call it a minimum wage, but it is certainly not a living wage. If you are held in one spot on this earth because of your economic status and cannot afford to leave town or even go across town, it is the same as being held on the plantation by the slave master.

When my eyes are on the eyes of a brother often in passing on the streets, I, sometimes see staring back at me this expressionless mask of fear and perpetual grief. But a glance and nod are an assuring recognition that we share the same grief, and that we are in this nightmare together.

Jackson, however, retains a strong belief in the ability of the slave to endure, overcome, and triumph. He says, *"We must pick up the fallen; there will be a special page in the "book of life" for the slaves who have crawled back from the grave.* This page will tell of utter defeat, ruin, passivity and subjugation in one breath and in the next overwhelming victory and fulfillment.

This is the narrative style for Jackson – clear, concise and carefully orchestrated, just like his thinking. His tone is a paradoxical combination of anger and love; it is rational and instructive, like abolitionist literature and slave narration. In addition, it seeks to capture the reader's imagination that pains their heart, our hearts to tears! Knowing that we are the hunted and can be felled by the assassin's bullet at any given moment, always sharing the same recognition that we are always is the cross hairs of the gun.

Jackson's language and tone makes an appeal to his audience to hear our voices past, to recognize how we are trapped within a neo-slave mentality, a mentality "cramped within the cloud of ignorance." Sometimes he speaks directly to slave mothers in general – and his mother in particular – for he acutely feels the impending doom for women with sons and daughters, while knowing that this impending doom, this sudden loss of life, was the state of affairs for all slave mothers, past and present. Who will become the next victim of the fatal bullet from the modern-day slave patroller?

In Incidents in the Life of a Slave Girl, Harriet Jacobs states that *"the awful manacles of slavery were the pelting storm of a slave mother's life" (156).* She concludes that some *"cloud of despair prevents a mother from protecting her own; her children who have been snatched by the evil hand of their slaver never allowing the mother to wipe their tears from their crying eyes."*

Conversely, we were all brought to tears as we heard the painful and heartbreaking cry of George Floyd as he cried out for his mother ten times as he took his last breath. It was heartbreaking to hear, and it broke our hearts. I will say again, we have always been in a perpetual state of grief while languishing in those slave castles in Africa, packed into the bowels of ships and arriving on these shores of injustice.

Jackson is qualified to write his narrative because he was a captured neo-slave who transformed himself into an intelligent captive. Like authors of slave narratives, he was compelled to tell of his treatment. Jackson's works recount the firsthand experiences of a genius in a closed and ruthless environment. He was a neo-slave under the gun, behind walls, under surveillance of the overseer, encaged in solitary confinement. He was the unbroken slave, always, and a heartbeat away from a tragic death. Jackson explains, *"In their most vicious moment I would be placed in an isolation cell within a cell. The inner-door would be locked and welded shut and there would be no one to talk to just the sound of screaming voices of men being beaten or retreating from intolerable pain into a cacophony of madness"* (XXI).

If one has ever visited the slave fortresses, Elmina Castle and Cape Castle on the Ghanaian Gold Coast, one would see cells firsthand that fit Jackson's description. There they were called the "breaking room." These cells had no windows, no light, no ventilation, and one had to go through two steel doors to gain access. They were the homes of the unbroken captured slaves who refused to be shipped abroad. These slaves were left in isolation to suffer a slow, suffocating death simply because they chose not to become a slave. They refused to walk through the Door of No Return onto the slave ships that would cast them into the pit of hell. If you ever choose to travel to Africa, and if you ever want to feel the horrors and the excruciating pain felt by your ancestors, visit the slave castles. I guarantee you will fall to your knees and grieve for those that came before you. I felt heart wrenching grief as I sat there in silence, the doors shut. I felt their pain but heard their chants and felt the strength of those souls who refused to wear the mantra of the enslaved. I take those unforgettable feelings to my grave, for they are forever etched in the core of my being.

Despite Jackson's circumstances in incarceration, the solitary confinement and prison guards' brutality, Jackson does not relent. His determination to survive echoes the determination of slaves to endure brutal conditions. Jackson explains, *"We will not be pushed out of this existence. The floor and ceiling are trembling. They are fighting above me now. In hand-to-hand combat we always win; lose sometimes when pigs give the white cons knives or zip guns" (20)*. Despite all the bedlam, in the rigor and accuracy of his ideas and vision, Jackson discovers a common ground in the audacity of his undertaking. He created a literacy work of art, Soledad Brothers, under the most dehumanizing and life-threatening conditions. The conditions under which Jackson launched his undertaking were unimaginable, yet he managed to survive and create art, which was an extraordinary feat. Of course, this had been done before by courageous slaves. Jackson realizes the toll neo-slavery has taken on his life in the quote below:

The slaves they fall victim to the full fury and might of the system's repressive agencies. Believe me, every dirty trick of deception and brutality is employed without honor, without humanity, without reservation to either convert or destroy a rebellious slave. I am by nature a gentle man. I love the simple things of life, good food, good wine, an expensive book, music, and beautiful black women. I used to enjoy a walk in the rain, and summer evenings. All of this is gone from me; all the gentle, shy, loving, characteristics of a black man have been wrangled unceremoniously from my soul. The bullets and blows have generated in me a cold flame that will live to grow until it destroys my tormentor or myself. (56)"

One only has to traverse the time-stream to imagine how a captured slave must have yearned to fell the pleasure of a walk in the rain, to enjoy good food, palm wine, a beautiful black woman to enjoy a sunset as a free person, instead of all the years in his or her life darkened by the early morning shadows of slavery. Such was the life of a slave. Such was Jackson's life as a neo-slave. Never able to enjoy their space in time in the time space continuum.

Conversely, the future can only be better than the past when we honestly admit, acknowledge, and recognize the sins of the past and correct them in the present, for they are forever intertwined. Americans cannot ask for absolution of their sins until they recognize they have committed some of, if not the most atrocious sins against humanity. The world got a glimpse of your atrocity as we watched life being drained from George Floyd's body. We all heard his dying voice pleading for life, asking his dead mother for help. We are demanding that his voice merges with the voices from our treasured past. Today we are hearing our next generation's voices and they now hear the voices of their ancestors. Darnella Frazier heard the voices as she stood courageously and recorded for posterity the modern-day lynching of brother George Floyd. We have suffered for too long and the voices of our ancestors are calling from the ripples of time, it sounds like this; it pains us to dwell on our past, we drink deeply from this pain. Our recall must be nearly perfect. Time has faded, but yet the ripples of time remain continuous and nothing has really changed. Now we must add the name of Jacob Blake, Breonna Taylor, Daniel Prude. How many more must die at the hands of these vicious, soulless fiends?

We want you to feel the first kidnapping, live through the middle passage, while remembering the millions of souls who have watery graves at the bottom of the Atlantic because of a need to balance the slave ships. Hear the voices from our black bodies whose blood soaked the soil of America with our corpses; cotton and corn growing from our chest. Hear the cries of our voices as we were burned alive and hung from the trees entrenched in American soil. Hear the cries of countless mothers as they had their babies snatched from their arms to be sold off as another man's property; hear their cries as they claim the bodies of their sons and daughters who were gunned down in the streets like stray dogs. Understand that these thousands of histories are all one moment, a collective breath, collective stories, collective suffering from black bodies bound together in the ripples of time.

My young brothers and sisters, merge your minds, open your ears to hear and your eyes to see through the uncounted generations and feel all that they have felt – pain! However, listen to them, they are also telling you; never allow yourselves to be counted among the broken souls. The ruinous effects of slavery and black colonial existence will try to break your will. Stay hungry for freedom, we have been lied to and insulted with false truths too many times. They will never be satisfied until they push you out of existence. We must learn to understand today and yesterday so that we remain on solid ground while planning our tomorrows, with a clear understanding of our historical past which dictates our present-day conditions and will dictate a clear path to freedom.

Allow your spirit to guide you. George Jackson said: *"Our voices must always pick up the fallen, there always will be a special place in history, in the book of life for slaves who have crawled back from the grave."*

In one breath Jackson writes about utter brutality and subjugation but also exhilarating victory and fulfillment, because we still stand and continue to endure the most horrific brutality inflected upon the bodies of human beings. But always remember, our bodies are a temple, to be taken back. You have already awoken it now, all you must do is to keep it alive, nourish it properly and feed the mind and spirit while protecting it from the traps set by our captors. What you need to guide you is in you. Your light is your guide and your power. Remember your ancestors, and you will know you are a star child, and the universe is your home. The center of the circle is the home of your home. Dwell there, ever in your heart, and we will always overcome the evildoers who wish to inflict pain on our black bodies. We are the original children of the Black Mitochondrial Mother. Hold her dear to your heart and we will always prevail.

CHAPTER 4

THE CHAMELEON TURNS RED:
THE RISE OF DOMESTIC WHITE TERRORISM IN AMERIKKKA

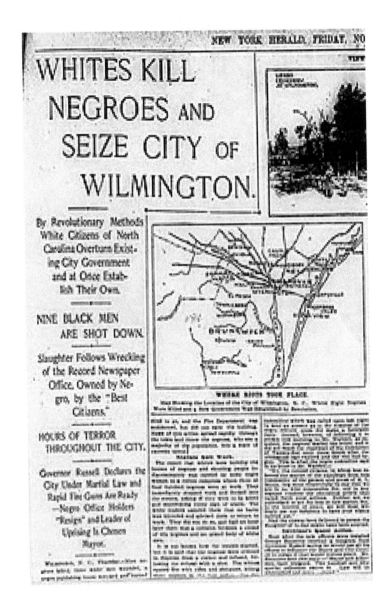

An estimated 100-200 Blacks Murdered
in massive voter suppression, in Opelousas, La.

The Opelousas Massacre 1868

It is now 6 a.m., the sun is rising, and slavery has ended. That is six hours in cosmic time and 251 years in earth time. President Abraham Lincoln, General Ulysses Grant, General William Sherman, Fredrick Douglas, Henry Harland Garnet, Nat Turner, Harriet Tubman, Harriet Jacobs and all those gallant warriors of freedom cast a new dawn for those wretched creatures who had suffered at the hands of slavery. The 13th, 14th and 15th amendments were supposed to ensure freedom for our wretched people. Forty acres and a mule were to allow black families to start building transitional and generational wealth to close the wealth gap between White America and its newly-freed black citizens. During and after slavery, post-Reconstruction freed slaves had assumed they would gain equal rights of citizenship. They assumed they would have and enjoy the right to vote and to hold public office. The storm clouds of white terrorism were looming over the horizon, however.

What the newly-freed slave would confront was the rising tide of white grievance and white privilege since they were competing with poor whites for jobs, while whites with political power felt threatened by the newly-emerging black electorate. This threat to white privilege, which would level the playing field unleashed the beginning of a new form of attacks on black bodies. During slavery, the terror on black bodies were more measured because their bodies were commodities of value. Once slavery ended, the violence was no longer measured. It unleashed a new and more vicious form of white domestic terrorism and mob violence introduced into the ripples of time.

The 1868 Opelousas massacre in Louisiana would become one of the first incidents of white domestic terrorism on the newly freed slaves. The objective was to stop blacks from voting and halt local black political progress in its tracks. The dispute over an article published in the local newspaper provoked one of the bloodiest white domestic terror attacks during the post-Reconstruction era. This attack was a wanton disregard for the newly won political gains of the former slaves after the Civil War and the end goal was to restore white privilege in the South. Suppression of the black vote would become the strategy of white supremacists through the ripples of time and would continue through the age of Donald Trump.

This is a white man's government. We regard the Reconstruction act of Congress as a usurpation, and unconstitutional, revolutionary and void and-Democratic Platform: Published in

Harpers Weekly, September 1868

The Opelousas massacre of 1868 remains one of the most brutal examples of African American voter suppression by white domestic terrorists. It occurred in the run-up to the 1868 presidential election, which pitted conservative Democrat Horatio Seymour against Ulysses Grant. The number of casualties estimated from this terror attack ranged well into the hundreds. Killings were a prelude of the physical brutality to be experienced by black bodies in the South during Post-Reconstruction. It also underlined the importance of partisan media in shaping the postwar political discourse as a tool to be used while shaping public opinion much what we are witnessing today with Fox news spin machine.

Using the biblical proverb. Mathew 12:30 (Motto: *"He that is not for us, is against us."*) After the upheaval of the Civil War, newspapers became a hotly contested space for Democrats and Republicans to communicate their competing visions for the political, economic and social futures of some 4 million formerly enslaved black people. Republicans at the time used their newspapers to advocate expanding Black people's rights and privileges. But throughout American history, political parties have used partisan newspapers as propaganda weapons to influence their electoral base, starting with the Federalist party's *Gazette of the* United Democratic papers were aligned with the slogan of their party's presidential nominee Seymour: *"This is a White Man's Government,"* one that hoped to keep Black Americans in perpetual bondage—or at least perpetual servitude.

In Opelousas, the tides of change were sweeping throughout the region. In April, Louisiana's new state constitution, one of the most far-reaching pieces of Radical Reconstruction legislation was passed on the strength of the Black Republican vote. It granted full citizenship to Black men with equal civil and political rights, while banning segregation in public schools and on public transportation. The state's white planter class, beset by labor shortages, saw their world order crumbling as formerly enslaved people gained new rights and exercised those rights in their attempts to level the playing. In July, the 14th amendment gave former enslaved equal status under federal law. This was damaging to the white male white supremacist ego and would challenge their understanding of white privilege. *"The April election returns left white leaders fully cognizant of the radical Black voting strength and the future implications that strength had for the Democratic party,"* wrote Carolyn DeLatte, an early historian of the Opelousas massacre.

This recognition is the same fear expressed by Donald Trump and the 2020 Republican Party as they utilized various methods to suppress the black vote in the presidential elections. Nothing has changed in the ripples of time, only the color of the Chameleon. While Black voters, immediately after the Civil War, were largely Republican, they were not a monolithic group. Some did join the Democratic party—a fact that, in St. Landry parish, caused conflict on both sides. In early September 1868, a rumor circulated among local Democrats that Republican Blacks were going to reclaim Black Democrats for the party, if they had to do it "at the point of a bayonet." These rumors led to a mostly peaceful standoff on September 13, 1868 between Black Republicans and white Democrats, where leaders of each party gave speeches and negotiated a peace accord between the two parties that banned guns at gatherings. It also required the editor of the *St. Landry Progress*, Emerson Bentley, to refrain from making "incendiary" comments about the Democrats in the paper or in speeches.

According to the award-winning investigative reporter Farrell Evans, Emerson Bentley was an 18-year-old Ohio native who also served as secretary of the local Radical Republican party and taught at a Methodist school for Black students. Deemed by local Democrats a "carpetbagger," (a derogatory term used for Northerners who came South after the war to profit economically or politically),

Bentley regularly received threats. But he expressed religious motivation for his politics, crediting his "Christian spirit, and a desire to do something for the general good."

On September 19, 1868 Bentley broke the truce by lambasting Democrats in a Progress editorial. "*The assembly of armed men from all parts of the parish did not indicate peaceful intentions, but a total blindness to the interests of the people,*" he wrote. Declaring a measure of moral authority over the Democrats, Bentley added that Republicans "*do not plot in the dark; we do not assassinate inoffensive citizens or threaten to do so; we do not seek the lives of political opponents; we do not seek to array one class* against another; but we do intend to defend our just rights at all *hazards.*" In the article, he appealed to Black Democrats to rejoin the party that didn't seek to intimidate them with violence. On September 28, Bentley was teaching at the Methodist church on the outskirts of Opelousas when three local members of the Seymour Knights, a white supremacist organization, confronted him about his "incendiary" article.

Before leaving, the Seymour Knights forced Bentley to sign a retraction of the story. When word spread about the attack, Republicans, fearing for their lives, assembled in Opelousas. Rumors spread among white citizens that armed Black locals were plotting an uprising. After signing an affidavit with legal authorities about the attack and then hiding overnight in a barn behind the *Progress* office, Bentley left town. Eluding a white mob with help from numerous Republican party safe houses, he eventually made his way to New Orleans. As Bentley fled, white mobs began a killing rampage that lasted several weeks, targeting Opelousas's Black citizens—ostensibly to keep them from organizing. "*Colored men were not allowed to stand in groups upon the sidewalks,*" according to the New Orleans Advocate. *"Each day new victims fell."*

In St. Landry parish, dozens of black bodies were found scattered in shallow graves. The Republican Party estimated casualties at between 200 and 300, while Democrats put it between 25 and 30. An Army investigation reported 233. The mass desecration and murdering of black bodies became the weapon of intimidation and fear. Voter suppression and white domestic terrorism would become the modus operandi for white supremacy politics.

Over time, the real agenda—of demolishing St. Landry parish's Republic party's black political base—became clear. Several white party leaders were hunted and killed, with one corpse displayed outside the local drugstore as a warning. Mobs destroyed the *Progress* office's press and ransacked the Methodist school. *"The*

Negroes all over the Parish have been disarmed, and have gone to work briskly," declared the <u>Franklin Planter's Banner</u>, a Democratic party paper. *"Their Loyal League clubs have been broken up, the scalawags have turned Democrats…and their carpet-bag press…have been destroyed."* Republicans who weren't killed fled or switched parties. The reign of white domestic terrorism was escalating, and black bodies were executed on the cross of white privilege and grievance in Amerikkka.

Even though the Civil War ended, and slaves were emancipated, Reconstruction failed to implement the newly-won human and civil rights of the formerly enslaved. Post-Reconstruction would not bring to the former slaves the rewards of self-determination and full citizenship. It would not level the playing field; it would not begin closing the wealth gap, and certainly not protecting black bodies from white domestic terrorists. Instead, they would suffer a full-fledged assault on their aspirations and newly formed communities, unlike never before. The Chameleon emerged once again but in a different color.

White Terror Reigns: Black Bodies Under Assault

The dawn of expectation during Post-Reconstruction would end by 6:15 a.m. in cosmic time and 12 years earth time. The storm clouds of a new white nationalist terrorism were looming on the horizon. John Wilkes Booth, a white terrorist and agent of the South, assassinates President Abraham Lincoln. Andrew Johnson assumes the Presidency and scuttles Sherman's 40 acres and a mule law and plans for Reconstruction. Properties were seized from the newly-freed slaves and returned to former Southern slave-owners.

President Andrew Johnson

The White Knights of the Camelia, the Redeemers, and the KKK began merging forces with former slave patrollers. They collectively organized armed raids and orchestrated acts of terror against the newly-freed slaves, their communities and their properties. The former slave patrollers had moved into the KKK. The weasel clause in the 13th amendment was used to criminalize free slaves who, if not working, were charged with loitering or vagrancy, which became a felony. The birth of forced labor and chain gangs would become a part of this new institutionalized racism and the criminalization of the Black Body.

The storm clouds of white supremacy burst and by 8 a.m. the storms of white domestic terrorism and white grievance politics had arrived. Opelousas, Louisiana was the beginning. Its next major victory was in Wilmington, North

Carolina in 1898, in which the first overthrow of a duly elected government on American soil was carried out by white supremacists.

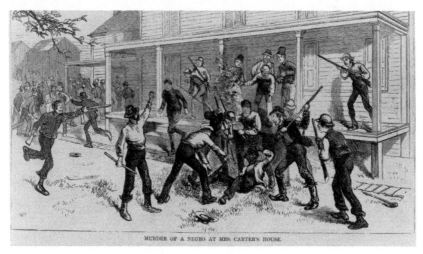

White Terrorists brutalizing Black Bodies during the Wilmington Coup

Above all and in retrospect, this was the spirit of the times. In 1877, immediately following the end of Post-Reconstruction, the Federal government restored white supremacist control of the South and adapted a "laissez-faire" policy toward African American human rights. The federal government and the lack of enforcement of the 14th and 15th amendments betrayed the ex-slave's quest for freedom while their black bodies became cannon fodder to white domestic terror attacks. These counter-revolutionary actions were initiated by President Andrew Johnson, who had collaborated with white supremacist congressmen and senators representing the Southern states. As a result, blacks were once again deprived of their civil and human rights and reduced to a status of quasi-slavery or neo-slavery. Therefore, a tense atmosphere of white supremacist ideology caused fear within the newly emerging black communities. This bred a new form of lawlessness—the era of white supremacist, white domestic terrorism and mob violence had begun.

During slavery, the value of the African American body was dictated by fair market value as property (private property). After emancipation, the slave lost its value as property and therefore their body became a target of white supremacist terror attacks. The consequences were deadly. African Americans as freedmen, became property owners and the holders of public office, and they now became the victims of mass violence, mass murder and lynchings.

White domestic terrorism...how it looked then......

According to Robert A. Gipson in <u>The Negro Holocaust</u>, "*In the last decades of the nineteenth century, the lynching of Black People in the Southern and border states became an institutionalized method used by whites to terrorize Blacks and maintain white supremacy:* (p.2). This mindset, this whiteness or white terror was a means by which white Amerikkkans exerted social control over African Americans. This practice was a uniquely Amerikkkan one. In <u>Lynch Law</u>, written by *James E. Cutler*, he states "*lynching is a criminal practice which is peculiar only to the United States." (p.1).*

Moreover, most of the lynching was by hanging or both. Other gruesome forms of violence included burning at the stake, dismemberment of body parts as trophies; maiming, castration and other unimaginable brutal methods of physical torture. Often, these heinous crimes were committed in front of hundreds, sometimes thousands, of whites in a festive atmosphere where food and refreshments were served to whet their appetites for black blood. Never was this atmosphere so poignantly described as in Chesnutt's <u>Marrow of Tradition</u>: "*White savages dancing in hellish glee around the mangled burned bodies of their black victims" (266).*

Lynching, therefore, was a tool used by white supremacists in tandem with grievance politics, both political and economic, to maintain control of a caste system in the South. According to The Crisis, the official organ of the NAACP during the Du Bois era, *"There were on average over two hundred known lynchings a year from 1912 to 1931.* In its early stages lynchings were a reflection of white grievance politics carried out by random acts of terrorism. However, as ex-slaves began to ascend to the political office and enjoy relative economic prosperity, white privilege needed cover to execute its terror attacks on the ex-slave in particular and the black community in general. Thus, the image of the burley black beast lusting after and raping the white female body became the rallying cry to excite the mob. It was a cry that gave cover to the destruction of black economic progress and prosperity. This claim of sexual contact between the black man and white woman, of this hypersexual and imagined lascivious lust for her body remains one of the most durable tropes of white supremacy. Indeed, it was a convenient cover exercised by white supremacist to intimidate, maintain control and strike fear into the heart of the black community

Anti-lynching crusader Ida Bell Wells was one of the voices from those ripples of time. She called out the brutal lynchings and attacks on black bodies and black communities. Born into slavery in Holly Springs, Mississippi in 1862, she moved to Memphis at the age 18, and worked as a teacher. At age 22, she sued the Chesapeake & Ohio & Southeastern Railroad Company for forcibly removing her from a train after she refused to be reseated in a segregated car. Though she ultimately lost the case, the effort foreshadowed her lifelong fight against racial injustice. An avid reader and writer, Wells became a popular columnist in Black newspapers in Memphis, and eventually rose to editor and part-owner of the local Free Speech and Headlight newspaper. She used the newspaper as a platform to criticize racial inequality extensively. When Thomas Moss, Calvin McDowell, and Henry Stewart—three Black men and friends of Wells—were brutally lynched in Memphis in March 1892 for defending their grocery business against white attackers, she immediately published an editorial in the Headlight , urging Memphis's Black community to *"save our money and leave a town which will neither protect our lives and property nor give us a fair trial in the courts, but takes us out and murders us in cold blood when accused by white persons."*

More than 6,000 African Americans heeded the call, but Ms. Wells stayed to promote the movement she had begun. In May 1892, she published another editorial that challenged the claim that *lynching was necessary to protect white womanhood.* In response, Memphis's white newspapers denounced and derided Ms. Wells as a *"black scoundrel." On May 27, 1892, while she was visiting*

Philadelphia, a white mob attacked and destroyed the Free Speech and Headlight office and threatened her with bodily harm if she returned. [231]

Our beloved sister relocated to New York, where she continued her anti-lynching efforts by writing for the <u>New York Age</u>, publishing several anti-lynching pamphlets, and embarking on a speaking tour through the Northern states and Britain, where she decried the atrocities of lynching and urged federal and international intervention. She ultimately settled in Chicago, married, became Mrs. Wells-Barnett and raised five children while collaborating with leaders like Frederick Douglass and W. E. B. Du Bois. From this, the NAACP was born. Wells-Barnett helped organize legal aid and publicity for victims of the 1918 terror attacks and the Red Summers, especially the White Terror attack on the black community in East Saint, Louis which left an estimated 300 blacks brutally murdered.

In the preface to her 1892 pamphlet<u>, Southern Horrors,</u> Sister Wells described the goal of her life's work: *"The Afro American is not a bestial race. If this work can contribute in any way toward proving this, and at the same time arouse the conscience of the American people to a demand for justice to every citizen, and punishment by law for the lawless, I shall feel I have done my race a service. Other considerations are of minor importance."* [234] Wells-Barnett died of natural causes in Chicago in 1931, as the terror of the lynching era was escalating throughout the country. Wells certainly was at the forefront in diminishing the argument that the black man was a beast and had an insatiable appetite for the white female body, the racist myth of the African American male's unquenchable desire for white women's bodies, which became a strategic position in the defense of lynching as a justifiable terrorist tactic.

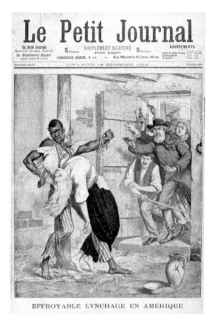

EFFROYABLE LYNCHAGE EN AMÉRIQUE

Ultimately, it would be this strategy that would spearhead the white supremacist assault on the black community in Wilmington, NC, as well as those in Atlanta, GA, Springfield and Chicago Ill, and Tulsa, Oklahoma, to name a few. The tactic is simple: make accusations of rape, which is secure from further investigation. Political or economic motives are camouflaged behind the cry of rape. Indeed, who would question this brutal assault upon the pillar of white man's purity - his white womankind? All acts of violence to protect her honor are therefore ordained by law which became the smoke screen for white terrorism.

As the white supremacists firmly entrenched themselves and solidified their power base in each locality in the South, they gained tight control over public office, **the courts, the police and public opinion.** Post-Reconstruction was the counter revolutionary period in which white supremacists reestablished their power while repelling black insurrection. The birth of the Klu Klux Klan and other white supremacists used lynching and mob violence, a domestic terrorist strategy, against blacks who had assumed public office and property rights. The restoration of white privilege was on the march.

In most cases, those participating in lynching and other white terror attacks were never indicted. The judge, prosecutor, jurors and witnesses – all white – were always in collusion with the perpetrators. Institutionalized racism was taking hold of the criminal injustice system. Arthur Raper in *The Tragedy of Lynching* states that "*at least lest on-half of the lynchings are carried out with police officers participating and the other half either condone or wink at the mob action*" (p.134). The slave patrollers have now taken on a new form – the policeman – as a means to brutalizing and maiming black bodies.

No one knew these ripples of time better than African American author, Robert W. Chesnutt. Naturally, a man of Charles Chesnutt's genius, a student of history and a literary genius, had studied this peculiar form of white terror. He knew that many whites, after Reconstruction and during the last three decades and the early 20th century, feared that African Americans had forgotten their place, and that the white man's pre-eminent position, ordained by God, needed protection. It would be during these times that the demons of racism and racial hatred would firmly entrench itself in in the American psyche.

White terrorism was an expression of fear of black assault on white woman, and so the white supremacist leadership used this false narrative – the black rapist – to fan the flames of hatred amongst the ignorant white masses, In Chesnutt's novel, *The Marrow of Tradition*, he lucidly characterizes this strategy with two of his fictional characters, Colonel Belmont and Captain McBane, who plotted the Wilmington Massacre. Their words were prophetic: *This is the age of crowds and we must have the crowds with us. We must play the crowds.* Much like Trump and his MAGA crowd today – same demons, different generations, different ripples of time.

It should be noted, this strategy of fanning the flames of mass hysteria to camouflage the use of mob violence and white terrorism for political gain was exposed in Chesnutt's novel. The white Supremacist leadership strategy in Wilmington, NC was to seize power from the black community through mob violence and terrorism in order to overthrow a duly elected multiracial government. In the age of white supremacist, counter-terrorist movements, the state and federal government authorized violent seizures of power and promoted the fabricated specter of black criminalization (rapes of white women) as a shield through which power might be taken.

This method of approach was never so obvious as one of Chesnutt's themes in his novel. Sandy, a trusted black servant, had been accused of assaulting and robbing Mrs. Ochiltree, a white affluent Southern "Lady". Carteret (one of the principal Wilmington conspirators) says this *"is something more than an ordinary crime, to be dealt with by the ordinary process of the law. It is a murderous and fatal assault upon a woman of our race, upon our race in the person of its womanhood, its crown and flower.* According to the narrative, if such crimes are not punished with swift and terrible directness, the whole white womanhood of the South is in danger. *"Burn the Nigger,"* said McBane, *"it is an assault committed by the black race, in the person of some nigger"* (182). Carteret continued, *"Hold on, let us plan this, there's more at stake in this matter than the life of a black scoundrel. Wellington (Wilmington) is in the hands of Negroes and savages. What better time to rescue power from the hands of scoundrels?*

The Lawless World of White Terrorism, the Wilmington, NC Massacre, 1898

By 6:45 a.m. the storms of white domestic terrorism had begun. The Wilmington, North Carolina massacre of 1898 was the tipping point. Indeed, Wilmington followed Opelousas as the beginning of massive organized white domestic terrorist attacks against newly emerging African American communities in general. It only took eight hours cosmic time or 33 years of Earth Time for the forces of the old confederacy to mount their assault on black bodies and their newfound freedom after the end of the Civil War.

Hear the voices cry out from Wilmington especially that of Robert Chesnutt, the first black literary writer of his times. In Chesnutt's *The Marrow of Tradition*, you hear the historically accurate account of the Wilmington, North Carolina coup d'état of 1898. This attack on the pillars of democracy was the first and only coup engineered by the white supremacist Democrats, who overthrew a legitimately elected government on US soil. This was a well-conceived plan to restore white supremacists to office. The citizens of Wilmington had elected African Americans and their white progressive allies into office, and their political agenda served the needs of the entire Wilmington community.

The destruction of the Black Newspaper office in Wilmington, N.C.

Armed White domestic terrorist with Gatling Machine Gun

During the reign of terror **this campaign featured white police, the new form of slave patroller**. They rode into Black homes and whipped Black men, threatening them with death for attempting to vote. On election day, armed white mobs gathered outside Wilmington polling stations, threatening any Blacks who tried to cast a ballot. The result: Democrats won every elected position in which they ran. The Chameleon's colors are a bit more subtle today: sabotaging postal deliveries, a limited number of drop off boxes for same-day ballots, photo ID requirements. Different tactics, same end game, i.e. the suppression of the black vote.

The Coup Left Lasting Scars

In addition to the killings, the mob forced virtually all of Wilmington's Black middle- and upper-class citizens to flee town. Once gone, the newly elected local government then began instituting Jim Crow segregationist policies. A new form of slavery had transformed itself then and now. The original Jim Crow was born out of Post-Reconstruction. Institutionalized racism was implemented, the police force became lily white. The coup decimated Black political and economic power in Wilmington for nearly 100 years. By 1902, the number of registered Black voters dwindled from more than 125,000 to about 6,100. After the coup, no Black citizen served in public office in Wilmington until 1972.

The alleged rape of a white woman by a black man camouflaged the coup. Chesnutt's own words spoke of the hanging and the violence that followed, and how it was a pretext for white men to grab power. In some eyes however, it was the white man's sworn duty to protect the white women of the South against brutal, lascivious Black men. The message was secondary to temporarily setting aside regular law in order to warn the black bodies of the swift and terrible punishment that would fall, like the judgment of God, upon anyone who laid hands upon the precious pillar of white womanhood.

Indeed, Chesnutt's voice from the past teaches us how this coup was a complete subversion of the principles of a free democratic election, but also how the term *whiteness* was instrumental in the results through a simple phrase… *domestic white terrorism*. The events preceding this attack were precipitated by a false claim of the rape of a white woman by a black man. The false imagery of the beastly nature of black men was front and center. Lest we not forget, the animalistic nature of black men was the creation of the Enlightenment Thinkers, who placed blacks at or below the same level of animals. Remember Shakespeare's *The Tempest*, how the lowly beastly Caliban longed to violate the sanctity of the Captain's daughter, the blonde fair maiden Miranda.

Both Wilmington newspapers in 1898 ran stories of the alleged assaults and fanned the flames of racial hatred against an innocent victim, all a part of this sickness occupying America's soil.

The seed of this racial hatred and the brutal treatment of black bodies in Wilmington can be traced to the end of the Civil War, the summer of 1865, just after the Civil War, Union commanders in the battered port city of Wilmington, N.C. appointed a former Confederate general as police chief and former Confederate soldiers as policemen. The all-white force immediately set upon newly freed Black people. Men, women and children were beaten, clubbed and whipped indiscriminately.

A Union officer with the Freedmen's Bureau maintained a ledger of daily police assaults: *A Black man whipped 72 times. A Black woman dragged for two miles with a rope* around her neck. A Black man, *"his back all raw,"* beaten by police with a buggy trace. *"The policemen are the hardest and most brutal-looking and acting set of civil or municipal officers I ever saw. All look bad and vicious,"* the Union officer reported.

Yesterday is Today, and the ripples of time show the image of a white police officer in Minneapolis pressing his knee against George Floyd's neck, with that unfeeling look as George Floyd pleaded for mercy. That image has opened a window onto America's unbroken history of brutality against black bodies.

Meanwhile the Grandfather Clause, which was passed in North Carolina but would not go into effect until 1900, was the mechanism by which the coup was sprung. The clause was enacted by seven Southern states between 1895 and 1910, with the aim of denying the vote to African Americans. It was similar to voter suppression techniques today. It stipulated those who had enjoyed the right to vote prior to 1866 or 1867, and their lineal descendants, would be exempt from recently enacted educational, property, or tax requirements for voting. Because the former slaves had not been granted the franchise until the adoption of the 15th Amendment in 1870, those clauses worked effectively to exclude Black people from the vote but assured the franchise to many impoverished and illiterate whites. Privileged and illiterate whites feared a loss of political and economic power in the face of ex-slaves ascending to the status of citizens.

As an example, African Americans in Wilmington had been elected to office in 1894, and another election was coming in 1898. In the meantime, the Secret Nine, according to Henry Hayden a historian and white supremacist sympathizer, interviewed participants and detailed how the local leaders who called themselves the Secret Nine, set up systems of night patrols. Hayden described how each block was assigned a lieutenant. Each of the city's five wards were assigned to a Captain, and atop the chain of command was a former Confederate Colonel who had once led the local branch of the KKK. This command structure was led by Alfred Waddell, a white supremacist.

Waddell's group drew up a **Declaration of White Independence**. It was a preamble that declared black suffrage unconstitutional. It rejected any notion of black rule, and it called for all jobs held by blacks to be turned over to whites. This was a total acceptance of white privilege, and it negated any closure of the wealth gap between the races. Furthermore, all political offices must be vacated and turned over to whites who already owned 93 percent of Wilmington's property. Finally, they demanded that Charles Manley, a black barber and owner of the black newspaper, the *Observer*, who wrote a scathing critique of the lynching of a black man accused of raping white women, leave town and never return. This declaration was given to the black ministerial alliance on the eve of the election. They were given 24 hours to meet all demands unconditionally or face the consequences.

Foundationally, the groundwork for white domestic terrorism and the coup had been laid – the alleged rape of a white woman, and the hanging of the accused black man. On the day of the election, white terrorists armed themselves to prevent blacks from voting (much like the events in Opelousas, Louisiana 30 years earlier), while they stuffed ballot boxes with votes. The grand theft was on. Like Trump's attempt on January 6th to incite

CONSTITUTION.

ARTICLE 1—The name of the organization shall be The White Government Union.

ARTICLE 2—The purpose of the organization shall be to re-establish in North Carolina the Supremacy of the White Race; to promote individual effort in behalf of the party and its candidates on the part of the voters, and to bring the head of the organization in the counties and State more closely and easily in touch with the Township Organizations, and the individual party voter.

ARTICLE 3—Neither oaths, grips, signs, nor passwords shall be allowed.

Any Union may, if it so desires, adopt a badge, button, insignia, or uniform.

ARTICLE 4—The organization shall be divided into County Unions and Township Unions.

ARTICLE 5—Every White Man who desires White Government in North Carolina, and is willing to use every practicable and honorable means to restore White Supremacy therein, and who proposes to support candidates pledged to effect that purpose, in the ensuing election, shall be eligible to membership of the township Union.

his armed insurrection, the difference being his Coup failed and the Wilmington Coup succeeded. Waddell gave the orders, *shoot to kill any black person found trying to cast their vote*. On November 10, before the election results were known, the election had already been stolen and the Coup had already succeeded. Waddell forces met at the Wilmington Light Infantry Armory, then attacked the <u>*Daily Record*</u>, black-owned newspaper, burning the building to the ground.

Within hours, the Coup was in full swing. The white domestic terrorists responded to the clarion call of its leader and on the morning of November 10th Reverend Kirk, the president of the black ministerial alliance recalls in his memoir, <u>Bloody Riot In Wilmington, NC</u>, "*Their preamble declared that this community would no longer be ruled by men of African origin; that our eyes are open to the fact that we must act now or leave our children to a gloomy future. The preamble also stated that from that day foreword only white men would hold public office and hold meaningful jobs; that we propose in the future to give employment only to white men.*"

The old South and the Chameleon of slavery again reared its ugly head of white supremacy and had taken on a new form, new shape and new color. To ensure their white supremacist children's future, Rev Kirk recalls the brutal assault on his community', after burning down the black newspaper office, they crossed the railroad tracks and went into what is known as Dark town. They brought in a Gatling gun and started killing men, women and children. The shrieks and screams of children of mothers, of wives were such that they caused the blood of the most inhumane person to curl and cringe. Rev. Kirk continued his eyewitness account; *They went into a colored man's house, shot him down, then took up a stick of wood and burst his brains out; then they went on firing, killing a great many of them; it seems as if every living Negro was fired upon. They went all day all night, while the city was under siege, it was under military rule.*"

House to House Terror Reigned

Indeed, this was a well-coordinated white domestic terrorist attack on black bodies and their community. It was an illegal power grab, white men with guns marching through the streets of Dark town, going door to door, firing at them as if shooting rabbits. As Rev Kirk recalled, *sixty or more shots would be fired at the target and it would be impossible for his escap*e. When the shooting stopped, an estimated 200 fatalities were counted. Some bodies were burned and charred beyond recognition. The previous statement was a vivid description of the white terrorist attack on black bodies and their community. Terrorism against blacks never ended with slavery. The ripples of time are replete with such atrocities. If we only recognize and reveal America's true history and character, only then can the healing start and reconciliation begin.

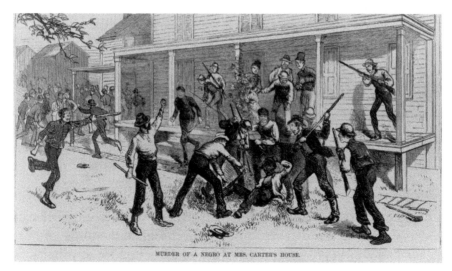

MURDER OF A NEGRO AT MRS. CARTER'S HOUSE.

White terrorists going house to house attacking black bodies

Conversely, the black survivors and community maintained that the event was a "massacre." A survivor of the incident who fled the city, Rev. Charles S. Morris, told his account of the event before the International Association of Colored Clergymen in January 1899:

"Nine Negroes massacred outright; a score wounded and hunted like partridges on the mountain; one man, brave enough to fight against such odds would be hailed as a hero anywhere else, was given the privilege of running the gauntlet up a broad street, where he sank ankle deep in the sand, while crowds of men lined the sidewalks and riddled him with a pint of bullets as he ran bleeding past their doors; another Negro shot twenty times in the back as he scrambled empty handed over a fence; thousands of women and children fleeing in terror from their humble homes in the darkness of the night ... crouched in terror from the vengeance of those who, in the name of civilization, and with the benediction of the ministers of the Prince of Peace."

Consequently, the final stages of this coup were executed on November 13, 1898 when the black and white public officials were forcibly and illegally removed from office. The mayor, police chief, health inspector, alderman and their policemen were removed and forcibly exiled from Wilmington. In their place were appointed ex-confederate soldiers and former patty rollers. Furthermore, the black owners of stores that had not been destroyed were driven out of town with guns pointed at their heads. Chesnutt's voice exposed this vulgar theft of power and wanton disregard for black life in an era when Black Lives did not Matter. He unearthed truth and gave it voice when all voice was silent..

When the <u>Washington Post</u> claimed it was a race riot caused by Negroes, Chesnutt let the world know that *"Upon a helpless people were unleashed a shameful form of terror that included an activated state militia who executed the use of rapid-fire colt machine guns mounted on carriages along with 12mm cannons"*. He let the world know that thousands were driven from their homes and out of Wilmington while their businesses and homes were destroyed or illegally confiscated.

After the coup, the mob swelled to nearly 2,000 men who then terrorized the city. Backed by the **newly instated racist police force and state militia and armed with guns and a military grade Colt Machine Gun** capable of firing 420 .23-calibre bullets a minute, the mob killed at least 60 Black residents, though many historians say the number could be well into the hundreds.

It was official, domestic white terrorism had officially merged with city and state policing. The **Wilmington City Police department and the North Carolina state militia** were now partners in crime. But this was only a dress rehearsal for the Red Summers when the blood of African Americans would flow even more in the streets of America.

The Prelude to Red Summer

Chesnutt's novel <u>*The Marrow of Tradition*</u> was the first literary work of art in novel form to spawn the term 'whiteness', with these three ingredients: white terrorism, property, and white power/privilege. These were the main ingredients involved in the Wilmington massacre. The terrorist mob violence used against the African American community in Wilmington, the removal of blacks from office and the destruction and confiscation of black-owned properties, and the brutality against black bodies was the storyline and truly represented the white supremacist methodology as they reclaimed white privilege and power.

Moreover, through the eyes and voice of Chesnutt we see a kaleidoscope of the true political landscape of the early 20th century America. It is a landscape that refuses to, under any circumstances, share power with the children and grandchildren of slavery. Their fathers and grandfathers, having endured the wrath of a system of slavery so hateful in its application of violence to black flesh, these bodies had to again suffer at the hands of white supremacists. All the gains made by the children of slavery during post-Reconstruction were being taken away.

Under those circumstances at the turn of the 19th century, a permanent pattern of racial violence in the form of white domestic terrorism began to emerge. White terrorist attacks were directed against entire African American communities in their attempts to close the wealth gap between the races.

Black efforts to combat racial violence against black bodies during the lynching era spawned many important Black organizations, including the nation's most effective and long standing, the National Association for the Advancement of Colored People (NAACP). The NAACP was formed in direct response to domestic white terrorist attacks in Springfield, Illinois, in 1908—an outbreak of violence that shocked America and demonstrated that lynching and white domestic terrorism was not only a tool of the South but was spreading throughout the country. When the NAACP officially launched in 1910, it made lynching a primary focus in 1912. By 1919, it had 310 chapters, boasting 91,203 members nationwide. Black scholar and activist W. E. B. Du Bois served as editor of the NAACP news magazine *The Crisis*. The NAACP would be a major force in the coming months as domestic white terrorism would continue to gather force and visit the city of East St. Louis, IL in 1917.

CHAPTER 5

THE BIRTH OF RED SUMMER:
THE EAST ST. LOUIS MASSACRE

THE BIRTH OF RED SUMMER
THE EAST ST. LOUIS MASSACRE, 1917

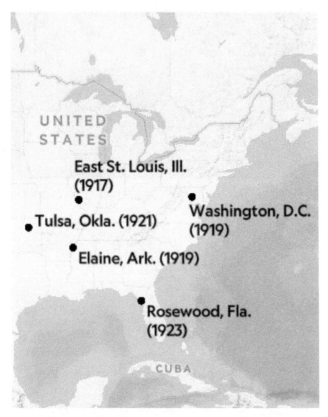

The rising tide of Red Summer and White Terrorism

A Black man lay half-conscious in the street after being beaten by a white mob during the East St. Louis Massacre of 1917. As the man tried to get up, a well-dressed white man standing behind him *"lifted a flat stone in both hands and hurled it upon his neck,"* wrote a reporter for the <u>St. Louis Post-Dispatch</u> on July 3, 1917. For 90 minutes on the evening of July 3, the reporter witnessed white mobs, according to his report *"destroying the life of every discoverable black man."* The gruesome displays of white domestic terrorism and racial violence would be among some of the worst the United States would ever see consistently over a stretch of time.

Black Man pulled off a trolley in East St. Louis and beaten to death.

Domestic white terrorists launched a reign of racial terror throughout the U.S. that historians say may have stretched from 1917 to 1943, ending with the city of Detroit. During that period, known as the Red Summers, at least 97 lynching's were recorded, thousands of Black people were killed, thousands of Black-owned homes and businesses were burned to the ground. The years 1919-23, labeled "The Red Summer" saw the greatest period of white domestic terrorist violence Amerikkka has ever known. Robert Gibson's chronology found in the *Negro Holocaust* makes the point succinctly: during that summer, there were 26 attacks against blacks in such cities as Chicago, IL, Washington, DC; Elaine,

Arkansas: Charleston, SC; Knoxville and Nashville TN; Longview Texas; and Omaha, Nebraska. Thousands of Blacks were killed in these attacks and tens of thousands were wounded and left homeless.

The Red Summer (African American blood flowing in the streets of America) label was the creation of James Weldon Johnson, an esteemed writer and composer who also wrote the <u>Negro National Anthem</u>. He was the executive director of the NAACP and led the fight for federal anti-lynching laws. Johnson so named the period because of the rise in domestic white terrorism from 1917 to 1923. To put it in proper historical context, whites felt threatened by the influx of blacks from the South. *"They wanted to keep blacks in subordinate positions, so they do not dare assert their equality or autonomy,"* said David Krugler, a professor of history at University of Wisconsin-Platteville.

The Red Summer also coincided with the resurgence of the Ku Klux Klan and that resurgence was propelled by increased Black resistance to injustice. Some called it the rise of the "New Negro," no longer subservient to the white power structure who wished to implement a new form of neo-slavery. Black soldiers returning from World War I were expecting the human rights they had fought for abroad—rights for which they were willing to die defending at home. Black veterans refused upon their return to accept injustice, inequality, and brutality by a white racist infrastructure. *"But by the God of heaven,"* wrote W.E.B. Du Bois, co-founder of the NAACP and author of <u>The Souls of Black Folk</u>, *"we are cowards and jackasses if now that the war is over, we do not marshal every ounce of our brain and brawn to fight a sterner, longer, more unbending battle against the forces of hell in our own land. We return. We return from fighting. We return fighting."* Our Black brothers were determined to reclaim and protect their black bodies and determine the freedoms of their own space and time.

The birth of Red Summer had its inception in East St. Louis on July 1, 1917. The massacre saw the indiscriminate killing of men, women and children. Mobs burned people and buildings while, shooting, and lynching. The estimated casualties ranged from 39 to over 200. According to firsthand accounts, the conflict started when armed black men shot two white police officers after mistaking them for armed night riders who had been indiscriminately terrorizing and shooting up black neighborhoods after dark.

Following the events in East St. Louis, a Congressional report, concluded that the Mayor Fred Mollman, the City Council and the Police Department bore responsibility for the conditions leading up to the massacre. The owners of the great corporations whose plants were in and around East St. Louis lived in other cities. They pocketed their dividends without concern for the municipal dishonesty that wasted the taxes, without a thought for the thousands of their own workmen, black and white, who lived in squalor, the victims of poverty, disease, and long hours of labor.

The greed that made crooks of the politicians made money grabbers of the manufacturers. They pitted white labor against black and drove organized labor from their plants. All this stirred the fires of race hatred until it finally culminated in arson and murder.

Mayor Mollman surrounded himself with advisers who were familiar with the game of politics and helped put him in office. They courted local leadership from the Democratic Party who feared the influx of blacks from the South who voted Republican and would shift the balance of political power in East St Louis. Their business first was to elect a man who would be subservient; one who would stoke the flames of racial hatred and might look the other way if a friend put a hand into the public treasury. They needed a man who would stand between them and the indignant taxpayer; someone who would promise fairness but perform for the economic interest of the rich; personally honest, perhaps, but weak and easily influenced by people who were able to dictate his policies and rob the municipality. In the history of politics in this country there had never has been a more corrupt administration than East St. Louis at that time. Such was the backdrop leading up to the East St Louis Massacre.

On July 3, Carlos F. Hurd, a staff reporter for the St. Louis Post-Dispatch, published the earliest and gruesome reports from the area. He reported that many white Americans, *"often dressed in suits and house clothes, roamed the streets looking for black residents to terrorize. He was even shocked by the calmness of their demeanor as they brutally killed black people."* These were not drunken, dispassionate trouble-makers; *"they were working people who were killing black people for fun. And they were doing so in the most sickening of ways."* The final death toll according to the NAACP was estimated between 100 and 200 blacks. They were buried in mass graves. (see image below).

Mass gravesite of black victims in East St. Louis

Hurd noted that the term "mob" did not quite make sense with the scene at hand. *"A mob is passionate. A mob follows one man or a few men blindly; a mob sometimes takes chances,"* he wrote. *"The East St. Louis affair, as I saw it, was a manhunt, conducted on a sporting basis. I saw one of these men, covered with blood and half conscious, raise himself on his elbow, and look feebly about, when a young man, standing directly behind him, lifted a flat stone in both hands and hurled it upon his neck,"* Hurd wrote.

W.E.B. Du Bois called the white terrorist attack "The Massacre of East St, Louis" in the September edition of, *The Crisis*, the official publication of the NAACP. He detailed accounts of babies that were torn from their mother's arms, much like during slavery, and thrown into burning flames. He also decried how some blacks were trapped in their homes and business as the structures were set on fire. Other accounts described execution-style shootings as black fled from their homes and place of business. One of the victims interviewed was Narcis Gurley, 71, shown in the picture below. She had lived in her home for 30 years and was afraid to leave her home as it was set ablaze by white terrorists. She was so fearful for her life that it was not until the blazing walls fell in that she fled with serious burns to her hands and arms. Indeed, this is one of millions of examples throughout the ripples of time of the desecration of our black bodies. The true scope and horror of this white terrorist attack on black citizens was given voice by W.E.B. Du Bois and suffrage activist Martha Gruening. They traveled to East St. Louis and interviewed victims and took the above photos for history to witness the desecration of black bodies and their communities, and to show the world the demons of white supremacy.

MARGIE OURLEY IT NEXT BIRTHDAY. LIVED IN HER HOME 90 YEARS. AFRAID TO COME OUT TILL THE BLAZING WALLS FELL IN.

Black homes and businesses destroyed.

These attacks were not only leveled against black bodies but also their businesses and homes. The picture above shows only a portion of the 200 homes and businesses destroyed by domestic terrorism on American soil against its citizens of color. The racial tensions in the U.S. and in East St. Louis were rooted in systemic inequality, and the antagonisms of white privilege and grievance. The area around East St. Louis had become a mecca for black Americans both fleeing the Jim Crow South and seeking economic opportunities in the booming World War I industries that were producing goods and services for the war machine. Tycoons like Andrew Carnegie and Andrew Mellon were heavily invested in the factories in the region, which was a mass production line and conduit for the wartime goods needed for America's efforts during World War 1.

"Thousands of black people from the South moved north to work in war factories. East St. Louis's black population, 6,000 strong in 1910, nearly doubled by 1917," according to the <u>St. Louis Post Dispatch</u>. These growing populations not only brought with them skills and a desire for mobility, but a new sense of power and collective numbers that created tense competition for employment, housing, and public resources in the city. White grievance was certainly front and center reflecting the tension between the races during these ripples of time as blacks sought to close the wealth gap between the races.

In fact, the city was a hotbed for racial tension and violence before the terror attacks. For years preceding July 1917, East St. Louis was experiencing political, economic and racial antagonism between white privileged political leaders who felt threatened by growing black votes and the political influence in the city. When white political leaders and their allies were met with resistance in securing political power over the growing black political machines in East St. Louis, terror and violence was increasingly used as a weapon.

The racially inspired terror attacks and — violence and riots meant to target a particular ethnic group — are rarely described as such. Just because these histories are denied or sweep under the rug only becomes apparent, we relive them in the moment in different ways. Many of the same struggles for political and economic freedom, social justice and the protection from the rule of law, that were alive in 1917, still exist today. Least we do not forget that East St. Louis is only a 20-minute drive to Ferguson Missouri where an unarmed Michael Brown was shot and killed by a cop Darren Wilson in 2014. The chameleon just keeps changing its colors in ripples of time.

Unfortunately, East St. Louis is not unique. There are sites of persistent racial trauma all over the country, traumas we have yet to fully expose and confront. By understanding and unearthing this history, we may come to terms with the never-ending struggle of justice for black Americans and the fights we have yet to wage in the United States.

*A fitting portrait of a sitting President, Woodrow Wilson ignoring the pleas of
Black America During the East St. Louis Massacre*

CHAPTER 6
THE REIGN OF DOMESTIC
WHITE TERRORISM SPREAD NATIONWIDE

Civil Rights Heritage Trial Induction Ceremony Honored Elaine 12

Black Prisoners Taken by National Guard

Washington, D.C., 1919. One of the first Black men killed during the Red Summer violence in the city was Randall Neal, a 22-year-old veteran who had just returned home from World War 1. According to the <u>Equal Justice Initiative,</u> Neal's killing sparked the "D.C. Race Riot of 1919," *which began on July 19. Black veterans organized and retaliated against the attack on Neal and others, as if in battle. In the negro district along U Street from Seventh to Fourteenth streets," reported the Washington Post, "Negroes began early in the evening to take vengeance for assaults on their race in the downtown district the night before."*

Domestic terror attacks were waged throughout the streets of the nation's Capital according to firsthand accounts, reaping a death toll of four and a list of wounded running into the hundreds, the *Washington Times* reported on July 22. *"Bands of whites and blacks hunted each other like clansmen throughout the night, the blood-feud growing steadily. From nightfall to nearly dawn ambulances bore their steady stream of dead and wounded to hospitals."*

President Woodrow Wilson ordered federal troops into the city to quell the violence. Certainly, we in the Black Community remember the same Woodrow Wilson who used the State Room in the White House to premier the Ku Klux Klan's movie, <u>Birth of a Nation</u>, a propaganda tool used as a recruitment drive for the Klan. The airing of this movie, with Wilson's blessing, grew Klan memberships close to 3 million. The movie storyline was of a beastly black man raping the frightened white damsel in distress. The world saw this perversion of reality as the black victim was hung for his crime. So sorry, back to the Washington D.C. attack on the black community. What is remembered during this ripple of time was gunfire, but it was friendly fire. Black men organized into sniper units, taking back their bodies and refusing to be brutalized by white fiends in human bodies. Stand your ground…and they did!

Another place in time, throughout the ripples of time where black bodies were denied their right to reclaim their bodies, their right to walk this earth as free and sentient human beings, tasting the sweetness of life instead of its strange, bitter fruit.

Elaine, Arkansas, 1919

Strange Fruit Hanging from a Popular Tree

Southern trees, bearing strange fruit, blood on leaves, and blood at the roots,
Black bodies Swinging in the Southern breeze

Strange fruit hanging from the popular trees

Them bulging eyes, And the twisted mouth, scent of Magnolia, clean and fresh.

Black bodies Hanging from the popular tree.

Strange Fruit Song by Billie Holiday

What occurred in Elaine, Arkansas was and is all our yesterdays. Its truth stood naked to the world, a story so horrific it also had to be told by Gerald Lambert, a white man and the founder of Listerine. Others also described the barbarism of cutting off the ears or toes from dead black bodies as souvenirs and dragging their bodies through the streets of Elaine; how soldiers brought a suspected union leader to his company store for interrogation, poured kerosene over his body and tossed a match.

Lambert owned 21,000 acres near Elaine and he, saw white men spread throughout the woods, firing at any suspicious person. *"A steel gondola car was hauled back and forth on the railroad track,"* he said, adding, *"the men inside firing from the shelter of the steel walls of the car,"* *shooting black* people.

In the summer of 1918, a new Union was founded by Black Delta native named Robert Hill. The union was called the Progressive Farmers and Household Union of America. Represented by a local attorney by the name of Ulysses S Bratton, the Union challenged the unfair practices of local landowners whose practices typified those of the sharecropping system, which kept the sharecroppers in perpetual debt. When the landowners refused to give the lawyer itemized records of their crops, a lawsuit was threatened, and what followed was one of the worst white domestic terror attacks in America's history of racial injustice.

Billie Holiday, a singer who was truly representative of the spirit of her times, captured the horrors and the brutality of white domestic terrorism during the era of Red Summer. Her rendition of *Strange Fruit* became the rallying cry for the protest movement against the horrors of white domestic terrorism personified in the hanging of black bodies. Though her song was released 16 years after the end of Red Summer, there were still lynchings and terror attacks during the period in which she made the song a national anthem to those who suffered such a horrific fate. In 1939, today was yesterday and all our todays are yesterdays, for 146,365 yesterday's we have been the victims of such egregious crimes. And until history uncovers these crimes against our black bodies and white America understands and owns the barbarity, nothing will ever change. The ripples of time. Count them – 146,365 days (and counting) of pure hell on these shores since 1619.

Elaine Arkansas was only one raindrop fertilizing the American soil with the blood dripping from our desecrated Black Bodies.

The magnolia tree is widespread throughout the South where much of this racial terrorism took place. It is the state tree of Mississippi and the state flower of Mississippi and Louisiana. It is a symbol of the beauty that the land possesses and is in direct contrast to the brutality inflicted on its Black Native sons/daughters.

So, my beloved people, that was how I was awakened from my nightmare during that ripple in time, another midnight of sorrow came once again, and I have no consolation but my flowing tears, and nothing to comfort me until our tormentors recognize the value of our precious bodies. My soul, which suffers through your pain, is once again saddened by the events in Elaine, Arkansas. Our sister Ida B. Wells' voice echoes the plight of millions of our souls who are subject to the violence of our tormentors. It was her voice that awakened me when I heard her say, *"Our country's national crime is lynching. It is not the creature of an hour, the sudden outburst of uncontrolled fury, or the unspeakable brutality of an insane mob. It represents the cool, calculating deliberation of intelligent people who openly avow that there is an "unwritten law" that justifies them in putting human beings to death without complaint under oath, without trial by jury, without opportunity to make defense, and without right of appeal."* As has been the case, America, ever since you brought us to these shores of horror and pain, we once again faced your demons from hell, this time in Elaine, Arkansas.

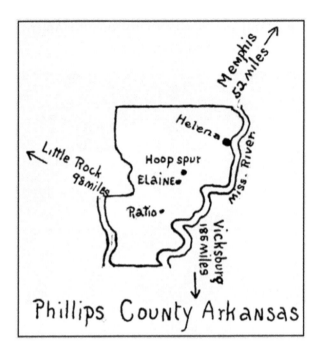

Phillips County Arkansas

The accounts that best captured the unfolding events of those sharecroppers under attack came from our beloved sister Wells. One of the convicted 12 wrote to her from prison, requesting help. Courageously, she dressed up as a sharecropper and went to Arkansas. There she interviewed the 12 prisoners accused of murder, their wives, and many others.

Wells gathered testimonies describing the sheer horror of the domestic terror attack and massacre from those who endured, lived and put a voice to their stories. She then chronicled and published the events in her book, <u>*The Arkansas Race Riots*</u>. One union member, Ed Ware, told her that *"Men had fired into the Hoop Spur church, killing several people, then burned it down the next day with bodies inside."* When he returned home, 150 men ransacked his house, seizing his union meeting minutes and his Masonic lodge books. As they surrounded his house, another man inside, *Charlie Robinson, tried to run away. He was elderly and handicapped and ran too slowly. They shot him and left him to die."* They stole all of Ware's personal belongings, including his cow, two mules, one horse, a farm wagon, his Ford car and various household goods. He lost 121 acres of cotton and corn.

Unlike Wilmington, North Carolina or Opelousas, LA, black bodies were not desecrated in Elaine in order to deny them the right to free and fair elections as guaranteed under constitutional law after the end of slavery. In this case, it was because our people wished to choose how the fruits, or profits of their labor would be equitably distributed to their families and their community. They exercised their right to self-determination while working towards their well-being, not that of the Planter Aristocracy. They were steadfast in their attempts to address and close the wealth gap created during slavery while leveling the playing field between the races.

Late in the evening of September 30, black sharecropper families came together to determine the rights for such control over their economic enterprise as sharecroppers. Gathering in the Hoop Spur church near Elaine, they came to discuss their membership of an organization called the **Progressive Farmers and Household Union.** Sharecropping or land leasing was another form of slavery, or neo-slavery. The progressive Union would allow it to negotiate and secure a better price for the cotton that had been planted and picked by sharecroppers and then forcibly sold to the landowners below market value. The 1919 yield had been extremely high and would produce a high degree of profitability, and in turn increase cash flow. The sharecroppers intended to hire a lawyer to make it so. It would help them secure a fair price for the cotton they picked, and then buy land. Unlike the narrative that would later be created, black people were simply demanding full rights of citizenship and justice, not only before the law but in line with the value of their labors. What transpired was that blacks who had returned home from the war and were emboldened by their experience, were demanding their rightful place in society. This was seen as a direct challenge to the white-dominated planter aristocracy in Phillips County.

Workers also had to buy food, clothing, household wares, tools, seeds and fertilizer at the plantation commissary, which charged exorbitant interest rates. The inflated prices always exceeded that which was paid for their labor. So was the system of sharecropping, just another form of slavery?

At 11 p.m. on September 30th, the terror attack began as a group of white terrorists burst into the church. When Black guards returned the fire, they killed a white agent of the Missouri Pacific Railroad. News of the shooting quickly reached the county seat of Helena. Immediately thereafter, the false narrative was created: blacks were allegedly uprising in Elaine and attacking whites. During the early morning hours of October 1st, the local sheriff sent armed white veterans from the American Legion post to suppress what was now called a black insurrection.

More importantly, calls went out to the governor for **federal troops**, and now the overkill was in motion. Military tactics were employed as all lines of communication in and out of Elaine were neutralized (telephone lines to Elaine were cut). Indeed, calls went out to over 1,000 white domestic terrorists, from all over the state, including Mississippi, to join those forces, including sheriffs and other police forces to put down the alleged insurrection. It was effectively an invasion of armed white terrorists from in and out of state. By day's end, countless black women, men and children had been slaughtered, some of their bodies desecrated beyond recognition.

It would not be until the following morning when Gov. Charles H. Brough of Arkansas and a World War I veteran, Col. Isaac Jencks, personally escorted 583 soldiers, including a machine gun battalion, from Camp Pike in Little Rock, the Arkansas state capital, to Elaine. This search and destroy mission would become a scorched earth strategy. First Colonel Jencks sent all the white women and children to Helena by train. He then ordered all blacks to lay down any weapon in their possession and authorized the killing of black insurgents who did not comply. Then the real massacre began for the next five days, Colonel Jencks and his troops, assisted by vigilantes, hunted black people over a 200-mile radius. They scorched and burned homes with families inside, and slaughtered and tortured other individuals. The troops were aided by seven machine guns.

On October 7, Colonel Jencks declared victory and began to draw down his troops. The captured men and women he deemed insurrectionists were taken to the Phillips County jail in Helena. On October 31, a grand jury indicted 122 black men and women for offenses ranging from murder to night riding. A jury convicted 12 black men of the murders of three white men, even though two of the deaths had occurred from white people accidentally shooting each other in a frenzy. The "confessions" of the black men had been secured through torture and intimidation. Black people were thus blamed, sentenced and jailed for crimes they did not commit. The fix was in and the defendants and the Black Community bore the blame.

TO THE NEGROES
OF PHILLIPS COUNTY
Helena, Ark., Oct. 7, 1919

The trouble at Hoop Spur and Elaine has been settled.

Soldiers now here to preserve order will return to Little Rock within a short time.

No innocent negro has been arrested, and those of you who are at home and at work have no occasion to worry.

All you have to do is to remain at work just as if nothing had happened.

Phillips County has always been a peaceful, lawabiding community, and normal conditions must be restored right away.

STOP TALKING!
Stay at home---Go to work---Don't worry!

F. F. KITCHENS, Sheriff   COMMITTEE
Edward Bevens J. C. Meyers S. Straub E. M. Allen
T. W. Keesee D. A. Keeshan Amos Jarman
H. D. Moore J. G. Knight Jno. L. Moore E. C. Hornor

Nicholls Print, Helena, Ark.

The white propaganda machine produced a narrative that resembled those during ripples in the time stream dating back to slavery. In their view *"a deliberately planned insurrection"* had occurred. Instead of slaves planning an insurrection from massa's plantation during slavery, it was black sharecroppers who had intended to murder the plantation owners to seize the land. The consensus blamed outside agitators for stirring up ignorant sharecroppers, because, according to The Enlightenment thinkers, blacks did not have the intelligence to identify the wrong suffering they were enduring. Fortunately, there were other eyes that laid bare the truth. According to several accounts from white witnesses, both vigilantes and the troops committed acts of barbarism. A local schoolteacher saw *"28 black people killed, their bodies thrown into a pit and burned,"* and *"16 African Americans killed, their bodies hanging from a bridge outside of Helena."*

A Memphis reporter described events on Oct. 2 after the troops had arrived. Troops and vigilantes, he noted, went into the canebrakes in search of "negro desperadoes," *leaving dead bodies "lying in the road a few miles outside of the city. Enraged citizens fired at the bodies of the dead negroes as they rode out of Helena toward Elaine."*

After killing the elderly woman, they pulled her dress over her body and dragged her body down a road," Krugler said. "The corpse was desecrated. This was done to send a message.

Our beloved sister Ida B. Wells described how many families described running into the woods for safety from bloodthirsty mobs, hoping to surrender themselves to the federal troops for safety. Instead, the troops either shot or arrested them. Vigilantes from Mississippi seized another union member, Lula Black, and her four children from her house, knocked her down, pistol whipped and kicked her, then took her to jail. Carrying an axe with their guns, they then moved to another home, where they murdered yet another union member, Frances Hall. In a final act of disrespect, they tied her dress over her head and left her body on the side of the road for several days. (See her picture in the frame above)

Seventy-nine-year-old Ed Coleman had remained at home with his wife when people fleeing Hoop Spur came to his house and warned them to leave. As they ran from the posse, *the Colemans saw his neighbor, Jim Miller, and his family burned alive in their house. After hiding for two days in the woods, the Colemans returned home to find dead bodies of women and children scattered about their community.* Families of union members found no welcome when they returned to their homes. *The wife of Frank Moore* had hidden for four weeks. When she came back to her neighborhood, a plantation manager, Billy Archdale, told her *"if she did not leave, he would kill her, burn her up, and no one would know where she was."* Most of those who survived found their homes emptied of possessions that later appeared in white peoples' homes.

Sister Wells provided hard evidence of the massacre in the Arkansas Race Riot, but it took the Supreme Court to expose the truth and bring it to national attention. In Moore v. Dempsey in 1923, the court overturned the convictions of six of the Elaine 12, arguing that the confessions had been secured through torture. The trial had occurred in a setting dominated by a mob spirit, violating the prisoners' right to due process. The decision by the justices was aided by two white men involved in the massacre who reversed their previous testimonies. They now verified that the planters had gone to the Hoop Spur church to destroy the union and that the posse had killed their own men, instead of the black people who had been accused. They described the wholesale massacre of hundreds of unarmed and defenseless black people, and the torture used to secure confessions.

On the other hand, the NAACP in New York, which had sent Field Secretary Walter White to investigate the events in Elaine, contested such allegations from the outset. White wrote in the *Chicago Daily News* on October 19, 1919, that the belief there had been an insurrection was "only a figment of the imagination of Arkansas whites and not based on fact." He said, "White men in Helena told me that more than one hundred Negroes were killed." This work also challenged allegations of an insurrection and documented the torture and other depredations the prisoners had suffered.

Within days of the initial shoot-out, 285 African Americans were taken from the temporary stockades to the jail in Helena, the county seat, although the jail had space for only forty-eight. Two white members of the Phillips County posse, T. K. Jones and H. F. Smiddy, stated in sworn affidavits in 1921 that they committed acts of torture at the Phillips County jail and named others who had also participated in the torture. On October 31, 1919, the Phillips County grand jury charged 122 African Americans with crimes stemming from the racial disturbances. The charges ranged from murder to night -riding, a charge akin to terroristic threatening (as defined by **Act 112 1909)**. The trials began the next week, with John Elvis Miller leading the prosecution. White attorneys from

Helena were appointed by Circuit Judge J. M. Jackson to represent the first twelve black men to go to trial. Attorney Jacob Fink, who was appointed to represent Frank Hicks, admitted to the jury that he had not interviewed any witnesses. He made no motion for a change of venue, nor did he challenge a single prospective juror, taking the first twelve called. By November 5, 1919, the first twelve black men given trials had been convicted of murder and sentenced to die in the electric chair. As a result, sixty-five others quickly entered plea-bargains and accepted sentences of up to twenty-one years for second-degree murder. Others had their charges dismissed or ultimately were not prosecuted.

In Little Rock and at the headquarters of the NAACP in New York, efforts began to fight the death sentences handed down in Helena, led in part by Scipio Africanus Jones, the leading black attorney of his era in Arkansas, and Edgar Mahaney. Jones began to raise money in the black community in Little Rock for the defense of the "Elaine Twelve," as the convicted men came to be known. The twelve men were: Fred Moore, Frank Hicks, Ed Hicks, Joe Knox, Paul Hall, Ed Coleman, Alfred Banks, Ed Ware, William Wordlaw, Albert Giles, Joe Fox, and John Martin.

At the same time, the New York offices of the NAACP, upon the advice of Arkansas attorney Ulysses S. Bratton, hired the Little Rock law firm of George C. Murphy, a former attorney general and candidate for governor, as counsel for the twelve men. Even at the age of seventy-nine, Murphy, a former Confederate officer and Arkansas attorney general, was considered one of the best trial attorneys in Arkansas. By late November, Jones was working with Murphy's firm to save the Elaine Twelve.

Their initial task was to appeal the sentences given to the Elaine Twelve and ask for a new trial based on errors committed by the trial court. Gov. Brough issued a stay of the executions to permit an appeal to the Arkansas Supreme Court after the motions were denied. For the next five years, the cases of the Elaine Twelve were mired in litigation as Murphy and Jones fought to save the men from death. They secured new trials for six of the men, known as the *Ware* defendants, based on the fact that the trial judge had not required jurors to indicate the degree of murder on their ballot forms. The convictions of the other six men, known as the *Moore* defendants, were affirmed.

The cases of the Elaine Twelve were litigated on two separate tracks. The re-trials of the *Ware* defendants began on May 3, 1920. During the trials, Murphy became ill, and Jones became the principal counsel. Hostility toward him was so great from local white residents that, out of fear for his life, he was said to sleep at a different black family's house every night during the trials. The convictions were again affirmed. Gov. Brough once again stayed their executions until the Arkansas Supreme Court could again review the cases. Ultimately, the *Ware* defendants were freed by the Arkansas Supreme Court after two terms of court had passed, and the state of Arkansas made no move to re-try the men.

The *Moore* defendants were granted a new hearing after the U.S. Supreme Court, in the case of *Moore vs Dempsey*, ruled that the original proceedings in Helena had been a "mask," and that the state of Arkansas had not provided "a corrective process" that would have allowed the defendants to vindicate their constitutional right to due process of law on appeal.

Instead of pursuing a new hearing in federal court, in March 1923, Scipio Jones entered into negotiations to have the *Moore* defendants released. To be released, the men would have to plead guilty to second-degree murder and a sentence of five years from the date they were first incarcerated in the Arkansas State Penitentiary. Finally, on January 14, 1925, Governor Thomas McRae ordered the release of the *Moore* defendants by granting them indefinite furloughs after they had pleaded guilty to second-degree murder. In the interim, Jones had secured the release of the other Elaine Defendants.

The murders, thefts, violence and terror continued long after the troops had gone, and the convicted men had been released. No white person was ever charged, or any trials held for anyone that took part in the mass lynching. Time and time again we witness the double standard in the legal justice system. The perpetrators of the crimes are found to be not guilty, while the victims of the violence receive no justice for the heinous acts committed against them, and sometimes they are charged with the crime committed against their own black bodies. The basis for these heinous crimes was the reassertion of white supremacy after veterans returned home from World War I. The white militias wanted to send a message that they were going to keep the Blacks in their 'place.' But what made 1919 unique was the willingness and fortitude of the Black sharecroppers and their community to engage in armed resistance against white oppression and domestic white terrorism.

ELAINE RIOTERS, WHO WERE BROUGHT
TO PEN TO PAY DEATH PENALTY IN CHAIR

Left to right: Ed Hicks, Ed Coleman, Ed Ware, Frank Moore, Paul Hall, Albert Giles, Joe Knox, Frank Hicks, Joe Fox, Alfred Banks Jr., John Martin and William Wordlow.

As I assess the damage done to our bodies throughout these ripples of time, I cannot help wondering to what extent do the American people truly understand the harsh brutalities black Americans have endured as human beings? The descendants of the massacre have begun to organize to make their stories heard, and The Elaine Legacy Center, in conjunction with the Dewitt Proctor Conference, held a Truth Hearing on February 8, 2019 where 12 commissioners heard several descendants convey powerful stories of the massacre handed down through their families. Many family members wept as they told of murder and the desecration of black bodies, land theft, forced migration and the horrors of living in a region where fear of retribution silenced people over generations. They, like so many black souls, seek redress, not in the form of apologies but a recognition of the harm done, and how generations continue to suffer the consequences of their actions. All we have ever wanted was simply the right to life itself.

Race relations in this area of Arkansas are currently quite strained for a number of reasons, including the events of 1919. The conference on the matter in Helena in 2000 resulted in no closure for the people in Phillips County. On September 29, 2019, a memorial to those who died during the massacre was dedicated in downtown Helena-West Helena. On November 5, 2019, the Elaine Twelve were memorialized on the Arkansas Civil Rights Heritage Trail in Little Rock.

Certainly, the desecration of black bodies is the benchmark for our suffering as they flow through generations the former enslaved. America cannot address its transgressions until it understands that the desecration of the body manifests

94

itself in the inequality, poverty, inadequate education, inadequate housing, inadequate healthcare, unequal access to the competitive job market, the racially biased criminal injustice system, and the limited life chances of black people. It is our psycho-social dilemma created from slavery as we struggle to close the wealth gap created out of slavery while contending with the intergenerational trauma of white domestic terrorism and police state sponsored violence.

Until the nation confronts and acknowledges this history, the past based on wanton violence and the degradation of the rights of its black citizenry, then nothing will ever change. The obligations of the past weigh heavily upon the present. Unfortunately, America has yet to reconcile its brutal past. Elaine was, as was Tulsa the largest massacre of black people in post-Civil War history, yet no federal investigation was ever conducted. A history buried among the many stories of American atrocities committed against black bodies and Native Americans. But I guess America's attitude, until she comes to terms with her sins, will be reflected in a statement by the former Republican Senate Majority leader Mitch McConnell. While speaking from the floor of the Senate in 2020, McConnell said he didn't see the need to apologize for "something that happened 150 years ago, for whom none of us currently living is responsible."

White supremacy has had a detrimental economic and psychological impact on African American families through the centuries. The legacy of slavery is reproduced with every generation in which certain classes of Americans have been denied the right to vote, the right to an education, the right to life itself. Along with that legacy, mothers and fathers still must pass along to their children the tools needed to navigate this violent world and make it home alive; by necessity they pass along the memories of those who did not. These memories, this vital information, can be all that parents have when the legacy of slavery has stripped them of everything else.

CHAPTER 7
THE DESTRUCTION OF BLACK WALL STREET
(MAY 31 TO JUNE 2, 1921)

The Destruction of Black Wall Street (May 31 to June 2, 1921)

Top left and Top Right:
Captured Black Citizens Taken to Interment locations

Middle photos, more black bodies marched to interment.

Bottom photos:
desecration of black bodies,
left photo charred remains, *right photo* lynching

The Destruction of Black Wall St.
WHITE DOMESTIC TERRORISM
MAY 31st – JUNE 2, 1921

The White Wind of Domestic Terrorism would blow racial hatred across Tulsa, Oklahoma in the summer of 1921. A Black elevator operator named Dick Rowland was arrested in Tulsa after a misunderstanding led to rumors that he had sexually attacked a white woman in an elevator. Though charges against Mr. Rowland were soon dropped and he was released, a white mob quickly gathered to lynch him. When the Black community banded together to help the young man leave town, the mob indiscriminately attacked the prosperous local Black residential and business district known as Greenwood. Over the next two days, the mob would kill hundreds of Black people, displace many more, and destroy the once vibrant Black Community called Black Wall St. No white terrorist was ever convicted in Tulsa, a city still haunted by the 1921 Tulsa Race Massacre, which left more than 300 Black people dead and more than 10,000 homeless.

White mobs destroyed 35 square blocks of Greenwood, a Black neighborhood that was so prosperous it was called "Black Wall Street."

Furthermore, the city of Tulsa represented another chapter in the devastating attacks against black communities in what historians call one of the worst episodes of racial violence committed against Black people in the country's history. The Tulsa Race Massacre began on May 31,1921.A mob of white men gathered outside the Tulsa courthouse, where Rowland was taken after his arrest. Black World War I veterans confronted the mob, determined to protect Rowland. A struggle ensued and a white man was shot. It sparked the murderous rage that would follow. Hundreds of white people marched on the Black neighborhood of Greenwood. Whites killed more than 300 Black people—dumping their bodies into the Arkansas River or burying them in mass graves. More than a hundred businesses were destroyed, as well as a school, a hospital, a library, and dozens of churches. More than 1,200 Black-owned houses burned. The economic losses in the Black community amounted to more than $1 million.

Walter White, who later became executive secretary of the NAACP, said in a NAACP report: *"One story was told to me by an eyewitness of five colored men trapped in a burning house. Four were burned to death. A fifth attempted to flee, was shot to death as he emerged from the burning structure, and his body was thrown back into the flames."* There were reports that white men flew airplanes above Greenwood, dropping kerosene bombs. *"Tulsa was likely the first city"* in the U.S. *"to be bombed from the air,"* according to a report by the Oklahoma Commission to Study the Tulsa Race Riot of 1921

B.C. Franklin, a lawyer in Greenwood and the father of famed historian John Hope Franklin, witnessed the massacre. *"The sidewalk was literally covered with burning turpentine balls,"* Franklin wrote in a manuscript later donated to the Smithsonian's National Museum of African American History and Culture. *"For fully forty-eight hours, the fires raged and burned everything in its path, and it left nothing but ashes and burned safes and trunks and the like that were stored in beautiful houses and businesses,"* he wrote.

Many black residents fought back, but they were greatly outnumbered and outgunned," according to Human Rights Watch, which in May of this year released a 66-page report entitled *"The Case for Reparations in Tulsa, Oklahoma: A Human Rights Argument."* At best, the Tulsa police took no action to prevent the massacre," according to the document. *"Reports indicate that some police actively participated in the violence and looting."*

Two weeks after the massacre, the Tulsa City Commission issued a report which was typical of the narratives issued in Opelousas, LA, Wilmington, NC and Elaine, Arkansas. It blamed the destruction on the Black people who lived there, not the white domestic terrorists. *"Let the blame for this Negro uprising lie right where it belongs—on those armed Negroes and their followers who started this trouble and who instigated it and any persons who seek to put half the blame on the white people are wrong,"* according to the commission. Once again, as has been the case throughout our history, the criminals criminalize their victims.

Black Wall Street burns

Greenwood, or Black Wall Street, as it was called, comprised 36 square blocks in North Tulsa. Its more than 600 businesses thrived beyond expectation. Certain whites were astonished, envious and aggrieved by its success. Known as Little Africa to the black community and Nigger Town to the KKK and other white supremacists, Greenwood's prosperousness was an affront to white privilege.

The Destruction of Black Wall Street (May 31 to June 2, 1921)

Earlier, many African Americans living in Tulsa were descendants of the displaced Maroons who were eventually defeated by President Andrew Jackson during the Seminole Wars, which ended in 1812. Forced to march from Florida, South Carolina, Georgia and West to Oklahoma on what we know as the *Trail of Tears*, many were settled on the barren Oklahoma land eventually found to be rich in oil deposits. It produced black millionaires and dozens of black businesses, which made Black Wall St. prosperous.

Black people owned oil companies and rigs. Many of them brokered oil, which created black-owned banks. Indeed, their resume was impressive, other businesses included bus lines, restaurants, chains of general stores, real estate companies, grain and feed stores, beauty salons, night clubs, hotels and movie theaters with seating capacity in the hundreds. The success of the grandchildren of slavery was astonishing and a slap in the face to white racist Oklahomans.

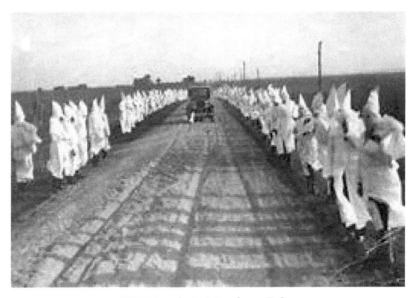

KKK Ready to March on Tulsa

For that reason, the Klan and state officials seized the moment to take down Black Wall Street. During this era, the KKK had influence in the state government here in America's bible belt. The KKK set out to systematically destroy a major black economic movement which could have emulated itself nationwide and demonstrated how to close the wealth gap while making Black communities self-sufficient. Using the alleged rape of the white woman as cover (just like in Wilmington, N.C. 23 years earlier), the KKK seized the moment. What ensued was one of the most shameful acts of violence by white domestic terrorists in America's history.

When Rowland was accused of assaulting the elevator operator, the African American community rallied around him. But when they forced the issue at the jail house, gunfire was exchanged between blacks and whites, and lasted for three nights and two days. And as was the case in Elaine, Arkansas white supremacist terrorist groups were brought in from out of state, numbering in the tens of thousands. Their para-military forces invaded Greenwood, using machine gun fire. And several airplanes were used for reconnaissance and to drop bombs on strategic targets.

Furthermore, over thirteen hundred businesses were destroyed, Black Wall Street was leveled to the ground, reduced to burned out rubble. Estimates of fatalities vary. There were roughly 12,500 black residents in Tulsa at that time. Close to 9,500 were rounded up and placed in concentration camps through the city. Some reports place the death toll in the thousands. Flatbed trucks were used to parade the stacked bodies around the city before they were taken to mass graves and dumped like garbage. The carnage was unfathomable, and the demons of racial hatred had been unleashed on Tulsa as white supremacists celebrated their destruction of Black Wall Street.

The *Tulsa Tribune* published the front-page headline "Nab Negro for Attacking Girl in Elevator." Later, Tulsa police commissioner J. M. Adkison and police chief John Gustafson were under pressure to keep law and order in Tulsa. Less than a year before, in August 1920, a white drifter, Roy Belton, had been ripped from jail by a white mob and hung in public for killing the town's favorite cab driver. Also in August 1920, in Oklahoma City, an eighteen-year-old Black youth, Claude Chandler, was lynched by a mob that featured the future mayor of Oklahoma City, O. A. Cargill.

This time, the police, fearing a lynching, moved Rowland from the regular jail to the top floor of the Tulsa County Courthouse for safekeeping. Meanwhile, the *Tulsa Tribune*'s afternoon edition fanned the flames with the headline "To Lynch Negro Tonight!" as an ugly mob began to gather outside of the Tulsa Courthouse.

As Rowland sat in jail, back at the offices of the Black newspaper, A. J. Smitherman of the Tulsa Star led an impassioned discussion about how to protect him. Smitherman's *Tulsa Star* promoted the idea of the "New Negro," independent and assertive. Smitherman had chastised Blacks for allowing the lynching of Claude Chandler the year before in Oklahoma City, and he urged the men in the room to protect Rowland and themselves.

W.E.B. DuBois had visited Tulsa in March as the NAACP protested the gruesome lynching of Henry Lowery in Arkansas. DuBois had already warned the Black veterans of World War I, in the May 1919 issue of the *Crisis*, that they would be "cowards and jackasses if now that the war is over, we do not marshal every ounce of our brain and brawn to fight a sterner, longer, more unbending battle against the forces of hell in our own land." According to the Tula's Historical Society, the events unfolded as followed, Later that afternoon at the Black-owned Williams Dreamland Theatre, sixteen-year-old Bill Williams watched as a neighbor jumped on stage and announced: "We're not going to let this happen. We're going to go downtown and stop this lynching." True to their word, an armed contingent of 25 Black men went to the Tulsa County Courthouse. Led by O. B. Mann, of Mann Brothers Grocery Store, and Black Deputy County Sheriff J. K. Smitherman (A. J.'s brother), they offered their assistance to Sheriff Willard McCullough, but he persuaded them to leave.

As the white mob reached nearly a thousand, a new contingent of 50 or more Black men, feeling anxious, arrived to protect Rowland, but they, too, were persuaded to leave at about 10:30 p.m. Then, as they walked away—according to Scott Ellsworth's interview with seventy-eight-year-old survivor Robert Fairchild—E. S. MacQueen, a bailiff and failed candidate for sheriff, grabbed a tall Black man's .45-caliber Army-issue handgun.

Then according to several chroniclers, "all hell broke loose," as the mob engaged the retreating Black men in a pitched gun battle that inched its way north toward the Frisco Railroad tracks that separated downtown from Deep Greenwood. The mob broke into downtown (white-owned) pawnshops and hardware stores to steal weapons and bullets. Tulsa law enforcement deputized and armed certain members of the mob. A disguised light-skinned African-American Tulsan overheard an ad hoc meeting of city officials plan a Greenwood invasion that night. Sheriff McCullough, hunkered down in the County Court House, kept Dick Rowland safe as the mob's fury was aimed at a Negro revolt in Greenwood. While most mob members were not deputized, the general feeling was that they were acting under the protection of the government.

The Destruction of Black Wall Street (May 31 to June 2, 1921)

After an all-night battle on the Frisco Tracks, many residents of Greenwood were taken by surprise as bullets ripped through the walls of their homes in the predawn hours. Biplanes dropped fiery turpentine bombs from the night skies onto their rooftops—the first aerial bombing of an American city in history. A furious mob of thousands of white men then surged over Black homes, killing, destroying, and snatching everything from dining room furniture to piggy banks. Arsonists reportedly waited for white women to fill bags with household loot before setting homes on fire. Tulsa police officers were identified by eyewitnesses as setting fire to Black homes, shooting residents and stealing. Eyewitnesses saw women being chased from their homes naked—some with babies in their arms—as volleys of shots were fired at them. Several Black people were tied to cars and dragged through the streets

The Oklahoma National Guard, called in by the governor to restore order, did so by joining the fray against the outnumbered and outgunned Black community. The Guard helped round up and disarm at least four thousand African Americans—men, women, and children—and marched them at gunpoint to makeshift detention camps at the Tulsa Convention Center and the McNulty Baseball Park as the mob in the early hours looted their homes.

Over the course of three days, dead bodies were stacked up on trucks and railroad cars and buried in secret around the city by white aggressors. Even afterward, few Black families had a chance to organize a funeral or mourn their dead. Many Black Tulsans simply disappeared.

Tulsa's Greenwood Cultural Center tabulates that in the span of 24 hours 35 city blocks of Black Wall Street were burned to the ground. The white mob blocked firefighters while 1,256 homes were destroyed and another 400 were looted. A massive share of people in Greenwood were left homeless. The destruction also included many businesses and community institutions: four hotels, eight churches, seven grocery stores, two Black hospitals, two candy stores, two pool halls, two Masonic lodges, real estate offices, undertakers, barber and beauty shops, doctors' offices, drugstores, auto garages, and choc joints.

Oklahoma's Tulsa Race Massacre Commission reported that 100 to 300 people were killed, though the real number might be even higher. "There's really no way of knowing exactly how many people died. We know that there were several thousand unaccounted for," Mechelle Brown, program coordinator for the Greenwood Cultural Center, told CNN during a 2016 interview.

Details are difficult to gather, because many survivors of the massacre fled the city. Among the counted dead was Dr. A. C. Jackson, a noted surgeon endorsed by the Mayo Clinic (the clinic acknowledged his prominence). Late in the battle as gunfire was sporadic, Jackson walked back to his home, after attending to victims, with his hands up. According to Tim Madigan's *The Burning: Massacre, Destruction, and the Tulsa Race Riot of 1921*, retired white Judge John Oliphant, Jackson's neighbor, testified that two young men trained their guns on the physician. "Here I am," said Jackson. "Take me." "Don't shoot him! That's Dr. Jackson," yelled Oliphant. It was too late. The most significant lesson it has taught me is that the love of race is the deepest feeling rooted in our being. . . . Every Negro was afforded the same treatment, regardless of his education or advantages. A Negro was a Negro on that day and was forced to march with his hands up for blocks. What does this teach? It should teach us to "Look Up, Lift Up and Lend a Helping Hand," and remember that we cannot rise higher than our weakest brother.

A Mississippi native who had come to Tulsa via Rochester Parrish has disappeared from the record. But the ethos and bond that empowered residents to rebuild the community was strong. The law firm of Spears, Franklin & Chappelle provided legal assistance to victims. These African-American lawyers filed claims against the city of Tulsa and against its new Fire Ordinance No. 2156, which would prevent most of the victims from rebuilding and the insurance companies from paying for damage caused by the massacre, even as white pawnshop and hardware store owners were compensated for damages to their shops. The lawyer leading the charge was Buck Colbert Franklin, the father of famed historian John Hope Franklin, the late professor emeritus at Duke University. He did not find evidence that the disaster was premeditated by city officials, but he thought they certainly took advantage of it to the detriment of the Black community.

Indeed, the KKK played its well-orchestrated hand well, with the blessing of local, state and some federal officials. White supremacists had succeeded in destroying Black Wall Street. Their movement had its beginnings in the destruction of Black economic and political empowerment in Wilmington, NC and Opelousas, LA. Now, the rising tide of white supremacy claimed another victory in Tulsa.

Undoubtedly, black voices such as Charles Chesnutt and W.E.B. Du Bois understood this rising form of white terrorism. It is pointedly expressed in their writings. In The Souls of Black Folk Du Bois addresses the inhumane ways of white savagery. *"We are not more lawless than the white race, we are more often arrested, convicted and mobbed by barbarous violence of the mob."* In Charles Chesnutt's <u>Marrow of Tradition</u> he wrote, *"The great steal was made, but their scheme still shows the mark of the burglars' tools. Sins, murderous barbarity, like chickens, come home to roost. The South will pay a fearful price for the wrong of Negro slavery; in some form or other it will doubtless reap the fruits of this latest iniquity."*

The end of post-Reconstruction and the dawn of the 20th century was exemplified by this disregard for black lives and the unleashing of these savage white terror attacks. White men were trying to restore their dominance while asserting the national ethos of segregation. It was the white man's plan to restore himself to dominance in Southern society. However legitimate the post-Reconstruction era may have been, the white male ego was moved to restore dominance to its proper place as ordained by God.

Furthermore, the insecurity of the defeated white male ego, after suffering a humiliating defeat during the Civil War, needed justification for reestablishing the moral and socio-economic fabric of the old South. White male hysteria was simply not that of rape and the assault on white women, it was about the vote, loss of political power and economic prosperity, all of which were threatened by black ascendancy. Black sexual assault was the cloak behind which disenfranchisement was hidden.

To this end, African American citizens, and former slaves for the first time, were made victims to this particular form of mass violence called white domestic terrorism. Certainly, during those enduring times while enslaved, they were exposed to the vicious and demonic nature of some white men, however, nothing compared to the wanton disregard for human life after slavery in its original form. In this hour, as the darkness of night descended on the grandchildren of slavery; as in the hours, days, weeks, months, years and centuries to come, when the depths of racial animus are stirred, the demons of racism are unleashed and the black body is no more than a lowly beast, set upon by another more brutal beast whose only interest is to kill, desecrate and destroy black bodies. Nothing compared to the wanton disregard for human life after the end of slavery's initial phase. Nothing changes in the ripples in time – only the Chameleon.

CHAPTER 8

A VOICE FROM THE RED SUMMER:
IF WE MUST DIE (CLAUDE MCKAY)

Claude McKay: Leading protest Poet of the Harlem Renaissance

In the historical context of Red Summer, white-supremacist violence against black bodies; McKay's poem was a call to rebellion against the atrocities committed by White Fiends.

IF WE MUST DIE

If we must die, let it not be like hogs
  Hunted and penned in an inglorious spot,
While round us bark the mad and hungry dogs,
  Making their mock at our accursed lot.
If we must die, oh, let us nobly die,
  So that our precious blood may not be shed
In vain; then even the monsters we defy
  Shall be constrained to honor us, though dead!

Oh, kinsmen! We must meet the common foe;
  Though far outnumbered, let us still be brave,
And for their thousand blows deal one death-blow!
  What though before us lies the open grave?
Like men we'll face the murderous, cowardly pack,
  Pressed to the wall, dying, but—fighting back!

The literary works of the American Negroes also ruthlessly exposed incidents in which the reactionary racial exponents freely accused the innocent Negroes of false crimes and used various kinds of legalized torture to put them to death and to massacre the unarmed Negroes. Many Negro authors, such as Langston Hughes in his novels "The Village"and "Father and Son", and Claude McKay in his poem "Torture", filled with indignation, thoroughly exposed the various criminal actions of the white racial exponents, who framed, tortured and massacred the innocent Negroes. In the southern part of the United States, there are various kinds of terrorist organizations which prosecute the Negroes. The most notorious is the Ku Klux Klan. In his book, "The Negroes' Reconstruction", Du Bois described the activities of the Ku Klux Klan as, "A group of organized, masked and armed men do what they please after dark in the village. On their way, they whip, shoot, harm and murder women, children and unarmed men, or they may chop off their four limbs. With brutal strength they break into homes where the people are asleep. They use pistols, rifles, knives and ropes to do what they please. Such criminal actions, which are witnessed by many, are used as a means in American presidential elections in the State of Louisiana." In the shocking "Scottsboro Case", in the City of Scottsboro, Alabama, a group of racial advocates accused nine young Negroes of the rape of two white women, even though these nine young people had never seen the two women before, and furthermore, one of the two women later denied the charge. However, these nine young Negroes were unreasonably convicted by the American reactionary authorities. . . ..

From The Messenger 1921

Through the ripples in time, I was able to witness the Red Summers and became so distraught at what I had witnessed, I laid my soul down to rest. I think my slumber may have lasted longer than it did; but I was awakened by a voice so eloquent and pained. It was the Jamaican poet, Claude McKay. When I checked my chronometer, it was 1919. By cosmic time it was about 8AM, only a few hours after the end of slavery and post-Reconstruction. In the flow of time, in that moment, as we experience the residue of slavery, constantly unfolding, I heard Claude McKay. His voice registered the same cries echoing throughout time, black bodies numb with pain, hearts broken with sorrows, continuously witnessing mangled black bodies as a backdrop to this historical stage called America.

I recalled before I fell asleep, slavery ending and President Grant along with General Sherman giving freed slaves 40 acres and a mule. Thoughts were that they were free citizens with all rights to vote and hold public office. They would have economic independence and build generational wealth. I recall the 13th, 14th and 15th amendments, which ensured their right to vote and full citizenship. I recall something called post-Reconstruction, in which the subjects were to enjoy all the rights of *We the People*. More importantly, I remember federal troops were sent to the South to ensure their protection and the implementation of all rights guaranteed by the constitution. I remember ex-slaves voted into office on a local, state and federal level. My sleep was induced by the assurance that the horrific nightmare of slavery had ended only to be awakened by the voice of Claude McKay.

To The White Fiend

*Of my black brothers **murdered** and **burnt** by you*

Like Men we'll face the murderous Cowardly Pack Pressed to the Wall, dying but Fighting Back

As I awakened, I appeared to be in a period they called the Red Summer. What happened? What had been so promising had turned into a nightmare? From the very beginning of Post-Reconstruction, white supremacy began to undermine ex-slaves' newfound freedom. Black codes were implemented. These restrictive laws were designed to limit the freedom of African Americans and ensure their availability as a cheap labor force after slavery was abolished following the Civil War. Slave labor became the meager wage. No wage at all!

The Emancipation Proclamation gave some 4 million slaves their freedom; the question of freed blacks' status in the postwar South was still very much unresolved. Under black codes, many states required blacks to sign yearly labor contracts; if they refused, they risked being arrested, fined and forced into unpaid labor, or neo-slavery. Outrage over black codes helped undermine support for President Andrew Johnson and the Republican Party. In April 1865, as the war ended, Lincoln shocked many by proposing limited suffrage for African Americans in the South. Days later, a Confederate agent, John Wilkes Booth, assassinated him; however, his successor Andrew Johnson would be the one to preside over the beginning of Reconstruction. It was during this period that

Johnson would roll back the core of Reconstruction and return land that had been allocated to former slaves but seized by the Union Army. He removed federal troops and allowed the rise of the KKK, which was the beginning of white terror attacks on the communities of ex-slaves. In the years following Reconstruction, the South reestablished many of the provisions of the black codes in the form of the so-called Jim Crow laws. Slavery had returned with a new face; the chameleon had changed colors.

Indeed, white landowners acted to control the labor force through a system like the one that had existed during slavery. To that end, in late 1865, South Carolina and Mississippi enacted the first black codes. Mississippi's law required blacks to have written evidence of employment for the coming year each January. If they left before the end of the contract, they would be forced to forfeit earlier wages and were subject to arrest. In South Carolina, a law prohibited blacks from holding any occupation other than farmer or servant unless they paid an annual tax of $10 to $100.00 a year. This tactic would begin the criminalization of the black body and would ultimately lead to forced labor and chain gangs.

Johnson's Reconstruction policies ignored the fact that Southern states were implementing their own black codes in 1865 and 1866. While the codes granted certain freedoms to African Americans—including the right to buy and own property, marry, make contracts and testify in court (only in cases involving people of their own race)—their primary purpose was to restrict black labor and prevent ex-slaves from building generational wealth. Some states limited the type of property that blacks could own, while virtually all the former Confederate states passed strict vagrancy and labor contract laws, as well as so-called "anti-enticement" measures designed to punish anyone who offered higher wages to a black laborer already under contract.

Forced labor was on the horizon. Blacks who broke labor contracts were subject to arrest, beating and forced labor, and apprenticeship laws corralled many minors (either orphans or those whose parents were deemed unable to support them by a judge) into unpaid labor for white planters. Having no voice in a political system in which blacks effectively had no control, the black codes were enforced by all-white police and state militia forces—often made up of Confederate veterans of the Civil War— and former slave patrollers, across the South. Neo-slavery was now in full force. These laws were aimed to criminalize black people. The chain gangs were born, and forced labor and slavery was reinvented. The chameleon had changed its colors and the brutality on black bodies was intensified with a growing system of institutionalized racism and social injustice.

In similar fashion, it became increasingly obvious to me that while sleeping nothing had really changed slaves were still slaves only in a different form, the chameleon had only changed its colors. The restrictive nature of the codes and widespread black resistance to their enforcement enraged many in the North, who argued that the codes violated the fundamental principles of free labor ideology. The fight was ongoing. This disease had to be eradicated. It was then that I realized that slavery was growing into a new systemic problem, institutionalized racism was beginning to permeate America's institutions. After passing the Civil Rights Act (over Johnson's veto), Republicans in Congress effectively took control of Reconstruction. The Reconstruction Act of 1867 required Southern states to ratify the 14th Amendment—which granted "equal protection" of the Constitution to former slaves—and enact universal male suffrage before they could rejoin the Union. The 15th Amendment, adopted in 1870, guaranteed that a citizen's right to vote would not be denied "on account of race, color, or previous condition of servitude." During this period of Radical Reconstruction (1867-1877), blacks won election to Southern state governments and even to the U.S. Congress. As indicated by the passage of the black codes, however, white Southerners showed a steadfast commitment to ensuring white supremacy and the survival of the planter aristocracy.

Nevertheless, Johnson continued to give white supremacists carte blanche on the complete disregard for the constitutional safeguards protecting the legal rights of ex-slaves. Once Johnson removed all federal troops from the South, the carnage of black life began. Reconstruction policies waned after the early 1870s, undermined by the violence of white supremacist organizations such as the Ku Klux Klan. By 1877, when the last federal soldiers left the South and Reconstruction ended, blacks had seen little improvement in their economic and social status, and the vigorous efforts of white supremacist forces throughout the region had undone the political gains they had made. White privilege would be restored, disenfranchisement of blacks would accelerate, and white domestic terrorist violence would become more commonplace. Discrimination would continue in America with the rise of Jim Crow laws and a new form of slavery called neo-slavery, replete with segregationist white supremacist doctrines, which would institutionalize racism and foment state-sponsored violence against people of color as we still witness today.

It should be noted that in 1907, W.E.B. Du Bois gave voice to the spirit of the times. His voice rang from the memorial site in Harpers Ferry, West Virginia, as he commemorated John Brown's attack on the system of slavery. This occasion was one of the first of his many speeches for the Niagara Movement, a black civil rights movement. If he were alive today, he would say to Donald Trump: *"The battle we wage today is not for ourselves alone but for all true Americans. It is a fight for ideals, lest this our common Fatherland, false to its founding, because in truth, the land of the thief, and the home of the slave,- a by word and a hissing among the nations for its sounding pretensions and pitiful accomplishments. Never before in the modern age have a great and civilize folk threatened to adapt so cowardly a creed in the treatment of its fellow citizens, born and breed on its soil.*

Later in his speech DuBois addresses the naked nastiness of America its Black Citizens stripping of their humanity. While stating ", *all we ask is justice, we are no more lawless than you; yet we are often arrested, convicted, murdered and mobbed more. We do not believe in violence, yet we are victims of the raid and the barbarous victims of the mobs."*

Such were the voices that awakened me from my slumber, voices from ripples in time, which continued to echo the heartfelt pain of a people shackled with the legacy of slavery. When awakened I was terrified at what I witnessed. It was the dawn of white terrorism in an America unmasked, which featured the advent of massive mob violence and white domestic terrorism unbridled and beyond regret. The mobs who attacked, burned and hung black bodies did so gleefully, a festive atmosphere in which hundreds attended with picnic baskets to witness the burning or hanging of black flesh. These frenzied, soulless human beings beaming with joy remind me of the mindless souls at a Trump Mega rally, dancing without face masks to the tune of the carnival barker; or the insurrectionist who stormed the Capitol while viciously and gleefully beating their victims with the handles of a Trump flag.

At this moment, in this space and time, the voice of Claude McKay grasps the spirit of the times, the sorrows and heartfelt pain of our tortured souls. The White Fiend is a brilliantly composed protest poem, written in Italian sonnet with a traditional 14-line rhyme scheme in the first half. The speaker's tone is that of anger and rage against white America. The rage and anger are the result of the savage mob violence perpetrated against black bodies.

Furthermore, the racially motivated white mob violence occurred during the early 20th century and was accompanied by American troops' occupation of Haiti in 1915 and President Woodrow Wilson previewing the Movie, *Birth of the Nation*, a Ku Klux Klan propaganda movie which was instrumental in boosting its membership into the millions. McKay's voice was in direct protest against the rise of white domestic terrorism. In the first half of his poem, McKay expresses the potential for black retaliation against the violence and repression. The tone is that of anger. The second half second half of the poem is more conciliatory, and the tone is that of love. The vehicle for this expression is one of pen and poetry. The higher moral standard will illuminate the world with light. His protest poetry replaces the gun with a pen, and swaps raging violence with luminous love.

Granted, McKay's aspiration to a higher moral standard was an example of character growth. However, the title itself is exemplary of the spirit of the times. *To The White Fiends*, infers racial tensions and animus. McKay skillfully names his enemies; he refers to white 'fiends' not 'fiend'. Not the single but the plurality, the combination of White Fiends(white men) is equal to the omnipotent oppressors wicked white whirlwind of Domestic White Terrorist with the power to inflict violence on the black body.

Consequently, the historical context of this violence influenced McKay dramatically. Racism, segregation, mob violence and blatant white terrorism is a part of the American social fabric. More than 29 acts of mob violence were committed against black communities, their people and property. Thousands of black bodies were brutalized during this period. Atlanta, St. Louis and Chicago were a few examples of sheer brutality committed against black bodies while the federal government turned its back instead of protecting the black communities. Jim Crowe and segregation ruled with an iron fist. Furthermore, as American troops occupied Haiti, we saw the birth of the Pan African movement, of which McKay was a part, as were most Harlem Renaissances writers at that time. The first part of McKay's poem was appropriate for those times.

Indeed, the first half of the poem the speaker sets up a tone of anger and the potential for black retaliation against these savage acts of violence. The speaker reminds his audience not to be so arrogant in one's thinking and one's power that there cannot be resistance or counter-violence. Stanzas two through four exude the rage over the terror attacks on black bodies during the Red Summer of 1918-1923. During this time many blacks were shot, hanged, burned and bodies mutilated beyond comprehension. McKay's emphasis on our black brothers murdered, burnt. Hence his emphasis on the power of retaliation through the gun and taking out ten white fiends for every one of his black brothers. As a result the first five stanzas there is a tone of anger, rage and retaliation; it is a wakeup call to the white fanatics called white fiends.

Meanwhile in stanzas five through seven, the emphasis is less on violence but more on the psychology of color. Blackness moves from objectification (black skin color) to subjectification (black soul). The speaker now infers that God will use this dark soul as a beacon of light. Moreover, McKay makes a mockery of his white fiends and their inferences on blackness as evil; if you (white fiends) believed blackness was evil you would be fearful of retaliation. However, the most important message in stanzas five through seven is the transformation of the tone, moving from anger and violence to God moving the black soul to become a beacon of light. As the speaker moves forward in this transition, the usage of the conjunction, but in line eight, swings the message and tone of the poem. THE value of the tonal transformation is found in the weapon of poetry, not the gun. God has now transformed the speaker into a weapon of love and reconciliation. *"But the almighty from the darkness drew my soul and said, even thou shall be a light."* The speaker has now been bequeathed by God to burn his shining light through poetry, to shed light on the brutal head of white terrorism and state-sponsored violence.

Hence, the speaker embraces a universal love of the greater good. He has removed his soul from the darkness of violence and hatred. In stanzas eleven and twelve, this black soul of darkness (retro violence) has been removed by god to enlighten who remain in darkness by continued engagement in white terrorism through mob violence. The speaker rises above their savagery and teaches them a higher moral principle. as thy dusty face I sat among the white, for thee to prove thyself a higher worth.

Consequently, the language of the speaker is now anointed with god's grace and love. The anger is gone and has been replaced by reconciliation and truth. The images become more biblical and figurative. He puts word in God's mouth. 'Thee' and 'Thou' appear in stanzas 9,11 and 12. The little lamp now becomes synonymous with Jesus as light of the world and is an excellent use of personification. The alliteration of 'black brothers burnt' is graphic and forceful imagery. Finally, the metaphysical burning of black bodies is replaced by the burning of the light of truth. And this light of truth sheds light on the atrocities committed against these black bodies.

Furthermore, the speaker, in the last two stanzas (13 and 14) will become one voice, or the African race will become many, given voice by many poets, and they will not only be the voices of burnt bodies but the burning light of truth; the burning lamp that will illuminate the moral high ground to the world. Africa and slaves of African descent must now become the truth bearers of the world. The transformation of dark and wicked souls (white fiends) is the responsibility of black voices. In stanza thirteen it states that before the world is swallowed up by night and this horrific time of racial violence, the black race must bring mankind out of the awful darkness and into the light. From rage to reconciliation, the hopes and desires of America must be reconciled for its sins. Or else, according to McKay, if White America fails to reconcile their heinous crimes (*for thee to prove thyself a higher worth, before the world is swallowed up by the darkness of night*), there would be no absolution of its sins and it would forever be cast upon the shores of eternal damnation.

Rosewood and Ocoee Florida:

The plague of racial violence spreads

Unfortunately, the call for white repentance by McKay fell on deaf ears of those who embraced white supremacy. In Rosewood Florida in 1923 and Ocoee, Florida in 1920 there were close to 250 black deaths at the hands of white terrorists, and entire black neighborhoods were destroyed. Rivaling the prosperity of the Florida town Eatonville, made famous by writer Zora Neale Hurston, Rosewood was a middle-class town of proud Black people who had developed their own community and built their own houses.

The "Rosewood Massacre" began on January 1, 1923, after a white woman named Fannie Taylor, of Sumner, Florida, said she had been assaulted by a Black man. Taylor allowed others to claim that she had been 'raped.'

"It was the one word that no one in the region wanted to hear, least of all the black residents of Sumner and nearby Rosewood," David R. Colburn wrote in the <u>Florida Historical Quarterly</u>. "What happened to Fannie Taylor on that cold New Year's morning will remain forever sealed in history, but the events that followed her alleged attack will not."

According to Colburn, "Within an hour of the allegation, news spread. "Bloodhounds tracked the scent of the alleged attacker to Rosewood, three miles from Sumner. Although Fannie Taylor never suggested that her attacker was a resident of Rosewood, the community would be permanently damaged by the events that unfolded during that first week of January 1923."

Hundreds of whites joined the domestic white terrorists already in Rosewood, and acts of systematic racial violence against blacks continued until January 8. More than 10,000 white men from across the state of Florida descended on Rosewood. Black men, women, and children hid in the swamps around the town.

"Before the week was out," Colburn wrote, "the mob returned to plunder and burn down the town of Rosewood and drive all the black residents from it forever." It is still unknown how many people were killed in Rosewood. In 1994, the Florida state legislature voted to pay $1.5 million in reparations to be divided among at least 11 survivors of the massacre to compensate them for loss of property. The Rosewood Massacre was dramatized in a 1997 film by director John Singleton.

The Ocoee massacre was another white terrorist attack on African American residents in the northern town in Florida, which occurred on November 2, 1920. Most estimates say 30–35 Blacks were killed, although it could be as many as 50. Most African American-owned buildings and residences in northern Ocoee were burned to the ground. Other African Americans living in southern Ocoee were later killed or driven out on the threat of more violence. Ocoee became an all-white town after the attack. As is the case in Florida today, the events in Ocoee occurred following efforts to suppress black voting.

In Ocoee and across the state, various black organizations had been conducting voter registration drives for a year. Blacks had been disenfranchised since the beginning of the 20th century. Moses Norman, a prosperous African American farmer, tried to vote but was turned away twice on election day. Norman was among those working on the voter drive. A white mob surrounded the home of Julius "July" Perry, where Norman was thought to have taken refuge. After Perry drove away the white mob with guns shots (killing two men and wounding one who tried to break into his house), the white domestic terrorists called for reinforcements from Orlando and Orange County. The whites, as was the case in Rosewood and Tulsa, destroyed the African American community in northern Ocoee and eventually killed Perry. They took his body to Orlando, desecrated and hanged it from a light post to intimidate other blacks. Norman escaped, never to be found. Hundreds of other African Americans fled the town, leaving behind their homes and possessions.

During these massacres, white terrorists murdered and maimed black bodies indiscriminately, unprovoked and with disdain for black life, said Alice M. Thomas, a Carnegie scholar and a professor in the School of Law at Howard University. *"They went into homes, stole personal belongings, and burned down homes. They used the massacres as a cover to murder without sanction, maim without sanction, and steal without sanction. No one, to this day, has been held accountable."*

Domestic white terrorism was now common in many parts of the country following the end of slavery. It was an intentional use of violence to intimidate former slaves and restore white privilege and white supremacy as ordained by God. According to their sense of reality, order had to be restored to the universe as dictated by the taxonomy of the Enlightenment thinkers. David F. Krugler, author of *1919, The Year of Racial Violence* stated: *"The motivation was to punish African Americans for economic success and take it away. In Tulsa, they burned* it *to the ground."*

This growing white supremacy doctrine institutionalized racist practices throughout the country and would deny African Americans access to the democratic process and the economic wherewithal to provide for self, family and community. Furthermore, the marriage between the state police apparatus, and the domestic terrorists like the KKK, would create the tools of police violence to enforce white supremacy while keeping the knee on the neck of those aspiring for a better life.

"I remember talking to an elder," said C.R. Gibbs, an author and historian of the African diaspora. *"He spoke with pride about guns brought in from Baltimore. Black people took up rooftop positions. They were determined to pick off members of the white mobs, [who had] infiltrated Black neighborhoods.* "The official death toll was 15. The total damage to property is unknown. The riot, Gibbs said, was fueled by *"not just blind race hatred, but resentment of social gains the Black community made just after World War I. When we embraced the capitalist aesthetic, folks lynched us. When we showed we were prosperous, people burned down stores on the premise we violated social codes and legal codes.* "Another place in time, throughout the ripples in time where black bodies were denied their right to reclaim their bodies, to reclaim their time and space, their right to walk this earth as free and sentient human beings with the right to taste the sweetness of life instead of its strange fruit, bitter fruit.

CHAPTER 9
FROM RED SUMMER TO EMMITT TILL
(THE LYNCHING ERA, DESECRATION OF THE BLACK BODY)

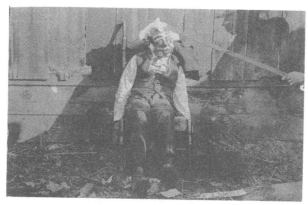

Unknown-body hung propped -up in chair, paint glue and cotton balls applied to face, head propped-up with steel rod

<u>Left photo</u>, Jesse Washington, Waco Tx.5/5/1916: body hung then repeatedly lowered into fire
<u>Right Photo</u>, Henry Smith, Paris Tx : Body parts taken as souvenirs

The front and back of a postcard showing the charred corpse of Will Stanley in Temple, Texas, in 1915.

From The Red Summer to Emmett Till - A Nation steeped in racial violence, a Mothers Broken Heart

Our beloved Mitochondrial Mother looks in horror as she has watched the desecration of her most beautiful work of art. During the infancy of the humanoid experience, she gave her first born protection from the dense foliage on the African Continent and from the intensity of heat from the sun. The Black body was a masterful creation. She gave humanity the melanin or melanic pigmentation and was advantageous in many ways: (1) It is a barrier against the effects of the ultraviolet rays of sunlight. On exposure to sunlight, for example, the human epidermis undergoes gradual tanning as a result of an increase in melanin pigment. It was a defense mechanism protecting her children from the cancerous effects from the intensity of the African sun during her children's infancy on the continent of Africa.

(2) It is a mechanism for the absorption of heat from sunlight, a function that is especially important for cold-blooded animals. (3) It affords concealment to certain animals that become active in twilight. Our skin became an excellent camouflage from those nocturnal hunters that would look to serve us up as a full course meal. (4) It limits the incidence of beams of light entering the eye and

absorbs scattered light within the eyeball, allowing greater visual acuity. (5) It provides resistance to skin abrasion because of the molecular structure of the pigment and this was important protection from the thick foliage on the African continent. Moreover, the crop of hair on the head was curly, thus preventing the sun from drawing out the moisture from the body as it bounced it constant rays of heat off the top of the head. Finally, she equipped the face with a round or flattened nose, acting as an air conditioning unit allowing more moisture flowing in and out of the body.

The idea here was that her children could eventually leave Africa and spread its seed around the entire world. Then, these different populations would eventually adapt to their new environments. Those who went North into colder climates no longer needed the dark pigmentation and their skin became lighter. No longer needing the curly hair to protect their bodies from the sun, their hair became straighter, and their noses became narrower; although constant gene flow and interbreeding between these different populations meant that everyone remained part of the same species, the same human family. The Mitochondrial Mother created a model, her first black body to ensure the survival of humanity.

But now, she is troubled, heartbroken as she watches the demonization, dehumanization, desecration and mass murders perpetrated against her work of art. She asks, "what is this thing called lynching? And why are these acts being carried out by my sons against thy brother, cast from the same mitochondrial DNA? My heart pains for my children". I answered: Mother, most lynchings involved the killing of one or more specific individuals, but some lynch mobs targeted entire Black communities by forcing Black people to witness lynchings and demand that they leave the area or face a similar fate. They claim white privilege and white superiority over their black brothers and exploit their bodies for their labor and financial gain.

Mother, your white sons left their homes in Europe over 600 years ago and traveled back to Africa, their original home, and placed their brothers in chains and spread them throughout the world as slaves. They justified their heinous crimes by dehumanizing their blackness as a sign of inferiority and their whiteness as a sign of superiority, while losing sight of the importance of your work. They forgot, had blackness not been a part of your genius, they would never have become the men whom they are today. The blackness was not a curse but a magic formula allowing your creation to spread throughout the planet called earth. So, let us take an excursion through ripples in the time space continuum so that you may see in depth how low some of your white sons have fallen into the pits of hell.

The best markers to follow are those set down by the EJI, or Equal Justice Initiative. Their trackers show the lynchings that occurred during the Jim Crow era. "Where?" she asked. These are difficult questions to pinpoint. The Alabama-based Equal Justice Initiative found that nearly 4,000 black people were lynched in a dozen Southern states between 1877 and 1950—a higher number than any previous estimates. These sometimes spontaneous but often organized domestic terror attacks on Black Bodies are just another chapter in the history of white domestic terrorism perpetrated by some of your white sons, Mother, against their darker brothers, your first creation. "Idiots," she shouted, "they have turned on their brothers, they are killing themselves".

Mother then asks, "How did it come to this?" I explained to her, from your white sons' mind's eye, whiteness became of greater worth than blackness, and that black people were demonized as beasts of burden and dehumanized to a level less than human. They wanted their black brothers to be only hewers of wood and carriers of water for them. They reduced our capacity to reason to that of a child, forgetting that it is black fingerprints which are found on the origins of civilization and all its wonders. But to them, Mother, they refused to recognize our worth, according to white writers, white historians, white philosophers and white molders of public opinion, nothing happened in the world of value or importance that could or should not be labeled white. "How ridiculous" our Mother stated ", my white child has lost his mind!"

So My Dearly Beloved Mother, we stood up, ripped away the chains and demanded our freedom. We had enough…it is their white terror tactics that you are witnessing, and that is in response to our insistence that we are equal. What you are witnessing, Mother, is their response, the total desecration of our black bodies, the endearing son of your creation. Hanging has only been one of the many heinous acts taken against flesh of flesh…. black flesh!

These examples of their cruelty are presented by the EJI, one of the organizations dedicated to the exposure of such atrocities committed against your flesh. You must understand Mother, your white sons formed white mobs frequently choosing to lynch black victims in a prominent place inside the town's African American districts. This tactic is done to provoke fear and submission to their wicked will. In 1918 in rural Unicoi County, Tennessee, a group of white domestic terrorists searched for a Black man named Thomas Devert who was accused of kidnapping a white girl. *When the men found Mr. Devert crossing a river with the girl in his arms, they shot him in the head and the girl drowned. Insisting that the entire Black community needed to witness Mr. Devert's fate, the enraged mob dragged his dead body to the town rail yard and built a funeral pyre.* The white terrorists then rounded up all 60 African American residents and forced the men, women, and children to watch the corpse burn. These African Americans and eighty Black people who worked at a local quarry were then told to leave the county within twenty-four hours. [179]

In 1927, John Carter was accused of striking two white women in Little Rock, Arkansas. The laws were rigged, dear Mother. You see, it is against the law for a black man to strike a white man, but it is the same law that gives the white man carte blanche to do as he will to your son and his black body. So, this next body seized during these ripples in the time-space continuum was that of John Carter. He was seized by domestic white terrorists; he was forced to jump from an automobile with a noose around his neck and shot 200 times. *The mob then threw Mr. Carter's mangled body across an automobile and led a 26-block procession past City Hall, through Little Rock's Black neighborhoods, and toward Ninth Street, which was the Black community's downtown center. At 7:00 p.m. at Broadway and Ninth Street, between the Black community's two most significant landmarks—Bethel African American Episcopal Church and the Mosaic Templars Building—rioting whites used pews seized from the church to ignite a huge bonfire on the trolley tracks. They threw Mr. Carter's body onto the raging fire, which burned for the next three hours.*

Do you now understand the ill-fated path of your white sons: some practice domestic white terrorism to subdue and terrorize his black brother, your first seed, into submission. The practice of terrorizing an entire African American community after lynching one alleged "wrong-doer", which in a lot of cases are false accusations of rape, demonstrates that Southern lynching during this era was not to attain "popular *justice" or retaliation for crime*. Rather, these lynchings were designed for broad impact—to send a message of domination, to infer total control of the black body and to signal that I have the power to desecrate that body as I see fit, to instill fear, and sometimes to drive African Americans from the community altogether, from their space in time. Once again, yesterday becomes today in the ripples of time.

Dear Mother These Precous Bodies Were Worth Fighting For

Mother, from 1915 to 1940, some of your white sons targeted Black Bodies who protested being treated as second-class citizens. African Americans throughout the South, individually and in organized groups, were demanding the economic and civil rights to which they were entitled after slavery. In response, some of your white sons developed terror tactics called lynching, while attacking entire black communities. *In 1918, when Elton Mitchell of Earle, Arkansas, refused to work on a white-owned farm without pay, "prominent" white citizens of the city cut him into pieces with butcher knives and hung his remains from a tree. [181]* In 1927, Owen Flemings refused to follow an overseer's command to retrieve mules from a flooded district in Millwood, Arkansas. *The overseer pulled a gun, which Mr. Fleming wrestled away from him and fired in self-defense. A mob pursued and quickly caught him. Alerted of Mr. Fleming's offense, the local sheriff told the mob, "I'm busy, just go ahead and lynch him." [182]* They did.

In Hernando, Mississippi, in 1935, Reverend T. A. Allen tried to start a sharecropper's union among local impoverished and exploited Black laborers. When white landowners learned that Reverend Allen was using his pulpit to preach to the Black community about unionization, they formed a mob, seized him, shot *him many times, and threw him into the Coldwater River. [183] Also in 1935, Joe Spinner Johnson, a sharecropper and leader of the Sharecroppers' Union in Perry County, Alabama, was called from work by his landlord and delivered into the hands of a white gang. The gang tied Mr. Johnson "hog-fashion with a board behind his neck and his hands and feet tied in front of him" and beat him. They took him to the jail in Selma, Alabama, where other inmates heard him being beaten and screaming. Mr. Johnson's mutilated body was found several days later in a field near the town of Greensboro. [184]*

Beloved Mother remember our travels through the time space continuum. Remember the dark night when we passed through slavery only to be awakened with the dawn of reconstruction: your black sons were freed only to be swept away by the terrible white winds of domestic terrorism destroying every black body in its path; remember Opelousas, LA, remember Wilmington, North Carolina, remember, Elaine, Arkansas. And I know you remember Tulsa, Oklahoma. Think of all the carnage you have witnessed, the destruction of your precious artwork and now we are in the moment on that time stream where we bear witness to lynchings. African Americans' efforts to fight for economic power and equal rights in the early 20th century—a prelude to the civil rights movement—were violently repressed by your white sons, white domestic terrorists who acted with impunity. Whites used terrorism to relegate African Americans to a state of second-class citizenship and economic disadvantage that would last for generations after emancipation and create far-reaching consequences into the time space continuum. We will visit a few more cities before we hyper-jump to the present.

Lynchings in the South, 1877 - 1950

According to the Equal Justice Report, it documents 4084 lynchings of Black people that occurred in Alabama, Arkansas, Florida, Georgia, Kentucky, Louisiana, Mississippi, North Carolina, South Carolina, Tennessee, Texas, and Virginia between 1877 and 1950. The data reveals telling trends across time and region, including that lynchings, which peaked between 1880 and 1940. Mississippi, Georgia, and Louisiana had the highest number of African American lynching victims during this period. The rankings change when the number of lynchings are considered relative to each state's total population and African American population. Mississippi, Florida, and Arkansas had the highest per capita rates of lynching by total population, while Arkansas, Florida, and Mississippi had the highest per capita rates of lynching by African American population.

Lynching Outside the South, 1877-1950

In addition to the 4084 documented lynching's committed in the South between 1877 and 1950, EJI has documented more than 300 racial lynchings of Black people in other parts of the United States during the same period. The vast majority of these 341 lynchings were concentrated in eight states: Illinois, Indiana, Kansas, Maryland, Missouri, Ohio, Oklahoma, and West Virginia. Though the numbers were lower, mirroring the lower concentration of Black residents in these states, racial lynchings committed outside the South featured many of the same characteristics.

When Black people migrated north and west and built communities outside the South in growing numbers during the lynching era, they were often targeted by white domestic terrorists in response to racialized economic competition, grounded in the expression of white grievance, white privilege and unproven allegations of crime, mostly the rape of a white woman, and violations of the racial order. As early as 1900, anti-lynching crusader Ida B. Wells-Barnett gave a speech continuing her denouncement of Southern lynching and noting the growing number of atrocities being committed in other regions. *"So potent is the force of example*," she told an audience in Chicago, "*that the lynching mania has spread throughout the North and middle West. It is now no uncommon thing to read of lynchings north of the Mason and Dixon's line, and those most responsible for this fashion gleefully point to these instances and assert that the North is no better than the South. [186]*

EJI found the highest numbers of documented domestic white terror lynchings outside the South during the lynching era in Oklahoma, Missouri, and Illinois. These totals were largely fueled by acts of mass domestic white terrorist violence against entire Black communities that left many people dead, property destroyed, and survivors traumatized.

Springfield Missouri

Lynchings outside the South were often brutal and brazen public spectacles. In April 1906, two Black men named Horace Duncan and Fred Coker were accused of rape in Springfield, Missouri. Though both men had alibis confirmed by their employer, a white terrorist mob refused to wait for a trial. Instead, they seized both men from jail and hanged them from Gottfried Tower near the town square. They then burned and shot their corpses while a crowd of 5,000 white men, women and children watched with satisfaction and glee. [189] Newspapers later reported that both men were innocent of the rape allegation. [190]

Okemah Oklahoma

In Okemah, Oklahoma, a Black woman named Laura Nelson and her teenage son, L.W., were kidnapped from jail before they could stand trial on murder charges in May 1911. Members of the white terrorist group reportedly raped Ms. Nelson before hanging her and her son from a bridge over the Canadian River. [191]

Marion Indiana

On August 7, 1930, a large white group of domestic white terrorists used tear gas, crowbars, and hammers to break into the Grant County Jail in Marion, Indiana, to seize and lynch three young Black men who had been accused of murder and assault. Thomas Shipp and Abram Smith, both 19 years old, were severely beaten and hanged, while the third young man, 16-year-old James Cameron, was savagely beaten but not killed. Photographs of the brutal lynching were shared widely, featuring clear images of the crowd posing beneath the hanging corpses, smiling and satisfied, but no one was ever prosecuted or convicted. [192] The vile and haunting images of fiends enjoying the carnage of human life inspired writer Abel Meeropol to compose the poem that later became the song Strange Fruit. [193]

Duluth Minnesota

Even in states with sparse Black populations and very few documented racial terror lynchings, attackers terrorized small and vulnerable Black communities. On June 15, 1920, in Duluth, Minnesota, a mob of 5,000 people lynched three Black men named Isaac McGhee, Elmer Jackson, and Nathan Green.

After seizing the men from jail, where they were being held on charges of assault, the white domestic terrorists ignored the pleas of a local white clergyman to spare the young men and hanged them from a light pole. [19]

Omaha Nebraska

Will Brown's charred body

White Domestic Terrorists Storm Courthouse

A crazed group of domestic white terrorists stormed the Douglas County courthouse on September 28, 1919, set it on fire, removed our African American brother, Will Brown, lynched and then burned his precious body. He became the victim of another false claim of rape by a white woman. It was later determined that the then political boss Tom Dennison and his allies encouraged the lynching in order to discredit Mayor Edward P. Smith, a liberal advocate for reform and better race relations. The terrorists beat Brother Brown, hanged him from a telegraph post, riddled his body with bullets, and then dragged his burning corpse through the streets until it was mutilated beyond recognition.

After this total desecration of a black body, the violence soon spread into a "riot" that destroyed property throughout Omaha's Black community. *Fragments of the rope used to hang Mr. Brown were sold for ten cents as souvenirs to white spectators. [196]* An infamous photograph of Will Brown's charred corpse is among the most inhumane images of lynching and the desecration of the black body in America that survive today.

After witnessing such barbarity and cruelty, our Mitochondrial mother turned to me and said: "I can no longer bear witness to things too horrible to behold my crying eyes. My eyes are saddened by the writhing forms of black dead bodies, disembodied heads dangling from ropes, with their eyes wide open, bulging, their tongues sticking out, limbs of bodies twitching, feet kicking, toes and fingers wriggling, and eyes looking every which way with pain and horror at what they see and are feeling; nostrils still breathing and lips still jabbering, and a heart that pumps blood intermittently as it drips and flows from the mouth and nose down to feed the vegetation below."

I tried to comfort our Mother, I took her in my arms, and I told her: behavior, attitudes and ideas affect our moral compass in life and are handed down through families from generation to generation. Our beloved Mother then looked at me and said, "Now I understand your suffering my child. This martyrdom is your final suffering before everlasting freedom from the final wheel of slavery. More and more after our excursion through the time continuum I feel your great suffering. Drawing much closer to your embrace, my son , I smell the blood on the chains, smell and witness the death and pain throughout the ripples of time, the disintegrating flesh all around me in the hull of the slave ship. I feel the lash eating my flesh. I feel the violation and the tearing of my womb by the slave master. I feel the moments of torment that cannot be lived unless it was lived, how yesterday becomes today in your fears and in your continued suffering, and yet cannot be forgotten and avoided." She looked at me with eyes full of sorrow and said, "I have heard the cry of all the George Floyds calling throughout the ripples of time", while placing her hand gently on my check and continued, "Never allow your spirit to be consumed with such darkness. Always rage against the dying of the light; always allow those that came before you – your ancestors – to remain your spirit guides, to light the path to redemption".

Our grandparents and great grandparents were that light. They still remind us of the Night Riders the sundown towns, the rapes, the lynchings, and the murders. Claude McKay's voice and that of Ida B. Wells tell our stories. The other side of these stories are those described by McKay, by Charles Chesnutt, by W.E.B. DuBois, stories of those particular white persons, who are a part of Trump's base in their 40-90 age group, whose ancestors were the perpetrators of such barbarity. The other side of their stories are the memories, traditions, and beliefs of the descendants of the perpetrators, the slave owners, the slave patrollers. The old Confederacy. These stories are that of your white sons, my dearly beloved Mother. They heard tales of lynching parties and the picnic-goers who came out in crowds to see the lynching spectacle. They jumped for joy and forged forward to get a severed body part as a souvenir from the body of their black brother. This is part of America's legacy, the demon that has passed from generation to generation and is dangerous to forget because tribal populism of America's dark side is still front and center in the American social fabric.

The names of the African Americans whose black bodies were lynched and killed that are published by the EJI are only the tip of an iceberg of the growing demon called white terrorism that was a way of life in the ripples of time after slavery. This record, these names, only represent the precious souls we could identify. There are hundreds of thousands that can never be identified, if we count the Trans-Atlantic Middle Passage. Then there are hundreds of millions whose names we will never know. This heinous thing called white supremacy has so brutally assaulted the bodies of our women during and after slavery. They, with the varying shades of color on our bodies, are a living record or testimony to such brutality. For African Americans, this list is a reminder of what we've gone through, and a glimpse of the causes of the fog of post-traumatic racial stress, which inundates our lives day in and day out.

Before departing, our Mother embraced me as only a Mother could, and she kissed me gently on my forehead and said: "I see the suffering my child has endured beyond endurance, but which has endured, a suffering of a people so great that some of the excesses had to be endured before and after to attain a greater happiness. You have been marked with that ability, that extraordinary gift for happiness and joy, and ecstasy of the spirit. It was excess left over from the suffering to come and the suffering that have gone on in the ripples of time. It was a divine conversion of that suffering into exhilaration, happiness and moments in paradise while alive; a sublime compensation for enduring the unendurable. It was like another life, a martyrdom and a crucifixion in the time space continuum. Your suffering gave rise to the birth of a new humanity – My Black Child has risen! I go now with peace of mind.

CHAPTER 10
EMMITT TILL: THE BIRTH OF THE CIVIL RIGHTS MOVEMENT EMMITT TILL MEDGAR EVERS

We Will Never Forget You

Cynthia Wesley   Carole Robertson   Addie Mae Collins   Denise McNair

Bombing of 16th St. Baptist Church

Emmett Till was just 14 years old in 1955 when a white woman echoed the time worn claim of black male aggression toward this thing called white female sanctity and her precious body. She accused him of wolf-whistling at her in a store in Mississippi. This alleged act of black aggression would cost the young black man-child his life when a few days later the woman's husband and his half-brother would beat and terrorize Till so severely that he was unrecognizable, before shooting him in the head. This was another brutal act of domestic white terrorism, but this one was so heinous that it aroused the consciousness of a nation and sparked the Civil Rights movement. The men responsible for the crime had multiple witnesses and mountains of evidence stacked against them but, as was always the case in the Jim Crow era, an all-white jury cleared them of all charges. Once again, the institutionalized racism in the American criminal justice system was in play. Soon the entire country would know Till's name and see the grotesque and desecrated remains of a black boy's body plastered across front pages. These images, as grisly as they were, caused hundreds of thousands of people to devote themselves to the impending storm called the Civil Rights Movement and embark on a mission to change the future of the United States forever.

Emmett Louis Till was born on July 25, 1941, in Chicago, Illinois. He was the only child of Louis and Mamie Till but never knew his father, who died in World War II. Till was raised by his single mother who often worked 12-hour days as a clerk for the Air Force to support herself and her son. According to his mother, Till was a happy and helpful boy, and she recalled how he once told her, "If you can go out and make the money, I can take care of the house." He did just that, by cooking and cleaning regularly. Nicknamed "Bobo", Till grew up in a middle-class neighborhood on the South Side of Chicago where he attended school.

But everything changed for Emmett Till in the summer of 1955. From the late 1800s to the 1960s, Jim Crow laws ruled. These laws had been in place since the Reconstruction period following the Civil War but were expanded and ramped up during the turn of the century with the Supreme Court's ruling in *Plessy v. Ferguson* in 1896. This ruling upheld the constitutionality of racial segregation and made laws establishing "separate but equal" spaces for whites and blacks. Once again, Black Bodies were restricted in how they moved, where they moved, and when they moved.

Signs such as this were commonplace in the South during the Jim Crow era. These laws prohibited blacks from living in white neighborhoods and instituted separate water fountains, bathrooms, elevators, cashier windows, and all public spaces. Thanks in large part to these laws, many blacks moved north to escape the Jim Crow South and settled in cities where the restrictions were not as tight, and the racism was not as all-encompassing as it was in the South.

Emmett Till's family was one that had moved north, and he would venture into the South in the summer of 1955. Till's great uncle Moses Wright journeyed from Mississippi to Chicago to visit the family, towards the end of his stay, Wright said that he was going to take Till's cousin, Wheeler Parker, with him on his trip back down to Mississippi to see relatives there. Till pleaded with his mother to let him go, she agreed. It was her son's first time visiting the South and Mamie made sure she brought him up to speed. According to Time, she told her son, "to be incredibly careful… to humble himself to the extent of getting down on his knees. As is always the case, a black mother had to embrace her son and give him the talk, how to act by showing deference and contrition to human beings who are encased in white skin.

Recounting her son's death

Retrieving his body from the train station in Chicago

Nevertheless, these pictures represent the outcome of the visit: the pain and the heartbreak shown by another black Mother who had to come to grips with losing a child to white domestic terrorism. According to reports, Till and a group of his friends entered Bryant's Grocery and Meat Market. Allegedly, Till bought some bubble gum and either wolf-whistled at, flirted with, or touched the hand of the store's white female clerk, Carolyn Bryant, whose husband Roy also owned the store. When Carolyn reported her story to Roy, he flew into a rage.

Roy Bryant had returned home from a business trip a few days after the alleged incident. After his wife told him what happened, Roy informed his half-brother J.W. Milam, and both headed to Wright's house where Till was staying. Early in the morning on August 28, 1955, the men forced their way into the Wright's home and demanded to see Till. When they spotted Till they dragged him out of bed and forced him into the back of their pickup truck. Wright's pleas went unheard as these two white terrorists had already decided Till's fate.

"He's only 14, he's from up North," Wright pleaded to the men according to PBS. "Why not give the boy a whipping, and leave it at that?" His wife offered them money, but they scolded her and told her to return to bed. Wright led the men through the house to Till when Milam turned to Wright and threatened him, "How old are you, preacher?" Wright responded that he was 64. "If you make any trouble, you'll never live to be 65."

In their blind, demonic and vicious rage, the men then kidnapped and savagely beat the 14-year-old black child. Once they ceased beating him beyond recognition, once they had totally desecrated his body, they shot him in the head.

Then to keep Till's body hidden, they tied a 75-pound cotton gin to his neck with barbed wire, hoping it would weigh him down when they tossed his body into the Tallahatchie River.

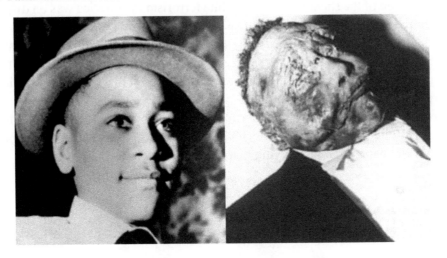

Emmett Till's murder served to motivate Civil Rights activists like never before. The shear racial hatred was on full display. Seeing to what extent the demons of racism would go in the desecration of another human being – a child – was unconscionable and beyond belief. The world saw just how sick and demented, and just how deep racial hatred was on American soil. One look at that child's face spurned a movement that still reflects in our hearts and in our minds the rejection of such barbarity.

Wright waited up to see what had happened to Emmett Till, and when he failed to return home, Wright set out in search for him. Three days later, Till's corpse was recovered from the Tallahatchie River. The boy was so savagely beaten, so unrecognizable that Wright could only identify him from the initialed ring that his mother had given him before the trip.

Mamie Till requested to have her son's remains sent back home to Chicago. Upon seeing her son's mutilated body, Mamie decided to hold an open casket funeral for her son so that the whole world could see what barbarity had been done to her son. The impact of Emmett Till's death and the subsequent murder trial, as reported by *TIME*, galvanized and gave birth to the Civil Rights movement. Mamie also invited *Jet*, an African American magazine, to attend the funeral and take pictures of Till's unrecognizable and desecrated body. They soon published the horrific photos, and the country took notice. The events that followed became an inflection point, a flash point in the struggle to free black people from this intergenerational attack on black bodies.

The exposure of the shear brutality of white terrorism in America was on display, as was the total inequity of race in the criminal justice system. Not even two weeks after his body was buried, Roy Bryant and J.W. Milam went on trial for the murder of Emmett Till. There were several witnesses to the killers' actions that night, and they were thus the obvious suspects for Till's murder and quickly apprehended. When the trial began in September 1955, the national and international press came to Sumner, Mississippi, to cover the events. Moses Wright, Willie Reed and others sacrificed their safety and lives to testify against the two white men in court, saying that the men were indeed Till's killers.

Moreover, prosecutors show the wheel used to weigh down the body of Emmett Till. Meanwhile, Carolyn Bryant gave a fiery testimony accusing Till of verbally threatening her and grabbing her. Bryant's statement was all that the all-white jury needed to hear. Once again it was the testimony of a lying and devious white woman who caused Till's gruesome murder, as have countless numbers of white women who have caused death and destruction throughout the ripples of time – Rosewood, Tulsa, Osceola, Wilmington, Omaha and the countless other occurrences during slavery when some fiends with white faces told white lies. Our Native American brothers and sisters knew…they said, "they always speak with forked tongue".

The all-white jury took barely one hour to exonerate Till's murderers as Bryant and Milam were acquitted of all charges, including kidnapping and murder. Less than one year later, in January 1956, Bryant and Milam would confess to murdering Till in a *Look* magazine article titled, "The shocking story of approved killing in Mississippi." The men got $4,000 for selling their story.

" In the article, the pair gleefully admitted to murdering the 14-year-old boy and expressed no remorse for their heinous crime. They said that when they kidnapped Till, they only intended to beat him up, but decided to kill him when the teen refused to grovel. Milam explained his decision to *Look*, saying: "Well, what else could we do? He was hopeless. I'm no bully; I never hurt a n***** in my life. I like n*****s – in their place – I know how to work 'em. But I just decided it was time a few people got put on notice. As long as I live and can do anything about it, n*****s are gonna stay in their place... I stood there in that shed and listened to the n***** throw that poison at me, and I just made up my mind. 'Chicago boy,' I said. 'I'm tired of 'em sending your kind down here to stir up trouble. Goddam you, I'm going to make an example of you – just so everybody can know how I, and my folks stand. "Because the men had already been tried and acquitted of Till's murder, their callous confession garnered no lawful punishment.

Just a few months after Emmett Till's murder, events were unfolding in Montgomery, Alabama. Till's memory and spirit inspired Rosa Parks to refuse to give up her bus seat. It started the Montgomery Bus Boycott which many people believe marked the start of the Civil Rights Movement. According to Reverend Jesse Jackson, Parks informed him that "I asked Miss Rosa Parks [in 1988] why she didn't go to the back of the bus, given the threat that she could be hurt, pushed off the bus, and run over because three other ladies did get up," Jackson said. "She said she thought about going to the back of the bus. But then she thought about Emmett Till, and she couldn't do it." The *Los Angeles Times* put it in perspective, saying, "If Rosa Parks showed the potential of defiance, [some historians] say, Emmett Till's death warned of a bleak future without it."

As Robin D. G. Kelly, chair of the History department at New York University told *PBS*: "Emmett Till, in some ways, gave ordinary black people in a place like Montgomery, not just courage, but I think instilled them with a sense of anger, and that anger at white supremacy, and not just white supremacy, but the decision of the court to exonerate these men from murdering – for outright lynching this young kid – that level of anger, I think led a lot of people to commit themselves to the movement."

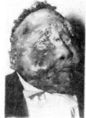

Close-up of lynch victim bares mute evidence of horrible slaying. Chicago undertaker A. A. Raynor said youth had not been castrated as was rumored. Mutilated face of victim was left unretouched by mortician at mother's request. She said she wanted "all the world" to witness the atrocity.

Mrs. Bradley got first look at brutally battered son in undertaker's morgue. More than 600,000, in an unending procession, later viewed body (r.).

The murder of Emmett Till left him unrecognizable, completely desecrated. Images of his face and remains were published in *Jet*. Even though the images of Emmett left his face unrecognizable to the world, to those of us who were black, we recognized him all too well, the pain and suffering, the brutalization and desecration of our bodies. The brutal hand of white domestic terrorism was all too clear. Claude McKay recognized it in his poem, "To The White Fiends". Billie Holliday and Nina Simone recognized it with their renditions of "Strange Fruit". And all the Mothers who have given their black babies the talk, they recognized it. We saw you, Emmett, and we have been on the march, on the move to defeat these rabid dogs in the name of freedom.

The Enduring Legacy of Emmett Till's Story

Indeed, to many, the story of Emmett Till represents a turning point in our historical struggle to combat the legacy of slavery. Scholar Clenora Hudson-Weems calls Till the "sacrificial lamb" of civil rights. Amzie Moore, an NAACP operative, believes that Till's brutal killing was the start of the Civil Rights Movement altogether. Till might not have been around to see the Civil Rights Movement and make the kind of changes that would have spared his life, but his death was instrumental in getting the movement off the ground in the first place as his brutal death was the tipping point for the moral compass of the nation.

Even decades after his murder, the story of Emmett Till's death continues to make headlines. In perhaps the most significant recent revelation, Carolyn

Bryant, the accuser, finally had a come-to-Jesus moment and admitted in 2007 to Timothy Tyson, a Duke University senior research scholar, that she fabricated much of her testimony at trial. One of the most damning things she said during Emmett Till's murder trial was that he made verbal and physical advances on her, but she admitted to Tyson, "*That part was not true.*"

At the time of her interview, Carolyn Bryant was in her 70s and seemed to feel some remorse for her part in the brutal murder — unlike her ex-husband, Roy. She told Tyson, "Nothing that boy did could ever justify what happened to him.

Medgar Evers and the Birmingham church bombing

As history continued to unfold, African Americans continued, their march toward freedom and white domestic terrorism only intensified. On June 12th, Medgar Evers, a 37-year-old black civil rights activist and head of the Mississippi chapter of the NAACP, pulled into his driveway after returning from a meeting where he had conferred with NAACP lawyers, he was struck in the back with a bullet that ricocheted into his home. He staggered 30 feet before collapsing. He died at the local hospital 50 minutes later. His assassin was Byron De La Beckwith, a known member of the KKK. After moving to Jackson, Evers was involved in a boycott campaign against white merchants and was instrumental in eventually desegregating the University of Mississippi when that institution was finally forced to enroll James Meredith in 1962.

In the weeks leading up to his death, Evers found himself the target of numerous threats. His public investigations into the murder of Emmett Till aroused the ire of the KKK. On May 28, 1963, a Molotov cocktail was thrown into the carport of his home, and five days before his death, he was nearly run down by a car after he emerged from the Jackson NAACP office. Civil rights demonstrations accelerated in Jackson during the first week of June 1963. A local television station granted Evers time for a short speech, his first in Mississippi, where he outlined the goals of the Jackson movement. Following the speech, threats against Evers escalated and he became the prime target of the KKK.

The strategy of the KKK was for the most part to now abandon their ritualistic and collective acts of terrorism. The violence meant to act as a form of social control and terrorism had now moved to small domestic terror cells. Individuals and small groups could plant bombs and orchestrate drive-by shootings, assassinations and the torching of houses. As these new tactics emerged the KKK and similar violent white hate groups went underground. We had now entered a new era of coordinated white supremacist domestic terror cells, coordinating attacks on black bodies and their communities.

Three months later, the Klan left its fingerprints on another heinous act of domestic white terrorism. At 10:22 a.m. on the morning of September 15, 1963, some 200 church members were worshipping when a bomb was detonated on the church's east side, spraying mortar and bricks from the front of the church and caving in its interior walls. The bodies of four young black girls (14-year-old Addie Mae Collins, Cynthia Wesley and Carole Robertson, and 11-year-old Denise McNair) were found beneath the rubble in a basement restroom. Ten-year-old Sarah Collins, who was also in the restroom at the time of the explosion, lost her right eye, and more than 20 other people were injured in the blast.

The bombing of the 16th Street Baptist Church on September 15 was the third bombing in 11 days, after a federal court order had come down mandating the integration of Alabama's school system. White domestic terrorists was determined to deter African Americans from gaining their full rights as citizens.

In the aftermath of the bombing, thousands of angry Black protesters gathered at the scene of the bombing. When Governor Wallace sent police and state troopers to break up the protests, violence broke out across the city. Many protesters were arrested, and two young African American men were killed (one by the police) before the National Guard was called in to restore order. Alabama Governor George Wallace was a leading foe of desegregation, and Birmingham had one of the strongest and most violent chapters of the KKK. The city's police commissioner, Bull Connor, a member of the White Citizens' Council was notorious for his willingness to use brutality in combating civil rights demonstrations and was remembered for turning dogs loose on children as water hoses ripped the flesh from their tender bodies.

Birmingham was named "Bombingham" precisely because of its reputation as a stronghold for white supremacy and that particular chapter's use of bombs as their weapon of choice. By 1963 Dr. King had made Birmingham the central focus of desegregation, and it became a central focus of the Civil Rights Movement. The consequences of such activity were the homemade bombs planted at churches and homes as the reign of domestic white terrorism dominated the landscape. Many of the civil rights protest marches that took place in Birmingham during the 1960s began at the steps of the 16th Street Baptist Church, which had long been a significant religious center for the city's Black population and a second home to Dr. King.

Though Birmingham's white supremacists (and even certain individuals) were immediately suspected in the bombing, repeated calls for the perpetrators to be brought to justice went unanswered for more than a decade. It was later revealed that the FBI had information concerning the identity of the bombers by 1965 and did nothing, because J. Edgar Hoover, then head of the FBI, disapproved of the civil rights movement and was complicit in the cover-up. It would be the same Hoover who would unleash the COINTELPRO (Counterintelligence Program) on the BPP five years later, and the same Hoover who had worked tirelessly to have Dr King and Malcom X and Fred Hampton neutralized by any means necessary.

PART TWO

CHAPTER 11

RIPPLES IN TIME AND ME

Left: Just released as political prisoner (1977)
Top Middle: Africa Bound (2015)
Top Right: Bobby Seale
Bottom Middle: Speaking at Yale University (1968)
Middle Right: Speaking at NY 21 rally (1969)
Bottom Right: .Berkeley CA Chapter (1968)

*Indeed, the European racist and ethnic groups practices thus have confiscated the quasi-totality of habitable lands of this planet, in only four centuries, and it categorically refuses the re-introduction of ethnic heterogeneity in all countries in which it physically destroyed the native former inhabitants. In each of the lands where genocide was practiced, **their main conquered population becomes subordinate to the newly created laws and state institutions conceived toward this end**. Yet when the process of eliminating the native population is complete, like a snake who has finished swallowing its victims, a collective feeling of guilt, which is hard to suppress, grips the consciousness of the conquerors and gives rise to an expiatory literature, in the form of legends of founding nations in which the conquered people are charged with all sins. **The conquered become heathens saved by the sanctimonious white European ethnic groups. The murderous Europeans in this way regain a pristine conscience**.*

- **Cheikh Anta Diop**

It was always clear that something inside was calling, a restlessness unexplained. The signs became more apparent on the evening news. First, it was Brown vs. the Board of Education decision, which challenged the systemic racism in America's educational institutions. Three years later I saw the gruesome body of a boy named Emmett Till. His face still haunts me today. Can you imagine a child my age seeing another child's face so disfigured, so brutally beaten, a bullet hole in his head, he no longer looked human? I ask my dad how and why. I could not imagine how the hate in another man's heart could spawn such an atrocity. What motive would drive such action?

I ask myself – *how did I get here how did I arrive at this particular point in time, a political prisoner in maximum security awaiting trial in the Marin County courthouse? How did an honor student an independent field major at UC, Berkeley wind up with a life sentence?*

In order to seek clarity, I allowed my mind's eye to multi-verse, to travel the ripples of time, which took me to the inception point on this plant. I entered this time-stream born into this world by Bertha and John Turner, two of the most beautiful humans I ever laid eyes on. Both were from a rural farming community in Trigg County, which is located during that time in tobacco country in Cadiz, Kentucky. My Father was from Rocky Ridge and had three sisters and one brother. My grandparents lived a harsh life, as did most blacks who were the victims of the sharecropping system after slavery and post-Reconstruction. Instead of promises made to ex-slaves during post-Reconstruction, they found themselves cast into another inferno of hell called Jim Crow. I remember my dad was always eager to escape such a meager existence, and he always shared stories of cultivating tobacco and having to live in less than favorable conditions. He constantly reminded me of cleanliness because he grew up on dirt floors and outhouses used as toilets, out of necessity.

My mom had nine sisters and four brothers. My grandparents had a plethora of grandchildren, of which I was the fourth oldest. My fondest memories during childhood were those particular moments in time. Climbing apple trees, eating apples and throwing them at the hogs. Retrieving eggs from the hen house, while sharing in an orgy of love from all those 20-plus family members who were under one roof in a four-room house.

It was during this time I began to see the world through the lens of racial discrimination. My grandmother would spend endless hours washing clothes, and more clothes, an endless flow that never stopped. I noticed because I would draw water for her from the well and pour it into a huge black kettle in the middle of the side yard from the house. Underneath this kettle sat a bundle of wood, which I would cut and feed to the fire throughout the day. Each morning, with baskets packed full of white folks' clothes; washed and neatly ironed, I would accompany my young Aunts Hilda and Eunice down a dirt road into town. I remember this road as clearly today as I did then. You could see the heat wavering in front of you like ripples about two feet above the top of the road. My feet would always caress these ripples of heat because I loved to traverse the days without any shoes.

Once we arrived at our destination we would always walk into the yard and proceed to the back of the house. This seemed odd to me, this huge white house, replete with columns and occupied by white faces. I would always ask my Aunt Hilda, why we were going to the back of the house. Furthermore, why are you saying yes mum to this strange-wrinkled woman with smelly hair? I questioned why we could not go through the front door.

My grandmother was the first to give me The Talk and she ended it with you are a Child of God and let no one tell you different. You are a blessed child, and we are a blessed people. I will never forget that conversation, and from that day, I saw racism and white people for who they are. A spiritless people who preyed on the labor of its black victims. I watched my dearly beloved Mom Bob wash their clothes from sunrise to sunset while being paid a meager wage of one dollar a week in order to help my granddad, who was paid 50 cent an hour at the local overall factory. They fed and clothed the family that they loved so dearly. I did not find out until later that my grandmother had purchased the house I loved, from a benevolent white man whom she paid from the fruits of her labor. She paid him from the money she earned by washing his clothes and others.

To put it differently, it would be my grandfather, Daddy Elliot, who made it quite clear that racism was an ugly disease and whites were the root cause of this evil. I would always sit at his side in his yard under a tree where he would smoke his corn pipe while sipping his corn whiskey. It was then I noticed a curious habit: he would always take snipes at white people as they drove by. Words of disdain flowed from his lips, and he made it quite apparent he was not feeling them. He would always tell me they were devils and were never to be trusted. I later found out why. My Aunt Hilda shared with me stories of night riders on horses who would nightly terrorize the small enclave of blacks in Cadiz, Kentucky. Every night, black folks had to be indoors by sundown or face the threat of being hung.

Moreover, all lights, or lanterns at the time had to be off, or face repercussions. My grandfather also shared stories of rapes and sexual abuse of our beloved black women. If there was a monetary debt owed to a white man that could not be paid, the debt was satisfied by the desecration and abuse of the black female body. He also let it be known that the shotgun at his side was for any of those fiends who would think twice about his girls. Nine beautiful girls with light eyes and long flowing hair, were potential prey for the lascivious and lecherous white man. Such were the roots of his deep-seated hatred for white people, and such was the awakening to me that America has a problem. And that problem is the deeply infested demons called racism and white supremacy.

For those reasons, my parents were determined to live a better life. My dad convinced my mom to elope. She was 16 and he was 20. You had to hear my grandfather, Daddy Elliot, tell the story. They had to drive to Missouri because they were considered minors in Kentucky. They drove all-night to marry and returned to Kentucky the following day. My grandparent's house was perched on a hill. You had to pull into the gravel driveway on an incline. My grandfather was sitting on his porch, corn pipe between his lips, and his jug of corn whiskey at his side. In his lap lay Betsy, his shotgun. As they approached him, he said "I had better see a marriage license or someone would not leave here in one piece". After the marriage license was produced, calm settled over Elliott Mayes and congratulations were in order.

My parents later moved to Indianapolis, Indiana and my father joined the army and was a part of World War II. His experience as a black soldier in a racist military shaped his life. It eventually had an impact on how I viewed the world dominated by racism and white supremacy. I often wondered why my father was so withdrawn. There was always certain sadness, a quiet rage that surfaced when he shared harsh misdeeds of white people. I finally pressed him on the hurt I saw in his eyes and the pain, which bled from his heart.

One day he blurted out, "a honky ain't shit." My Dad's generation had three names for racist white people: honkeys, crackers and old Fays. Each name expressed deep resentment for white people. My Dad shared with me the extent of racism in the military. They were constantly referred to as 'niggers' or 'boy' and were dehumanized in every conceivable way. Even though my Dad made Master Sergeant and drove trucks supplying front line troops, their down time was spent doing the heavy lifting for their white counterparts, cleaning toilets and any other demeaning task at hand.

Upon returning Stateside, he shared with me how he and his fellow black soldiers were threatened because they were niggers in a white man's uniform. They were cursed out, spat upon and more than once had to defend themselves from physical attack. From that moment in time, my Dad was heartbroken. He had fought for what he thought was his country but was threatened with death because of the color of his skin when he returned Stateside. I shed tears for my father and vowed never to trust a white man, and to never lay my soul bare to such a heinous and cruel hollow shell of a man.

Indeed, those moments for a child whose father shared his pain of being a black man in America left an indelible imprint on my memory banks. I believe at that time I may have been six or seven, but it became obvious to me the world was measured in terms of black and white. We lived in the projects called Lock field Gardens. Indianapolis was a racially segregated city. It did not take me long to realize there were two worlds: one black and one white, the haves and the have-nots. The Westside were the slave quarters, and the north side were the masters of the universe with all the wealth and trappings of white privilege.

One day I noticed in a newspaper these funny looking people in white sheets with hoods. I was dumbfounded. Why were these people wearing hoods? Unbeknownst to me I got a quick lesson in the meaning of the Ku Klux Klan. It was my dad who educated me, who taught me about these white terrorists who brutalized and hung my people in the South. I quickly recalled the conversations I had with my grandfather about the Night Riders. Moreover, the Klan had its roots in Greenwood, Indiana, which was roughly 20 miles from where we lived.

Not only were they dominate white supremacist groups, they also controlled the governorship and the political apparatus of the state of Indiana during those times.

My vision of the world was rapidly becoming shaped by racism and increasing social disparities in the 1950s. We were finally able to afford a TV. My dad and I would watch the evening news, and I would receive my education firsthand from a black man who had been abused, his talents pushed aside because of the color of his skin. He would always contextualize the news as it related to our historical experience. Neither of my parents finished high school; nonetheless they were the most thoughtful and intelligent human beings in my world. They were thoughtful, articulate, loving and protective of their only child. That was about to abruptly change. In the two years to follow, I was blessed with two beautiful sisters Marlonna and Rochelle Turner.

 They became the love of my life. I lived a happy childhood. I had a mother who probably was the most humane and loving person I have ever known. She was a strong Black Queen. She was royalty in the truest sense of the word. She was a person who would walk that last mile for her family. As when the lioness would stalk and hunt you down if, you abused her children. My Dad was quite thoughtful and instructive. My sisters were a bundle of joy. We were a poor but happy family, full of love, and living in the projects. But there was always a restlessness in my heart. Something was always tugging at my soul.

The constant tugging was from somewhere else. It persisted and it would always return to the face of the young Emmett Till. It was then I saw the ugly, unimaginable face of racial hatred personified by the demons in white America. Those demons began to occupy my mind, during my dream state as well as my waking consciousness. Questions arose. How could such demons possess and drive a person or persons to commit such atrocities. As I entered my 13th year on this earth, I began to feel the fear in my heart. It was a fear associated with possessing black skin in a hostile white world. It was then I began to understand that a black body could become a target and punching bag, an object to be vilified, spat on, brutalized and removed from the face of this earth. It was a frightening realization for one so young.

My Mother stood by my side and eased my pain as she always did when she sensed my hurt. I remember her telling me Emmett's mother was a strong black woman. As painful as it must have been for her, she allowed his face to be photographed for the world to see. She wanted the world to feel her pain. She wanted the world to see what racial hatred did to her son. She wanted the world to see how the demons manifested themselves in America's soul. I thought about my grandmother, my Aunts, and those white women. I thought about my dad and his treatment from the war; I thought about my grandfather's experience; I thought about my great-great grandparents who were slaves, those night riders stoking fear in their hearts; my ancestors' heartbeats as they lay in their own feces in the bowels of the slave ships enroute to a fate that launched us into 460 years of pure hell and darkness, fraught with unimaginable pain.

Now I saw white terrorism manifest itself in the disfigured face of Emmett Till. The image of his face broke my heart. My sense of purpose was beginning to take shape. Toward the end of the '50s, I became a high school student. Even though I always dreamed of becoming a doctor, I started taking notice of the civil rights struggle taking shape in the South in general, and Birmingham and Mississippi in particular. With my dad as my constant narrator and interpreter of the evening news, my consciousness was awaking, and my spirit became more restless.

I was beginning to see, feel to the core of my being, the darkness and evil demons of racism in America. In high school, America was portrayed as the torch of freedom and democracy, the civilizers of humankind. No longer was I willing to accept this lie. Truth was buried alive and I sought to unearth it. I began my quest to understand what would drive men to such madness. How could America be clean of such wickedness while doing bad things in her name? They claimed as a people their good deeds civilized the world. They claimed their bad deeds were done for good reasons. Really? Torture, hanging, kidnapping, murder, rape, flogging, genocide – all in the name of *goodness*? Slavery was an abhorrent evil. Thoughts of Emmett Till reminded me how the threads of slavery are too entangled to unravel in a day or a century. Freedom will be in chains for a while longer. America's sordid past must be unraveled, her true history and soul laid bare. The demons of racism exorcised! Her crimes committed against people of color must be told. I had to understand, better this thing called racism, this thing called slavery.

My journey would land me educational grants and test cases for the Affirmative action program at the University of California, Berkeley. This would become one of many life experiences where it was a responsibility to stand for, in a positive light, the descendants of African slaves. It was a blessing to have had the opportunity to attend UC Berkeley in the late '60s and early '70s. Berkeley was the hub of the Revolutionary movement during the '60s and it was an extraordinary experience. The energy and spirit of the times overwhelmed one's very being as the injustices of the American domestic and foreign policies were called to task.

Moreover, student protesters were becoming casualties of war. The Orangeburg Massacre, February 6th, was an incident of racial violence in which three unarmed African American students were killed and twenty-seven others injured at South Carolina State University when Highway Patrol officers opened fire on a crowd protesting segregation. The officers were acquitted of charges of using excessive force. The Orangeburg Massacre predated the better known 1970 Kent State shootings in which four unarmed white students at Kent State University in Ohio were shot while protesting the Vietnam War. Student activism was a life-threatening dilemma for students who would dare protest for social justice and freedom from police brutality.

I began to sense something special on this planet called earth. Most African nations were moving toward or had already experienced an anti-colonial revolution – Ghana, Algiers, Kenya, Congo and Nigeria. There was a rising African intelligentsia, and brilliant revolutionary thinkers, i.e. Amilcar Cabral, Kwame Nkrumah, Frantz Fanon and, one of the greatest of African intellectuals, Cheikh Anta Diop. Moreover, the ANC and Nelson Mandela were fighting the most brutal regime on the African continent, the apartheid government in South Africa. I later, would be blessed with seeing the faces of these brilliant leaders in Accra, Ghana at the W.E.B. Du Bois Convocation Center. There you will find the African Wall of Fame, honoring all the courageous and beautiful brothers who fought to restore freedom and Africa's place on the world stage.

Subsequently the putrid walls of colonialism were collapsing worldwide and in South and Central America, coupled with the illegitimate occupation of Vietnam. The revolution being waged by African Americans here in Amerikkka set the table for the most prolific social movement ever seen in this country.

Every day on the UC, Berkeley campus was an intellectual organism. Students from every political persuasion, formed political and social organizations, setting up tables with printed literature in Sproul Plaza. There were meetings, forums, films, classroom debates. The level of intensity and greatness of intellect in one location was unimaginable. Every social issue of the day was thoroughly scrutinized and dissected seven days a week for a minimum of eight hours a day. Students were often late for class and some days never made it, so tense were the debates.

Being one of 87 African Americans on a campus of 40,000 was a privilege and a blessing. At that time, I ditched my pre-med major and did a triple major in history, philosophy and political theory. We formed a Black student union, called the Committee on Liberation or Death (COLD) and began to press forward with social issues relevant to the African American in America and on the Berkeley campus in particular. Our principal issues were racial red lining in the community and in the admissions of African American students, and the need for an African American Studies Department on campus. After forming an alliance with the Third World Liberation front, consisting of Asian, Mexican American and Native American counterparts, we pushed forward with our demands. Having been the architect and founder of the African American studies program at the College of Marin in Kentfield California the previous year, I became one of the student activists and a player in future events on campus.

Date: October 10, 1969

'In this lengthy interview with the *Berkeley Barb* in October 1969, two activists within the TWLF—part of its Committee on Liberation or Death (COLD)—analyzed the gains and limitations of the strike from the winter.

John Turner and Oliver Jones attributed the failure of the strike to a lack of support for it among whites who, they noted, had rallied for the cause of People's Park in the months following the TWLF strike. They placed more value on People's Park than on the Third World Studies Department.

At this point in the struggle, Turner and Jones disparaged what they saw as *"mojo chauvinism,"* or what the Black Panther Party had identified as "pork chop nationalism": the development of a cultural nationalism that emphasized cultural pride (through hippie culture or the revival of African dress and customs) rather than the need for fundamental social and economic transformation.'

After the interview several members of the UC Black Student Union and I decided to go to the Sierra Mountains on a retreat. We spent several days in the Sierras backpacking as we developed and planned our strategy for implementing the African American Studies Department, while also developing plans for a student-led strike to shut down the University if our demands were not met. As we sat around the campfire exchanging ideas, a bulletin came over the short-wave radio: a third 16-year-old African American youth had been shot and killed by a white police officer in the Bay Area.

Obviously, the tenor of our conversation changed, for not only had this heinous crime taken place, but also the headquarters of the Black Panther Party was in imminent danger of attack. We had some serious decisions to make about the politics and position of the Black Student Union. Our group was of diverse political persuasions. Some adhered to Black Nationalism and were more akin to the teaching of the Black Muslim faith. Some supported the concepts of a cultural nationalist approach of the RNA or the Republic of New Africa. There were also those who considered themselves revolutionary and supported the Black Panther Party. Such was the beauty of the 1960s – young intelligent black students who were looking for ideas and strategies to change the world. My destiny was about to take a sudden undecided turn. We cut our trip short and returned to campus the next morning.

Back on campus we noticed that there was a growing militant mood from the students, both black and white. There were rallies which drew the usual 4,000 to 8,000 students, and marches were planned to address the murder of this young high school student. The overriding concern was how to support the BPP and how to shield it from attack by the police force. With the Black Student Union taking the lead, a defensive perimeter was set up around the Black Panther Party Headquarters in Oakland. One of the things that were in most students' book bags were gas masks, for it was not uncommon to be tear-gassed by the police. Demonstrations and marches were commonplace. Demonstrators even wore football helmets to blunt the blows of police billy clubs. In the truest sense of the word, Berkeley's campus was the eye of the storm, and every imaginable social issue was scrutinized. If there were an injustice it was called to question in the form of mass protest and demonstrations. Such was the life of a Berkeley student.

As one of the principles in the Black Student Union, it was my responsibility to take charge on this most eventful night. It would be my first chance of meeting Party leadership. We discussed the tactics and strategy of armed perimeter defense and where to station the unarmed participants. This meeting and conversation changed my life forever. It was under such circumstances that I met David Hilliard, Chief of Staff of the BPP. He ultimately bestowed on me the honor of forming the Berkeley chapter of the BPP. Even to this day, I hold him in the highest regard, a man who had to shoulder the responsibility of leading the Party in the absence of both Huey and Bobby who were political prisoners. My station was inside the Panther headquarters, equipped with a walkie-talkie and a .38 revolver. I was to instruct my fellow student compatriots, both black and white on the outer perimeter of the headquarters.

That night, as we waited for an eminent attack, it dawned on me that we were at war. For the first time in my life, I fully understood the ramifications of disarmament as a nation of African peoples, a people captured, disarmed, put in chains and exported to a foreign land to become the tool of labor for white people and cannon fodder for their racist brutality. The very basis of our slavery was disarmament. We were a captured people without the ability to protect and defend our family, our people, ourselves, and our community from our captors. Unless we drew a line in the sand, it would always be that way. That night was my epiphany, the tortured and disfigured face of Emmett Till flashed through my mind, the cries of those precious little girls, victimized by the bombing of the church in Birmingham by white supremacists, and the countless number of our ancestors' necks swinging from the limbs of oak trees fueled a rage I had never felt before.

The attack never came, and after two weeks of the same routine, all parties agreed that we had weathered the storm. The brothers in the Panther Party thanked us for our commitment. From that day forward, I had forged a bond with brothers and sisters in the BPP. They would eventually become my comrades in arms. I continued to meet and talk to David Hilliard and my respect for him continued to grow. I sensed in him a person of high moral character but there was also sadness in his eyes that reflected the enormous pressures he was under from day to day. It was the fear of being one step away from making the wrong decision, which could cause loss of life. He genuinely loved the Party and those under his command. However, make no mistake – there was also that eye of suspicion, for we never knew who an FBI plant might be, an informer, a running dog lackey who would sell his brother to Massa for an extra piece of cornbread.

Afterwards, life on the Berkeley campus for weeks and months to come became even more tumultuous. We continued moving forward with our demands for an Africana Studies Department and eventually called for a student-led strike. In late fall of 1969, we began to organize a student led strike and I did so while carrying 30 units and participating in planning and organizing what was to come. We formed an alliance called The Third World Liberation Front. The participants were led by the Afro-American Student Union and included The Asian American Political Alliance, The Mexican American Student Confederation, and the Native American Student Alliance. The white student support groups included the Viet Nam antiwar coalition, The Young Socialist Alliance, and the entire progressive segment of the student body politic. The strategy was direct action to force Roger Heyns, who was chancellor at that time, to the negotiating table and agree to the implementation of Third World College, controlled and taught by the ethnicities representing their particular interest.

The initial tactics to meet our objectives were informational and instructive. We did so by passing out informational packets at our tables sat up in Sproul Plaza, and at all campus entrances, with emphasis placed on the Telegraph entrance, which was the hub of the campus. We then held caucuses and focus groups in various classes, on the green inside Sather Gate, and in the various classroom buildings on campus. Afterwards we accelerated the process and began to hold massive rallies in Sproul Plaza, followed by organized marches throughout campus. Moreover, the plan was to set up picket lines in front of the entrance to the University and the entrance to all major buildings on campus. The strike was now in full swing and the eye of the storm had been unleashed.

During those times, the campus was like a war zone. Ronald Reagan was Governor of California, and straight on law and order. He viewed all protestors as left-wing anarchists, or black thugs, and hooligans. Sound familiar? Or shall I say his name, Donald Trump? Reagan in his determination to break the strike, kept state troopers and the National Guard on campus, waiting for the opportunity to pounce. When Reagan had enough, he let the chancellor know he was unleashing the hounds. They constantly used tear gas and terror tactics to disperse the picket lines while attacking mass demonstrators, much like Trump did outside the White House as he posed in front of the church for his infamous photo opportunity. It was during this when the National Guard tear gassed and attacked the peaceful Black Lives Matter Protestors.

UC had a student population of 40,000 and the city itself a population of 140,000 plus. Over half the students supported the strike and did so by putting their bodies on the line. The sheer numbers made it impossible to breach the strike, especially when a significant number of faculties supported the student demands. The formation of a Third World coalition was the impetus that finally pushed us over the finish line. The coalition consisted of Chicano, Native Americans, Blacks, Asians and Whites, and the solidarity shown eventually forced Roger Heyns to the negotiating table. The Third World Department would be forged; American Indian Studies, Chicano Studies, Asian American and the African American Studies Department. would emerge, and finally the board of regents acquiesced. We made history. We always said then and say today: people when united can never be defeated!

During this period of protest on the Berkeley Campus, I had felt a need to keep in touch with my newfound friends at Panther Headquarters. I would find myself late at night going down to their headquarters just to stand guard, for their lives were always one heartbeat away from being taken. I was always a welcomed guest, I guess because of our earlier commitment to help defend their lives. They knew my heart was as big as theirs. My heart bled for them. I developed an unwavering love for them, as they were always eager to risk their lives in service of the people, a people who throughout the ripples of time were uprooted from our homeland. Our ancestors were a hunted and captured people who have had to deal with the shackles of slavery, of institutionalized racism, and the day-to-day horrors of being captive in a brutal racist police state that terrorizes its black victims incessantly.

It was something surreal being behind locked steel doors with fortified steel walls, windows boarded up with four-inch gun ports, and sandbags at the base of all the walls. These young brothers and sisters, I admired to my core, they certainly, as far as I was concerned, were the best of our kind. Most came from the streets, and some were college students. And there were some who were college graduates. However, the one common denominator was they had learned the various revolutionary theories of all our great African Revolutionary thinkers as well as Marx and Lenin. The wall inside was replete with posters of Jomo Kenyatta, Patrice Lumumba and of course the venerable Malcolm X.

We would stay up all night debating political ideologies while keeping total visual focus on the movement in the streets. They taught me military strategy to use on campus during our strike, for on many occasions Governor Reagan would send in the National Guard and state police to break the strike. Football helmets and gas masks were the uniform of choice for the students. If we were not being tear gassed, we were being clubbed, but we developed a tactic to counter these acts of brutality, which I will not dare put on paper. However, eventually we won and today the fruits of our labor still stand. UC Berkeley has one of the more prominent African American studies departments in the country.

Founding the Berkeley Chapter of the Black Panther Party

It was during this period that a great honor was bestowed on me. David Hilliard, the Chief of Staff, had contacted me by phone and asked that I meet him at Central Headquarters on Shattuck Avenue. As I recall, I met with David, and Don Cox a brother with piercing green eyes like those of a big cat ready to pounce and who at that time was acting Minister of Defense in Huey's absence. It was then that I was asked to become a member of the Black Panther Party. The significance of this momentous event can only be measured by that particular moment in time and place. For me it was the eye of the storm looming on the horizon, and the thoughts of freedom and the liberation of my people became no longer an idea, but actionable strategies born out of historical necessity.

Indeed, this necessity was like a storm sweeping the black community. After the Panthers' armed invasion of the capital building in Sacramento, legitimately protesting the right to bear arms and challenging the passing of the Mulford act, which would deny these rights, the evening news captured these brazen and beautiful brothers adorned in black berets and black leather jackets, marching in unison. It shocked the nation and gave the black communities a pride never experienced in the history of this country. The Berkeley Chapter was established. Don Cox and Dexter Wood opened the San Francisco office, Aaron Dixon in Seattle, Washington. John Huggins, Bunchy Carter, Masai Hewitt and Geronimo Pratt in Los Angeles.

Within a two-year period, Bobby Seale and Huey Newton would grow a two-man party into a revolutionary movement steered by a political party unlike anything seen on the streets of America. From armed self-defense groups to the 10-Point Platform and Program, Huey and Bobby's mission, their vision, was our road map to freedom. The disarmed captives now were armed and ready for battle, a battle that was a war of liberation to free the people from an oppressive, racist system of white supremacy that was determined to keep us enslaved. Little did we know that the most vicious warmonger on the planet would ultimately unleash the hounds of war and destroy our party with a ferocity and viciousness unseen on American soil.

The Panther Party became the vanguard of the movement and all that happened during this period from a political standpoint had a strong support base out of UC Berkeley. Most campuses nationwide and its affiliate political groups would seek direction from Berkeley campus, and it had to come through the Berkeley chapter. I was becoming a warrior-scholar and my studies of history from a Third

World perspective led me to apply lessons learned on the African continent and Cuba to shape our political policy in Berkeley. Moreover, the emerging struggle in South Africa and the ANC led by the great Nelson Mandela only enhanced our position politically on campus.

We had speakers from Third World Countries, along with Dr. King and Hubert Marcuse. It made our influence insurmountable. We became a driving wheel in national demonstrations against the war in Vietnam. I travelled to campuses like Harvard, Yale, Cornell, Princeton, Columbia, and Howard to help organize black student unions (BSU) and put forth demands of an African American studies Department. More importantly I began to set up political defense committees for all political prisoners, i.e., Bobby Seale Defense committee and the New Haven Nine Panthers who was accused of the murder of Alex Rackley, an alleged police informant.

While back in Berkeley, we were orchestrating the development of the George Jackson Free Health Clinic, alternative primary schools for children, our breakfast program and eventually a community control of police initiative, which would be the first in the country to be implemented. All of this was in progress while maintaining honor roll status and becoming one of a few students chosen for the Independent Honors Studies Program in History. My thesis was "The disarmament of the African Nation and its Continuous Insurrection within the African Diaspora."

As I became more involved in my academic studies while continuing my involvement in the Berkeley chapter of the Black Panther Party, we became more of a focal point of the local, state and federal authorities. Sixteen members of the Berkeley chapter formed the nucleus of our cadre. We lived in three Panther Pads and in the chapter office, which was the old home of Bobby Seale in West Berkeley. We were followed everywhere, and at all Panther locations we had round-the-clock security in both the front and back of our locations. We always traveled in pairs and me with *two* bodyguards: even in classes.

Even though The **Black Panther Party Black Student Alliance** was started in 1972, The Berkeley Chapter of the Black Panther was the forerunner of this alliance. We were the Black Student Union on the Berkeley campus which was later transformed into the Black Panther Party. The goal was to unify students with their local black communities so that the schools and community would be more responsive to the needs of the Black Community. The Black Student Alliance initiated programs, which provided supplies and books to students at no cost, free childcare, food distribution, transportation services, and financial aid programs. Prior to this formation the Berkeley Chapter would also travel throughout the country to set up legal defense funds on the East Coast while organizing students on campus around the need to establish African American Studies Departments on campus.

In 1969, I met the individual who, other than Nelson Mandela, had the most profound effect on my life and my psyche. George Jackson, who was the General Field Marshall of the Black Panther Party and who would become my friend, my mentor my close comrade, was the spokesperson and leader of the prison movement and had challenged the institutionalized racism inside prisons in California. It was he and several prisoners who organized what was to become the Black Guerrilla Family, which ultimately became a conduit for freedom fighters to the Black Panther Party and the underground movement. In Soledad prison, white guards had shot and killed three black inmates who were attacked by white neo-Nazis inmates. No white inmates were killed, nor were they charged for assaulting their black counterparts. The next day a white guard was found dead. George Jackson, Fleeta Drumgo and John Clutchette, my brother in-law, were charged with the execution.

Because of the tense atmosphere created by these events they were transferred to San Quentin, The Soledad Brothers, as they were now known, were transferred from Soledad Prison to San Quentin Prison in the San Francisco Bay area, and their trial was moved to the state district court in San Francisco. They became a cause celeb and the focal point for protest and demonstrations across the country. In 1967-68 George had written a bestselling book called "Soledad Brothers". He was our Nelson Mandela. Naturally, being sent to the Bay area was a political blessing: UC Berkeley, the Headquarters of the Black Panther Party, and the most progressive and radical students in the world was a natural marriage for the Soledad Brothers and the unfolding revolution.

George Jackson's family had requested the Black Panther Party to assume command of the Defense Team and political apparatus to form a defensive perimeter around the Soledad Brothers. I was given the responsibility of heading this team. We then put together the logistics and support apparatus to complete the task. We began exchanging letters with George, and a bond of friendship was forged immediately. Our correspondence put us at a level of intellectual exchange of ideas for beyond our expectations.

The Soledad Brothers' first court experience was an omen of what was to come. The courtroom was packed, and when the guards bought in the brothers, the guards snatched papers out of Mr. Jackson's hands. When he protested, they started beating him with clubs. I along with three other comrades jumped over the rail and fought our way to his defense. I was handcuffed, beaten, and taken back to a holding area across from where they were holding George. We met in battle and our bond was forever sealed in blood. Later I received word through his sister Penny Jackson that he had requested that I co-author a book with him called <u>Blood is My Eye</u>. It was an honor and a privilege and certainly a challenge, especially researching information and engaging a brilliant mind in matters far beyond my capabilities. He was George Jackson, internationally acclaimed writer and General Field Marshall of an entire revolutionary movement. I was in awe of one so brilliant, so brave and so loving.

CHAPTER 12

THE BLACK PANTHER PARTY-COMMUNITY ORGANIZING AND SELF-DEFENSE

Freedom is not a static condition but 'perpetual, unfinished, and rooted in acts of continuous resistance - Amilcar Cabral

Panther Community Programs: Free Ambulance, Healh Care and Breakfast Programs and Liberation School for the Community.

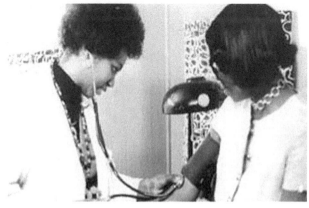

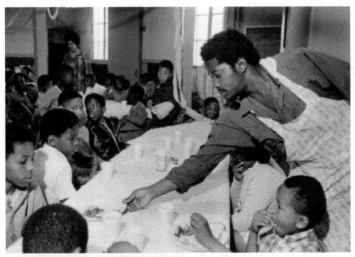

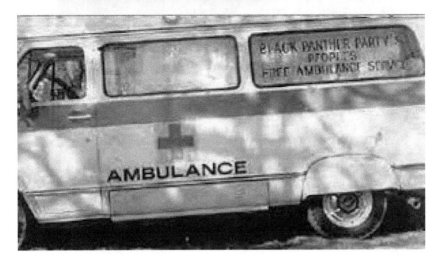

Ripples in Time: From Maroons to Panthers

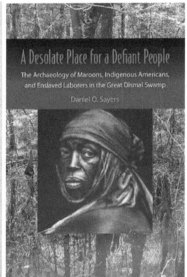

THE BLACK PANTHER PARTY
COMMUNITY ORGANIZING and SELF-DEFENSE:
ITS HISTORICAL ROOTS AND
THE IMPACT OF THE BLACK PANTHER PARTY

Introduction

To gain a better understanding of what the Black Panther Party was and the significance of our contributions to history, let us travel back in time to better gauge the historical significance of our contributions. Most people, particularly scholars, have focused on the public identity of the Black Panther Party (BPP) as a militant organization, but they have neglected the role of the BPP in grassroots community organizing. I demonstrate here that the BPP developed as a grassroots organization committed to social change through mass mobilization at the local level while demonstrating a steadfast determination to protect black people from police brutality while implementing programs that addressed the day-to-day needs of the people.

The origins of the BPP as a social and political movement are placed in the long-term historical context of community organizing in the African Diaspora, from the Maroon societies in the Western Hemisphere to the ideological framework developed by David Walker, Martin Delaney, Marcus Garvey and W. E. B. Du Bois. Such actions, processes, and rationales for community organizing and its protection were rooted in the struggle for the preservation of black culture, ethnicity, identity and socioeconomic wellbeing, as well as the struggle for citizenship, liberty, and dignity for black people in the racialized Western nation states.

I argue that the BPP created a major paradigm shift as a model for community organizing and protection against police brutality. One only needs to examine the typical models and strategies reflected in works like Mike Miller's Community Organizing: A Brief Introduction, to recognize the qualitative difference between form and substance. The typical organizational structure is based on traditional organizations and institutions. Furthermore, these faith-based, congregation-based, and institution-based organizations are rooted in the core values of the American status quo, controlled from the top down. On the other hand, the BPP's core values were quasi-Marxist, African-centered, and rooted in the socioeconomic conditions of the greater community.

With the implementation of the Ten Point Platform and Program as an alternative to the more conventional grassroots approach by handpicked organizers, the BPP addressed the causes and not the symptoms. I will show how the Party became the first and only political party founded upon the principles of a community-based organization with valuable community-based programs and mechanisms to protect the community against police brutality. The BPP became the first African American community-based party to actualize ideas and to operationalize practical applications. Our motto was *Practice is the Criteria of Truth.* It was the Panthers who developed a strategy of community participation that helped solve local problems. It was BPP members who went door to door, block by block, neighborhood by neighborhood, and city to city, in order to organize a grassroots movement that was connected to national programs, and thereby developed a blueprint for effective community organization. I draw attention to these overlooked legacies of the BPP in improving the black conditions in the U.S., and I conclude that the BPP's framework is still relevant today.

The legacy of the BPP has its historical roots in the long history of the struggle of African people throughout the Diaspora. Deeply rooted in the African sub-conscience is the collective will to survive. Indeed, what African people have given to and taken from centuries of development is a sense of collective responsibility. One can examine Olaudah Equiano's slave narrative to get a good sense of this spirit of collectivism with emphasis on the community organization strategies of the Igbo people prior to the slave trade. Everyone was cross-trained: carpenters were farmers and vice versa; everyone had a function that was for the common good. The community or village was organized to preserve the wellbeing, culture, and identity of its people.

The historical events unleashed by European colonialism would change the face of the African community forever. Institutions, belief systems, values, and culture, once in control of the indigenous people, would be destroyed and forces would create new internal dynamics. With colonialism came racism and acts of genocide, physical and mental. According to the great African scholar Cheikh Anta Diop, racial purity drives the conquering ethnic groups' refusal to mix with the indigenous people. This strategy of domination, based on the absolute separation of racial and ethnic groups, has always resorted to genocide to actualize its goals, as evident in the Americas, including Canada, Australia, and New Zealand. African people and those throughout the Diaspora, out of historical necessity and reality, had to develop a defense mechanism in order to survive this genocide of the, body, spirit and the mind. We organize to survive and to maintain that which is an essential part of our being.

From Maroon Society To Abolitionists: Foundations of the African Diasporic Community Organizing

For the captured Africans forced into the Middle Passage and slavery in the Americas, community organizing, and self-defense was the beginning of the fortification of that collectivism against the threat of extinction and dislocation, and against the shift from colonialism to neo-colonialism. With them came the spirit and action of resistance and the birth of the first Maroon communities who fled into the impenetrable swamps and hills of the Americas, running away from the slave plantocracy, in defiance of the colonial authorities. As organized communities of escaped slaves and their descendants grew, these Maroon communities were determined to fulfill the slaves' inherent desires to be free, and to secure freedom for their offspring. Once these communities were established it became necessary to establish defensive perimeters in order to protect the wellbeing of the community. The incessant flight from bondage of slavery to political and economic marginalization in the present stands for an intrinsic aspect of the Diaspora. It was from these Maroon societies, or self-liberated communities, that enslaved Africans drew inspiration to pursue freedom by any means necessary. Community organization and the preservation of Africana culture and ethnicity therefore had their roots in maroonage. In North America, these communities were called Maroons, in Spanish-speaking America they were called Palenques, and in Portuguese-speaking America they were called Quilombos. This heritage would ultimately become a model and example for the Black Panther Party.

Going forward, the Maroons' struggle for freedom was carried on by the abolitionist movement in North America. The abolitionist movement would create self-contained communities organized around the preservation of life and underground culture of the enslaved. David Walker, Martin Delaney, and Henry Highland Garnet became the voices of these growing communities.

David Walker was one of the early fathers of the African American liberation struggle, whose rhetorical strategy was Black Nationalism, self-help, self-education, self-liberation and self-defense. He was born in Wilmington, North Carolina in 1785, to a free mother and a slave father. Boston became his home in 1827, when he became involved in the abolitionist movement and its peculiar brand of community organizing. The most militant voice among the early African American protest leaders and writers, he called for resistance and community organizing in his *David Walker's Appeal in Four Articles,* published in 1829; *Together with a Preamble, to the Colored Citizens of the World,* and *Those of the United States of America,* a document patterned after the United States Constitution.

Indeed, Walker's Appeal was a call to arms to the greater community of slaves and free men, to organize a resistance movement, to educate our lowly brethren, to lift each other and form a nation. Within the structural framework of his Appeal, Walker infused biblical and historical analogies and a variety of rhetorical devices, including various forms of warning admonishments, threats of slave revolts, and divine prophesies:

"Would they be able to drag our mothers, our fathers, our wives, our children and ourselves around the world in chains and in hand cuffs as they do to work their farms, dig up gold and silver for them and theirs? This question I leave for you my brethren to digest; and may God alone force home to your heart. Remember that unless you are unified keeping your tongue within your teeth, you will be afraid to trust your secrets to each other, and thus perpetuate our miseries under the Christians. Never try to gain our freedom or natural rights from under our cruel oppressors and murders until you see your way clear — when that hour arrives and you move, be not afraid or dismayed." 7

No wonder Walker became a leader, the quintessential community organizer and freedom fighter. His appeal to organize resistance against the brutal hand of slavery would be published in the *Freedoms Journal*, the first African American newspaper to be published in the United States. Black ministers were now preaching Walker's Appeal to their congregations. Moreover, Walker would use his business acumen and skills to sew the Appeal inside garments that would be smuggled into the South. David Walker became the first African American to attempt to organize a nationwide community of slaves and freemen. His efforts would cost him his life. He is believed to have been poisoned "three months after the publication of his pamphlet's third edition, possibly as a result of large rewards offered by Southern slaveholders for his death." 8

Walker would not die in vain; his influences and themes of community organizing, self-defense, and black nationhood would be found and highlighted in the writings of Maria Stewart, Henry Highland Garnet, W. E. B. Du Bois, and Marcus Garvey, among others. In his *Condition of the Colored People of the*

United States, published in 1852, Delany emphasizes the need to organize family first, then community, to form the backbone of a nation within a nation. His commitment to social, political, and economic advancement and the preservation of one's culture was predicated on the art of the preservation of family, community, and race. It starts with the defense of the threshold. If a white person crosses your threshold with the intent to harm life, limb, or family, it is your duty to defend yourself and your family by any means necessary.

Yet it was Henry Highland Garnet who, in his <u>Call to Rebellion</u> speech given at the National Negro Convention in Buffalo, New York in 1843, continued to ignite the freedom struggle with his fiery rhetoric. This speech would define him as the blatant radical community organizer regarding the tactics and strategy of the freedom movement. It would put him at odds with Frederick Douglass, who was more prone to allow slavery to run its course and integrate the slave population into American society. Garnet, like his predecessors, wanted to organize the free blacks and slaves to rebellion and form a nation within a nation. He made the point succinctly in his Address to the <u>Slaves of the United States of America</u>:

"Brethren and Fellow Citizens: - your brethren of the North, East, and West have been accustomed to meet in National Conventions to sympathize with each Other, and to weep over your unhappy condition. In these meetings we have addressed all classes of the free, but we have never until this time, sent a word of consolation and advice to you. We have been contented in sitting still and mourning over your sorrows, earnestly hoping that before this day your sacred liberties would have been restored. But we have hoped in vain. Years have rolled on, and tens of thousands have been borne on streams of blood and tears, to the shores of eternity. While you have been oppressed, we have also been partakers with you; nor can we be free while you are enslaved. We, therefore, write to you as being bound with you." [9]

Garnet closes his address: *"Awake, awake; millions of voices are calling you. Your dead fathers speak to you from their graves and remember that you are FOUR MILLION!"* Garnet's call for national mobilization would inspire the abolitionist movement and would ultimately inspire W. E. B. Du Bois's call for mobilization of the "Talented Tenth."

Certainly, one of the most brilliant African American scholars and literary geniuses, Du Bois (1868-1963) had a heavy hand in developing the concept of community organizing. A towering black intellectual, scholar, and political thinker, Du Bois advocated direct political action, civil rights, and community organization as a tool for grassroots education. He argued that social change could be affected with his elitist army called the "Talented Tenth." He stressed waging war with the double consciousness (the European and African psyches) in each of us while stressing the reintroduction of Afrocentric values. According to Du Bois, the two realities are antagonistic and without harmony. The black person sees himself only through illusory and manufactured revelations of the other world; a white racist world that has created concepts, images, and myths while reconstructing history to totally denigrate, debase, and destroy the psyche of the black race in its attempts to justify his most egregious crimes against black humanity. This act of mental violence, genocide, and terror destroyed the harmony of self and the self-realization and re-capturing of the African spirit.

Hence, Du Bois' theory of Double Consciousness gave birth to the Talented Tenth, born out of historical necessity to teach the teachers so that the teachers would organize the community and teach the masses. Once slavery was abolished, this awesome task had to be guided by exceptional men. Having suffered the crippling cruelties of slavery, the descendants of Africa were left without any social, political, or economic infrastructure to provide the basic needs to survive. Mass organization, massive educational projects, polemical writing, and astute leadership were necessary to set the tone for destroying the myths of black inferiority. In *The Souls of Black Folk* (1903) Du Bois makes the point so eloquently:

"The inferiority of the black race even if forced by fraud; a shriek in the night for the freedom of the race who are not yet sure of their right to demand it. This is the tangle of thought and after thought wherein we are called to solve the problem of training them for meaning of life. Thus, two thousand Negroes have gone forth armed with the sword of truth while ready to give it voice." [10]

Indeed, this voice offered was given a different posture by Marcus Garvey, a profound force during the Harlem Renaissance. A contemporary of Du Bois, the Jamaican Garvey influenced the hearts and minds of millions of people of African descent. As a quasi-community organizer, Garvey founded the Universal Improvement Association (UNIA).12 His organization had over a million members, but UNIA had no viable and functional community action programs addressing the day-to-day needs of the people. There was no political agenda addressing specific policies that would have a positive effect on the community as a body politic. UNIA was primarily a cultural and economic nationalist organization with the desire to return to Africa all people of African descent.

Indeed, according to Garvey in "The Dream of a Negro Empire," it was the purpose of the Universal Negro Improvement Association to have established in Africa the brotherly cooperation that would make the interest of the African native and the American and West Indian Negro one and the same, that is to say, we shall enter a common partnership to build up Africa in the interest of our race. In theory, UNIA's agenda was to better the condition of African people socially, politically, and economically. Moreover, this transformation was to take place in Africa and not permanently in the colonies (inner cities) of America. Unlike the BPP, however, UNIA never applied its philosophy into practical application; the idea remained abstract and was never actualized.

The Historical Footprints of the Black Panther Party

Nowhere has the torch been carried with such ferocity than with the BPP. Combining all the heretofore-mentioned elements, the Party would become a major force in the history of the Black Liberation Movement, aimed at **actualizing** the ancestral dreams for self-liberation, self-empowerment, self-defense, community organizing and the yearnings of freedom for and full citizenship for blacks in a country that they built with the sweat, blood and minds of their ancestors. The Black Panther Party created a **major paradigm shift** as a **model for community organizing and self-defense. It became the first and only political party founded on the principles of a community-based organization with viable community programs and built-in protections for the community.** Moreover, the **BPP** *was* **the community**. Its membership reflected and embodied the thoughts and aspirations of the people. Bobby Seale and Huey Newton, the party's founders, were inner-city brothers who had acquired a college education but still hung out with their partners from their neighborhood. Both Huey and Bobby reflected the mindset of most African American youth growing up in the black neo-colonies. They were the brothers on the block. They stood for the brothers who hung out on the corner, who passed the bottle of WPLJ (White Port and Lemon Juice), – the poor man's champagne. They stood for the young black students at Merritt Jr. College. Black Nationalism coupled with a more radicalized campus mentality based on a Marxist internationalist worldview was typical of their mindset. Combining these two worldviews, Chairman Seale and Minister Newton set about recruiting, politically educating, and organizing the neo-colony population, in particular the unemployed "brothers" and "sisters" in the hood.

These attitudes were carried over into the Panther Vanguard ideology and hierarchical structures. The concept of developing political cadres within the neo-colonies gave the BPP its infrastructure. Its Ten Point Platform and Program would actualize this political ideology into viable community programs. Ultimately, BPP programs would be implemented in over 80 cities with 20,000 Panther organizers on the ground organizing their communities while implementing BPP programs nationwide. What made the BBP so different from other political organizations at that time were the sheer numbers dedicated to the implementation of the Ten Point Platform and Program and protecting its integrity with our lives. The Ten Point Program from October 1966 read as follows:

1. *We want freedom. We want power to determine the destiny of our Black Community.*

We believe that black people will not be free until we are able to determine our destiny.

2. *We want full employment for our people.*

We believe that the federal government is responsible and obligated to give every man employment or a guaranteed income. We believe that if the white American businessmen will not give full employment, then the means of production should be taken from the businessmen and placed in the community so that the people of the community can organize and employ all of its people and give a high standard of living.

3. *We want an end to the robbery by the white man of our black Community.*

We believe that this racist government has robbed us and now we are demanding the overdue debt of forty acres and two mules. Forty acres and two mules were promised 100 years ago as restitution for slave labor and mass murder of black people. We will accept the payment as currency which will be distributed to our many communities. The Germans are now aiding the Jews in Israel for the genocide of the Jewish people. The Germans murdered six million Jews. The American racist has taken part in the slaughter of over 50 million black people; therefore, we feel that this is a modest demand that we make.

4.   *We want decent housing, fit for shelter of human beings.*

We believe that if the white landlords will not give decent housing to our black community, then the housing and the land should be made into cooperatives so that our community, with government aid, can build and make decent housing for its people.

5.   *We want education for our people that exposes the true nature of this decadent American society. We want education that teaches us our true history and our role in the present-day society.*

We believe in an educational system that will give to our people a knowledge of self. If a man does not have knowledge of himself and his position in society and the world, then he has little chance to relate to anything else.

6.   *We want all black men to be exempt from military service.*

We believe that black people should not be forced to fight in the military service to defend a racist government that does not protect us. We will not fight and kill other people of color in the world who, like black people, are being victimized by the white racist government of America. We will protect ourselves from the force and violence of the racist police and the racist military, by whatever means necessary.

7.   *We want an immediate end to POLICE BRUTALITY and MURDER of black people.*

We believe we can end police brutality in our black community by organizing black self-defense groups that are dedicated to defending our black community from racist police oppression and brutality. The Second Amendment to the Constitution of the United States gives a right to bear arms. We therefore believe that all black people should arm themselves for self-defense.

8.   *We want freedom for all black men held in federal, state, county and city prisons and jails.*

We believe that all black people should be released from the many jails and prison because they have not received a fair and impartial trial.

9.   We want all black people when brought to trial to be tried in court by a jury of their peer group or people from their black communities, as defined by the Constitution of the United States.

We believe that the courts should follow the United States Constitution so that black people will receive fair trials. The 14th Amendment of the U.S. Constitution gives a man a right to be tried by his peer group. A peer is a person from a similar economic, social, religious, geographical, environmental, historical and racial background. To do this the court will be forced to select a jury from the black community from which the black defendant came. We have been and are being tried by all-white juries that have no understanding of the "average reasoning man" of the black community.

10.   We want land, bread, housing, education, clothing, Justice and peace. And as our major political objective, a United Nations-supervised plebiscite to be held throughout the black colony in which only black colonial subjects will be allowed to participate for the purpose of determining the will of black people as to their national destiny.

In each city where BPP chapters were established, the chapter/office created a community center which was the focal point of all community programs and activities. The number of party members in each chapter determined the number of Panther Pads needed to house members. The location selected for these entities generally came from the most depressed and highly populated areas in the African American communities. After the selection was made and the properties secured, the chapters' members would obtain a city map and map out areas of two square miles around the properties to canvas, recruit and politicize the community around the Ten Point Platform and Program. Using this strategy and with their people- oriented programs, the Party solidified a powerful base of community support.

Yet, in order to truly grasp the significance of this paradigm shift in community organizing one must examine the level of commitment by BPP members to the cause. This is a subject that has always been overlooked. In order to build a grassroots movement of such magnitude, people had to change their daily lives and routines. Once you became a Party member you had to leave your former life behind. If you lived with your parents, you had to move out. If you were a college student and lived on campus you had to move off campus. If you had your own house/apartment, it became a Panther Pad. Newly formed Panther Cadres lived in these Panther Pads or Safe Houses. Structuring their lives around the Program to be implemented in each community in each city became the new normal. Once you became a Panther, it was 24/7.

This new normal would change your life forever. Once you made the commitment to the liberation struggle, your outside social life ended. Those who were over 21 were no longer allowed to frequent nightclubs or bars. Those who were underage were not allowed to attend dances or parties. Once committed to the revolution you pledged not only in word but in action, to break all bonds which tied you to the social order and to the social norms with all its laws, moralities and customs, and all of America's generally accepted conventions. And then there were those who were chosen to do so, to blend in with the enemy as sleeper cells in order to destroy the enemy when needed.

Within the walls of Panther Pads and community centers we became our best friends, our comrades in arms, devoid of any contacts with the outside world in any meaningful way. We had no time to cultivate or maintain friendships outside of the cadres. Our everyday practice had to reflect our dedication to the revolution. The degree of our friendship and revolutionary love was determined by the degree of dedication shown toward the cause of our revolutionary struggle. The revolutionary despises public opinion. It despises and hates the existing social morality in all its manifestations. For the cadre. Morality is everything which contributes to the triumph of the revolution. Immorality and criminality are everything that stands in the way,

It is superfluous to speak of revolutionary bonds among revolutionaries committed to a common bond, unless there is unity of purpose. The whole strength of Panther commitment was based on this principle. Every evening after completing our assigned task during the day, each Panther Pad, Safe House, or Community Center location would conduct criticism and self-criticism sessions. We who had the same revolutionary passion and understanding would deliberate all important matters of the day together and come to unanimous decisions together and draw conclusions on critical analysis and not subjective feelings. This was another unique characteristic of the BPP, a community-based organization using the tool of criticism and self-criticism to rid oneself of the self-first motives of a capitalist society, which placed selfishness over the common good of the community. All decisions reached from such meetings were to enhance individual growth and be self-critical, and all collective decisions were made to strengthen the Party and enhance the programs serving the African American communities. It was always about going from a lower to higher level of consciousness on a daily basis. .

This was the uniqueness of the BPP as a political organization based in communities throughout America. Effectively, the Panthers blended into the communities, became one with the people; they became next-door neighbors to the people they were serving. Every member of a Panther Pad had a duty to perform. Some might be tasked with the night watch duties, ironically to guard the premises from police attack. Those assigned to the breakfast program were up at 5 a.m. And, as a part of the health Cadre, the Free Health Clinic opened at 10 a.m. There was also the shoe or clothing drive, which began at 9 a.m. Members of the information cadres sold newspapers on street corners or went door to door in the communities educating the people about the BPP Program. Finally, there were the stokers, the presenters who traveled from college to college, speaking at fundraiser events, organizing Black Student Unions and Black Studies Programs.

These activities reflected the typical day in the life of a Panther, a quintessential community organizer serving the needs of the people while addressing the aspirations of the community. Indeed, according to Louis Heath, one of the reasons for the BPP's extraordinary popularity in the black communities during the late 1960s was its various community service programs. These programs ranged from self-defense and security from police-state harassment to the provision of liberation schools and free health clinics. One of the signature BPP programs was the Free Breakfast for Children Program that fed hundreds of thousands of black kids per day. The health clinics also established a viable base of strong community support. 15

The day-to-day life of a Panther was a perilous one. When we left our Panther Pads, safe houses or Community centers we had to travel in groups. Whenever the cadres left to carry out their daily functions in the various programs they always traveled together. In my travels I was always accompanied by a bodyguard and the person selected would be determined on the degree of danger involved in my movements. Two of my favorites were David and Richard, both from Miami, Florida. We were constantly under surveillance by the police and every available opportunity they would, pull us over when we were driving and try and provoke an incident. Richard was the more intellectual of the two and was always quite engaging in his intellectual curiosity, to the extent that at times I would have to remind him of the task at hand. Nevertheless, he was a beautiful young brother who was deeply committed to the revolution and was willing to stop a bullet for the cause of freedom. I had much love for both. I knew their hearts and I knew that they would go to war at a moment's notice.

Once all daily assignments were completed all Panthers would retire to their safe havens, checking in with the watch commander to let them know everyone was accounted for. We would then secure our locations, most of which had reinforced steel walls around windows and doors. Some had sandbags, and other locations had trap doors leading into tunnels that were forged into sewer systems. After dinner we would have political education classes and our criticism and self-criticism sessions would begin. After we finished, what social life we had would ensue within the walls of the safe haven. A little music – Marvin Gay, "What's Going On," or James Brown, "I'm Black and I'm Proud" or the Stylistics, "People Make the World Go Around". Panthers had a drink called Bitter Dog; I will not bother you with the ingredients, but it worked. We danced a little, made love, and discussed our chances of seeing the morning light. After we shut it down, those who were assigned to night watch would take their posts. Back window, front window, side windows – locked and loaded as sleep fell over the Panther Pads in the hope of seeing another day. Such was the case at Panther locations throughout the country.

Even though we were a national organization and had revolutionary love for all Party members, the heartfelt love was felt most among the comrades living in your immediate Panther Pads and Community Centers. The closeness was measured by the level of commitment, the sweat and tears shed in a common struggle for a common purpose…serving the needs of the people. We always greeted each other lovingly with the phrase "Power to the People", followed with a warm embrace. During the early morning those who had completed night watch would be treated to the smells of morning breakfast being prepared by sisters Betty, Deborah, Vanita, Sheeba and Tweety, who were making preparation for the patter of little feet and the rush of children from the Community anxiously awaiting breakfast from our Free Breakfast Program. For some it would be their only meal of the day and we reveled in the thought that we were able to provide such a service. At the close of day Robert, our sergeant at arms, would have weapons drills and everyone had to master the art of breaking down and cleaning various weapons blindfolded.

After breakfast, the assigned Office Manager or Watch Commander would log the daily assignment instructions for the Chapter. At times, Deborah, my other half, would take such responsibility and she would alternate responsibilities with sister Vee who was as capable. Sheeba ran the Clinic and was always accompanied by a male Panther; more often than not, Richard was her travel buddy. Robert and Michael often headed the information Cadre and would station the rank-and-file members to the various major intersections in the

Berkeley community, including the U.C. Berkeley campus to sell Panther newspapers and educate the people around the Ten Point platform and program. The last assignment was always a tricky one for me. My beloved parents had given my 14-year-old sister, Marlonna, permission to move to Berkeley, California from Indianapolis, Indiana to be with and be protected by her big brother whom she loved dearly. Imagine the level of trust my parents must have had for their son to look after their young teenage daughter, knowing what the stakes were and the danger she would encounter. To this day we remain inseparable.

Under those circumstances I kept her in the office as much as possible and enrolled her at Berkeley High. After school was out, Marlonna was assigned to the Watch Commander, typing and answering the phone. But of course, being the feisty young teen she was, she wanted more action. She became our community rep, working closely with the families within our four-square block area, always in the company of Richard, my most trusted young Panther. She became awfully close to Momma Smalls, who ran the West Berkeley Community and whose six children were the leaders of our Panther Cubs. On some Saturdays, the kids who participated in the Breakfast program would attend liberation school. Afterwards, dressed in their navy-blue shirts/blouses and black pants/skirts, they would march through the neighborhood singing liberation songs. These same Panther Cubs were also our eyes and ears. They formed bike patrols and would cycle around the neighborhood, and when a police car was spotted they would peddle to the center, yelling out, "The Pigs are coming!" Or, they would say, "Beware, the pigs were parked down the street." Such was the relationship with the community we served. We loved them dearly and it was a reciprocal love, a heartfelt love beyond description.

As our notoriety spread we became the focal point of many rallies and programs sponsored on campus, especially issues dealing with police brutality and racism at home, and anti-imperialist wars of national liberation throughout the Third World. We sponsored the visit of Angela Davis when she was a professor at UCLA; Herbert Marcuse, the great German philosopher, Marxist and existentialist; and Dr. Martin Luther King Jr., to name a few. It was from the UC Berkeley campus and the Greater Bay Area community that my political outlook would develop. Indeed, the West Berkeley 10th Street office and the former home of Chairman Bobby Seale, a courageous and beautiful brother and certainly a decent human being, became known as the spot. It was only fitting that it would become the hub of such activity. Fate would also have it that my first national assignment would be flying to New Haven, Connecticut to organize Yale

University and help develop infrastructure for the National defense of Bobby Seale and the New Haven Nine (Panthers accused of the murder of Alex Rackley, an alleged informant who had infiltrated the Black Panther Party).

The added value of the proximity of the UC Berkeley campus to the Berkeley chapter, we were never short on resources. The chapter's composition was that of some UC Berkeley students and we used our contacts on campus to funnel money and material resources into the African American communities of West and South Berkeley. The Free Breakfast Program and the George Jackson Free Health Clinic were built from the ground up with monetary aid from the support network put in place.

In an interview conducted by a national educational publication with Doctor Tolbert Smalls our Health Care Director, gave insight to our community-based Health Clinic: *"The Berkeley Panther Group was under the leadership of John Turner, and the person who did a lot of the grassroots work was Sheeba Grayson—who I believe you've talked to. They were instrumental in getting the building, getting a plumber to come in and fix things in the rooms. The clinic opened in 1971. At the time the clinic opened, I was working there Mondays, Wednesdays and Fridays—Monday afternoons, Wednesday afternoons and Friday mornings...I was going to prisons to visit Angela Davis, and Friday mornings to visit George Jackson at San Quentin prison. Prior to the opening of the clinic, I used to do house calls for all the Panthers—I took care of everyone from the babies to the leadership. They would call me, and I would do house calls. After the free clinic opened, there were fewer house calls because I could see people inside the free clinic. The free clinic was very well thought-up. The Berkeley Public Health met with us and they did all our gonorrhea cultures and syphilis tests; I got the lab tech at the center I worked out of the health center and, Henry Smith – we called him "Smitty" – did our electrophoresis. We were doing hemoglobin electrophoresis on our sickle cell patients—it was state-of-the-art. I got all the doctors—Joe Selvie, an epidemiologist, and Bruce Bee and two other physicians who were ophthalmologists. At full capacity we were working five days a week; it was a busy clinic. I would sometimes be there at two o'clock in morning; I remember seeing several people one night. It served a lot of the needs of the community in Berkeley. I worked there from 1970 to 1974."*

Indeed, the George Jackson Free Health Clinic was our crown jewel. Dr. Smalls was a hardworking and dedicated brother for the Community. Sister Sheeba was my right hand. She ran the clinic with a high degree of efficiency and was truly a dedicated Panther of the West Berkeley Chapter. Her other half was a down-home brother named Mojo out of central headquarters in West Oakland. Sheeba eventually gave birth to their Panther baby who was christened Attica after the courageous brothers who were killed during the Attica prison uprising. This chapter also helped facilitate a national campaign to educate the public around sickle-cell anemia, the blood disease responsible for killing tens of thousands of African Americans nationwide. These programs allowed the BBP to create a different political subculture. The epitome of this subculture was representative of the Oakland/ Berkeley California community. This community was the hotbed of the revolution and the "Eye of the Storm."

In addition, the Berkeley Chapter used the campus as a staging area to recruit more community activists for any and all political issues surrounding the black community. We organized boycotts and marched for community control of police and won a ballot initiative to curb, control, and monitor police violence in the African American community. The community control of police became part of a community review board that monitored the behavior of the police department. A program similar to this certainly is a blueprint activists need to emulate for controlling police behavior today. Moreover, we would go door to door and set up self-defense groups throughout the community. In retrospect, because we had inside information on police movement in Berkeley it gave us a degree of protection that most Panther offices did not have.

The success of our Party was phenomenal and was even more evident between 1968 and 1969, known as the Year of the Panther. Our membership exploded and we opened 23 new offices as we galvanized mass base support from the anti-war movement. Our struggle was moving from lower to higher level of political consciousness as we built a mass-based anti-imperialist movement. What we witnessed was the intersection of the Civil Rights movement, the anti-war movement and the Black Liberation movement. Before they knew it, we were linking up with white student radicals grouped in the Students for a Democratic Society, the Peace and Freedom Party, The Young Lords, AIM (The American Indian Movement) and Black Student Unions throughout the country. While we confronted the ills of social injustice, we had continuous confrontations with the police state, and it became the standard of our daily political life.

Finally, the Berkeley Chapter of the Party was charged with the responsibility of organizing and maintaining the defense committee for one of the most celebrated political trials in American history, George Jackson and the Soledad Brothers. The BPP certainly reflected a paradigm shift in community organizing in the African American community. From our Panther Pads in West Berkeley, we directed the ebb and flow of revolutionary activity from our base of operation. For the first time in African American history, highly intelligent and young (some in their teens), African American men and women with a political agenda were rallying the masses around viable programs that served the interests of the black community. As the BPP grew in stature they galvanized the political consciousness of the African American communities around its Ten Point Program. From a national perspective, this had never been done.

The Beginning of the End

For those reasons, the agenda of black independence and community action programs, protected by the politics of self-defense soon made the BPP an enemy of the state. As the youth revolt against the Vietnam War grew, our heroic stance drew many activists of all nationalities towards our revolutionary politics. We sent 'stokers' (speakers) to major college campuses to address college students and educated them between the connection of an American Imperialist war of aggression against the Vietnamese people and the neo-colonial war of white terrorism waged against black people in American cites. Moreover, our propaganda machine was in full operation. At its peak, The Panther weekly newspaper reached a circulation of 250,000 per week, a measure of the support that we generated amongst our political base, both the Black Community and beyond. However, we now had the attention of Richard Nixon who swept to power in the 1968 presidential election.

It would be this trio of President Nixon, his Attorney General, John Mitchell and J. Edgar Hoover, director of the FBI, who would form the nucleus of the plan to take down the Party and effectively destroy the revolutionary movement during this critical moment in American history. Nixon encouraged police across the country to attack, murder and frame Panthers nationwide. The entire state apparatus, from the FBI down to state and local authorities, were coordinated in the ferocious attacks. Legal niceties were dispensed with; this was fascist, authoritarian justice emanating from the police state apparatus. As the time stream moved across the American landscape, the original slave patrollers had morphed into a highly specialized and deadly militarized killing machines. In 1968 we became increasingly under attack. The Panther Party was squarely in the crosshairs as casualties mounted, as did the number of political prisoners. What the Black Lives Matter Movement of today is witnessing pales in comparison to the sheer brutality and assassinations we suffered at the hands of the Nixon/Hoover Gestapo fascist forces.

Within two years, 28 Panthers were dead. Many others caught up in long, drawn-out court battles. Newton's epic series of appeals against his framed murder conviction became the era's cause *célèbre*, with "Free Huey" becoming the battle cry as would "Free Bobby" and "Free the Soledad Brothers" later. Our support continued to grow during this period of repression. The severity of the repression drew the public's ire, and the number of political prisoners forged more allies. The Prison movement grew out of these confrontations with the police state's apparatus of repression.

However, as the attacks intensified, we became hard pressed to fend off state violence and broaden our circle of allies while maintaining our identity as the staunchest revolutionaries still standing. During these difficult times our International Revolutionary allies forged links to an underground apparatus. The Cubans provided military training and political asylum to Panthers fleeing US authorities. Assata Shakur, a ranking Party leader from the Harlem, NY Chapter was one of the NY 21 who were arrested and framed on conspiracy to coordinate bombings of three police stations and the Queens, NY board of education. Shakur fled captivity and went underground, eventually finding sanctuary in Cuba. Our greatest internationalist achievement was the establishment of an officially recognized embassy by African, Cuban and Chinese Governments located in Algeria where our international section was headed by Kathleen and Eldridge Cleaver.

It was during this time that I met Brother Fred Hampton, our charismatic leader out of Chicago. He came to the Bay Area to organize coalition groups there, and we facilitated these endeavors by organizing meetings on the UC Berkeley campus. It was Hampton, not Jesse Jackson, who set up the original Rainbow Coalition. We formed coalitions with the Young Lords (the Puerto Rican movement), AIM, (the Native American Indian Nation), Brown Berets (Chicano movement), The Young Patriots and The White Panther Party, who were poor whites out of the southern Appalachian and northern ghettos. At age 17, Hampton was a rising star, a black youth headed for greatness. He graduated from Maywood High School with honors, a Junior Achievement Award, and three varsity letters. Four years later he was assassinated. His charisma was responsible for organizing a 500-member youth group as director of the

Maywood NAACP. His progressive political stance, however, was offensive to the more conservative Maywood community of 27,000. Chairman Fred would eventually move to the West Side of Chicago where he would organize the local chapter of the Black Panther Party as Panther chief. There he became one of our most effective organizers and one of the most eloquent speakers in the Black Panther Party.

Subsequently, during the Year of the Panther, the political landscape would change forever. Today's Black Lives Matter movement may march for social justice and challenges police brutality and the criminal justice system, but it does not have a face nor a political party with a fixed location that can draw the ire of the police state. BLM activists have experienced only limited violence – teargas to the nostrils or a baton to the head. By the spring of 1968, the intersection of the civil rights and the anti-war movement, along with the Black Liberation Movement meant that the Black Panthers became victims of state-sponsored violence of a ferocity, brutality and repression never before seen.

Five years earlier, Malcolm X and Medgar Evers had been assassinated, followed by the murders of Jimmie Lee Jackson, and the three civil rights workers in Mississippi – James Chaney, Michael Schwerner and Andrew Goodman. These acts of white domestic terrorist violence would culminate in the Birmingham bombings, which took the precious lives of babies, and the brutal assault of John Lewis and the civil rights marchers on the Edmund Pettus Bridge. All these events were spread out over 42 months (about three and a half years) and would segue into 1968 with extreme violence perpetrated against the movement and the Black Panther Party. For a period of 18 months a reign of terror unseen in American history would be unleashed against the Black Panther Party.

On April 4, 1968, Martin Luther King Jr. was assassinated in Memphis, Tennessee while supporting the rights of garbage workers. King's politics were beginning to swing to the left. He became an anti-war activist, and he also began to challenge the military industrial complex, calling it a threat to the common good of all Americans and the Vietnamese people. He was also getting more involved in the labor movement, becoming an advocate for union rights of workers. Many thought King was overstepping his boundaries, including some in the civil rights movement. During his last visit to UC Berkeley, months before his assassination, he shared his changing views and was convinced it does not do any good to integrate a lunch counter if you cannot afford the meal. He also shared his love and respect for those of us who were in the Party, but he could not justify sending his people to a certain death by advocating armed self-defense. It was ironic to some, that the assassins should then take his life a few months later. However, we were not surprised. His newfound voice and left-leaning political position posed a greater threat than ever to the fascist police state apparatus. Hoover finally got his wish – his chance, too – and silenced the man whom he loathed.

Two days later Panthers would clash with Oakland police in a violent episode that forever changed the political landscape of the Party, the revolutionary movement and the city from which it grew. On April 6, 1968, with hands in the air, Bobby Hutton, the Panthers' first recruit and the group's treasurer, was shot dead by Oakland officers. He instantly became a martyr for many in the black revolutionary movement. "Lil Bobby", as he was affectionately called by his comrades, became the first fatality of the Black Panther Party, at the age of just 17. In Oakland, tensions between the Panthers and the police were frayed beyond repair, and an explosion of racially charged violence was inevitable.

Two days after King's death, the expectations in Oakland were realized. A confrontation between the Panthers and the police culminated in a shootout that lasted 90 minutes. A tear gas barrage led to the Panthers' surrender at Union and 25th street. Four people, including two police officers, were wounded. One person, Lil Bobby, was dead. According to the police version of the story, Hutton, came out of the house armed and tried to flee before being shot. According to Cleaver's interview with *The Chronicle*, he said Hutton *"had his hands high in the air until he died."* Hutton's funeral on April 12, 1968, at Ephesian Church of God and Christ in Berkeley was attended by about 1,200 people, including the esteemed actor Marlon Brando. It was preceded by a news conference held by Bobby at the site of the shooting. Bobby gave a heartfelt message at the funeral: *"Bobby Hutton was a living example of infinite love for his people ... and their peace and freedom."* Looking down at the open coffin, Bobby added, *"We salute you, Bobby."*

Bobby Hutton to the right of Bobby Seale before his assassination

After his release from jail, Cleaver would go underground and reappear in Algiers, North Africa where the Party would set up an international branch of The Black Panther Party. Three months later, the first attack on a Panther office would occur in Seattle, Washington, followed with the arrest of Brother Aaron Dixon, who at that time was the captain of the Seattle Chapter. What would follow would become the frontal assault of J Edgar Hoover's COINTELPRO counter-insurgency war on the Black Panther Party.

Counter Insurgency War Against the Black Panther Party
Cointelpro the Assasination of Chairman Fred Hampton

Chairman Fred Hampton at the Chicago Chapter

Cointelpro Manifesto

Prevent the Coalition of militant black nationalist groups. In unity there is strength, a truism that is no less valid for all its triteness. An effective coalition…might be the first step toward a real "Mau Mau" in America, the beginning of a true black revolution.

Prevent the rise of a "messiah" who could unify, and electrify, the militant black nationalist movement. Malcolm X might have been such a "messiah"; he is the martyr of the movement today…Elijah Muhammad is less of a threat because of his age. King could be a very real contender for this position should he abandon his supposed "obedience" to "white liberal doctrines" (nonviolence) and embrace black nationalism. Stokely Carmichael has the necessary charisma to be a real threat in this way.

J. Edgar Hoover created COINTELPRO to infiltrate and to neutralize the BPP. In 1968, the United States Government unleashed violent attacks against the BPP. The party members, its leadership, and its community programs became targets for total annihilation by the state police apparatus. Philadelphia, New Orleans, Los Angeles, Baltimore, Philadelphia, New York, Chicago, and the Bay Area alone, there were over 51 attacks on Panther offices, Panther Pads and individuals, as well as over 1,000 arrests. There were 31 known assassinations as COINTELPRO unleashed over 7,500 agents provocateurs and informants throughout the county, infiltrating and undermining the party while provoking incidents of violence. These tactics would cause total disruption, confusion, and chaos, and ultimately destruction within the Party. We became the victims of the most brutal and well-orchestrated form of state-sponsored violence and terrorism ever unleashed against Black bodies who were representative of American citizens fighting for and demanding social justice and equal treatment under the laws of the United States Constitution.

On December 3rd Brother Fred Hampton had given a memorable speech where he was at his heartfelt, instructive best. It was directed toward his rainbow coalition groups to unify around a common cause. The following day, on December 4th, 1969, this beautiful revolutionary soul of the Black Panther Party was assassinated while sleeping in his bed. In the pre-dawn hours Chicago police, under the direction of the Cook County State's Attorney's Office under the explicit direction of Edward Hanrahan, J. Edgar Hoover and Richard Nixon, raided the headquarters of the local chapter of the Black Panther Party. When the smoke cleared, Chairman Fred Hampton and party member Mark Clark were dead. Four others lay seriously wounded, including sister Deborah Johnson who was eight months pregnant with Fred's son, who today carries his father's name and is just as caring, and wonderful a human being. Those of us who got to know this beautiful man-child were taken aback by his wit, his charm and his wisdom beyond his years. He was chatty, and his smile would accentuate the dimples in his cheeks as he enthusiastically greeted those who professed a strong revolutionary love for the people.

On that fateful night, officers assigned to Cook County State's Attorney Edward V. Hanrahan approached the dwelling with a warrant authorizing a search for illegal weapons. Gunfire — police claimed they faced a barrage from inside the apartment — erupted shortly after the raid began at 4:45 a.m. When the smoke cleared, Chairman Fred, 21, and Brother Clark, 22, were dead. Four other Panthers and two police officers were wounded. Seven Panthers in the Panther Pad were charged with attempted murder. The *Chicago Tribune* editorialized that the Black Panthers "have declared war on society" and as a result "forfeited the right to considerations ordinary violators of the law might claim." The headline over the editorial: *"No quarter for wild beasts.* "It was part of a coordinated assault hatched by the FBI and the Nixon administration Justice Department. Black Bodies once again were demonized and murdered with impunity.

Harold Bell, one of our wounded comrades, testified that everyone immediately surrendered. Bell and two others, including sister Deborah Johnson, were ordered out of Hampton's bedroom, where he lay motionless and bloodied. Then, according to Bell, "Police fired from point-blank range into Hampton's body." Bell's testimony about Hampton's execution-style death has been supported by Deborah Johnson and other survivors. Johnson testified that, after emptying his gun into Hampton's bed, the cop walked away muttering, *"He's good and dead now."*

Why didn't Hampton get out of bed and try to resist? About three hours before the shooting, at 1:30 a.m., Brother Fred was in bed talking to his mother on the telephone, when he fell asleep in mid-conversation. Sister Deborah tried to wake him but to no avail. During the raid others tried to wake him, not knowing that the most despicable person on this earth, William O'Neal, a Panther informant for the FBI, had drugged him earlier. He aided and abetted this betrayal of trust. He drugged Fred and had given the FBI drawings of the apartment and identified where Fred would be sleeping. Mark Clark and Fred never had a chance. Fred's body was riddled with 83 bullets and our hearts were broken. Panther paranoia became the norm. We were always expecting the next raid and wondering who would be exposed as the next informant, the next William O'Neal.

Now we know two weeks before the attack, O'Neal provided the FBI with a detailed floor plan of Panther headquarters, complete with an "X" over Fred Hampton's bed. Most of the shots were fired at that spot. To understand the gravity of this betrayal could only be understood by Panthers who were charged with the responsibility of ensuring that our comrades were safe and would see the light of another day. Those Panthers throughout the country, who on a nightly basis, were assigned to secure the life of their comrades while sleeping were appalled and crushed to know that O'Neal's betrayal was so precise that it included drawings and the exact spot where Chairman Fred laid his body down to sleep. It was utterly despicable, this act of betrayal. It was a violation of a sacred trust. When you pledge to defend and protect your comrades, especially when they lay sleeping, they entrust their lives in your hands. When that trust is violated and costs human lives, you deserve to burn in Hell. You no longer deserve the right or privilege to walk this earth.

Under those circumstances, it was truly heartbreaking for me because I had met with Chairman Fred as he was known to us, a few weeks earlier. I was looking forward to working with him more closely. As I reflected on the events that had occurred, especially that of running dog lackey and informant William O'Neal, I thought about comments made to me by our General Field Marshall George Jackson, who had a keen sense of history and reminded me as such. He pointed out that within the neo-colony there had developed a continuation of the freak sub-culture that perpetuates our neo-slave condition. *It causes us to betray each other*, it is a sub-culture that works in the shadows with our oppressor. It was blacks who killed Malcolm, informed on Nat Turner and Denmark Vesey. And later it would be O'Neal and Gloves Davis whose hands were on the triggers that assassinated Chairman Fred Hampton. To validate his point, Jackson reminded us that the slave rebellion planned by Gabriel Prosser was thwarted by a slave acting as informant. According to *Jackson, this freak sub-culture has always produced traitors who turn on their own people.*

O'Neal was one such neo-slave, instructed by the slave master to carry out the FBI's "divide-and-conquer" plan. The bureau feared a pact being forged between the Panthers and Jeff Fort, head of the Blackstone Rangers, the most powerful gang in the Chicago black neo-colony. Part of the COINTELPRO strategy was to cause a rift between Forte and our Party. An anonymous letter was sent to Forte and it read as follows: *"The brothers that run the Panthers blame you for blocking their thing and there's supposed to be a hit out for you.... I know what to do if I was you."* This letter-writing scheme was part of O'Neal's work for COINTELPRO.

Following the lethal raid, O'Neal was rewarded with a $3,000 bonus, according to FBI Agent Robert Piper, who wrote in a memo: *"Our source [O'Neal] was the man."* From the voices traversing the ripples of time, in 1828, David Walker, in *Appeal in Four Articles* condemned and attacked the ignorance and treachery of black men conspiring against one another in the interest of the oppressor. This same mentality manifested itself in the black revolutionary struggle during the 60s and 70s: in Walkers own words, *I am persuaded that many of my brethren, particularly those who are ignorantly in league with slave holders or tyrants, who acquire their daily bread by the blood and sweat of their more ignorant brethren and are too ignorant to see an inch beyond their noses.* Whether during slavery or neo-slavery, the William O'Neals of our freak sub-culture will always be the despicable ones, the outliers, the traitors, the soulless vampire preying on the blood of their brethren.

Words from one of the last speeches of Chairman Fred

"We always say in the Black Panther Party that they can do anything they want to us. We might not be back. I might be in jail. I might be anywhere. But when I

leave, you'll remember I said, with the last words on my lips, that I am a revolutionary. And you're going to have to keep on saying that. You're going to have to say that I am a proletarian, I am the people."

The Spin Machine and The Subversion of Truth

As Panther chief in Chicago, Chairman became one of our most effective organizers and one of the most eloquent speakers in the Black Panther Party. His abilities were never more apparent while engineering the development of the Rainbow Coalition of people of color, including poor whites, while orchestrating a tenuous peace among the Chicago gangland community. His powers of persuasion, his rhetorical skills, and his ability to build coalitions placed him at the top of Edgar Hoover's and Hanrahan's hit list. His targeted assassination was a severe blow to the Panther Party and his Rainbow Coalition. The state apparatus feared his ability to wield this coalition into a formidable force that would become a threat to the white power base in Chicago.

In attempting to resolve this issue of coalition building amongst the growing revolutionary organizations, the raid on Chicago Panther headquarters must be put into context. At this point in time and for reasons just mentioned, the FBI supervised a nationwide effort to destroy the Black Panther Party as it was no longer seen as an organization spouting the paranoid rantings of leftists, but a fact documented in the *Staff Report* of the US Senate Church Committee. The report stated that the FBI's COINTELPRO (Counter-Intelligence program) used "dangerous, degrading or blatantly unconstitutional techniques to destroy the BPP for fear of its growing influence on other left-wing radical groups. During the COINTELPRO years, the FBI paid out more than $7.4 million in wages to informants and provocateurs, more than twice the amount allocated to organized crime informants. Operating out of 41 field offices, COINTELPRO agents supervised agents-provocateurs, placed *"snitch jackets"* on bona-fide Panthers by having them mislabeled as informants, and drafted poison-pen letters in attempts to incite violence against the Panthers and divide the party leadership.

The web of lies and the spin machine around the assassination of Fred and Mark were quickly debunked. The state told the *Tribune* that the officers had no idea Hampton or Clark were in the apartment. To buttress claims that police were under attack, Hanrahan and his aides released photographs "which they said conclusively proved the Panthers opened the battle by firing a shotgun blast through the apartment door," according to the *Tribune*.

But the prosecutor's attempt to manage the news backfired. The day after the *Tribune* published its story, the <u>Sun-Times</u> published its own Page One version. The photos released by Hanrahan's office did not display bullet holes caused by a Panther gunfire but were simply nail heads manufactured by the police, the *Sun-Times* reported. *Daily News* columnist Mike Royko wrote that he inspected the apartment *"more than once" and concluded Hanrahan's claim that police encountered gunfire from the Panthers "doesn't mesh with the condition of the place. "In fact, what was determined was the police falsified their reports and it was proven that the gunfire came from police weapons into the apartments."* Next, Hoover, Nixon and the counter-intelligence forces had their sights aimed at Los Angeles.

Los Angeles Chapter Under Seige

The state-sponsored, military-style attacks on Panthers would continue four days later. On December 8, 1969, for the first time on American soil, a newly created special tactical team unit would be used to attack American citizens. What today is commonly known as a SWAT team spearheaded the attack, which lasted more than five hours. The brothers and sisters under attack held for its duration and only surrendered when they ran out of ammunition. In 1968, as black insurrection was spreading across the country in response to police brutality, the Southern California Chapter of the Black Panther Party was formed to help combat the growing threat. The Party established monitoring patrols in Black neighborhoods and worked to ensure police accountability.

On December 8, 1969, the LAPD served a warrant to search Party headquarters at 41st Street and Central Avenue for stolen weapons. Though the warrant was obtained using false information provided by the FBI, police used it as the basis to ambush 11 Party members inside the building. More than 300 police officers, including the newly militarized Special Weapons and Tactics (SWAT) team, descended on the headquarters. Armed with 5,000 rounds of ammunition, gas masks, a helicopter, a tank, and a military-grade grenade weapons, they initiated a violent domestic terror attack against our Los Angeles Black Panther Headquarters.

Five hours and 5,000 rounds later, three Panthers and three law enforcement officers lay wounded. During the raging battle, Panthers withstood the SWAT assault, including bombs dropped on the roof of the building. The most intimate and riveting narrative of the events unfolding were given by Party member Wayne Pharr. His book, <u>*Nine Lives of a Black Panther*</u>: *A Story of Survival* and its account of the raid, was published in the <u>Los Angeles Times Magazine.</u> <u>It</u> reads as follows*: on December 8, 1969, Brother Wayne Pharr was abruptly awakened in the gunroom of Panther Headquarters on 41st and Central. He said he had fallen asleep after exploring the sewers – mapping the tunnels they would use as escape routes if they were attacked. Shotgun still in hand, he was awakened by shouts from Melvin Cotton Smith. "They're out there," Smith yelled. "Get up" "Out where" Pharr said in a dazed state of sleep, "It's 5:30 in the fucking morning." Accordingly, Smith was high on his adrenalin and began to grab weapons and ammo and, along with Pharr, shotgun in hand, headed toward the front door.*

Almost as soon as the SWAT team reached their destination, the door to Panther headquarters flew open without warning, and SWAT members, clad in black with automatic assault weapons in hand, opened fire. Pharr, with the instincts of a cat, much like a Black Panther, had already dove into a sandbag bunker flanking the door. A split second later, Smith emerged with a Thompson submachine gun with finger on the trigger. The Panthers had pounced. Bullets flew from the Panther frontal assault and connected with the chests of their targets who were wearing bullet proof vest.

The force of impact from a Thompson pinned the SWAT members in the doorway, creating a bottleneck. It gave Pharr time to adjust his focus on the direction of the invader's movement. Trusting in their military-style flak jackets, the SWAT team pushed forward into the teeth of Smith's Thompson in their attempts to return fire. What they failed to see was Pharr at the ready inside his sandbag bunker. Shotgun in hand, the brother opened fire, blasting round after round from the side of the intruders, as Smith continued to hammer them from the front. Be that as it may, it was later determined that Smith was an alleged informant working with the FBI.

The invaders had no choice but to retreat, dragging their wounded with them across the street, out of the line of fire. One of the most aggressive and heavily armed shootouts in American history had begun, pitting the newly constituted paramilitary police force: Special Weapons and Tactics, a.k.a. SWAT, against a beautiful and courageous group of young brothers and sisters of the revolutionary vanguard, a.k.a. The Black Panther Party. From a tactical standpoint, the LAPD considered the encounter a disaster and a political embarrassment. From our perspective, it was a rebuke and a resounding victory for the revolutionary vanguard. How could 300 men of a newly formed counterinsurgency force, heavily armed with the most advanced weaponry, not attain victory but were instead fought to a standstill…a draw, and public humiliation!

Out of the shadows would emerge Panther leader Elmer "Geronimo" Pratt, a decorated Vietnam war vet, who used his military training to successfully fortify the building while introducing the idea of creating underground tunnels from the interior basements into the sewer systems as escape routes. Ironically, Geronimo was the main target of the SWAT mission and his location inside the headquarters was like the target assassination of Chairman Fred in Chicago. Soon thereafter offices followed Geronimo's lead. Our Chapter in Berkeley, California initiated that process and became part of Party members' daily assignment, working as excavators connecting the tunnel to the city's sewer system. Ultimately, the FBI recognized Pratt's value to the Party and framed him for a murder he did not commit. He was tried, convicted and served 27 years. We both, at different points in time, were remanded to San Quentin and shared valuable time and kinship when given the opportunity. On June 10, 1997, Pratt was released from prison then moved to Tanzania and died in 2011 at the age of 63.

For five hours, the 11 courageous brothers and sisters demonstrated that when people are united for a righteous and common cause, they can never be defeated. It was only after they had exhausted all their ammunition that they waved the white flag. These comrades became a symbol of sheer courageousness on that fateful day. They symbolized a victory not only for Panthers nationwide, but the entire black communities throughout the ripples of time… for Opelousas, LA; Tulsa, Oklahoma; East St. Louis; IL, Elaine, AR; and the countless number of black people who bore the brunt of police brutality from white domestic terrorism throughout the time continuum. We will always SALUTE and HONOR your COURAGE!

Power to the People - a salute to the LA Panther Heroes

General Field Marshall George Jackson: A Message to the Black Community Huey P. Newton Minister of Defense: A Message to the Panther Party

After the commando-style attack, the Chicago Police apparatus coordinated with an FBI informant on a mission to kill Black Panther Chairman Fred Hampton and Mark Clark. Following the operation against the LA office and the black revolutionary struggle, George Jackson, the General Field Marshal of the Black Panther Party, gave an emboldened warning: ***Our savior is the Black Panther Party. Don't avoid them and allow them protection among the people in the slave quarters. They are our brothers. Sons and daughters.***" Jackson continues to express his undying love for the Party. *"If we allow the slave masters' fascist*

machine to destroy these brothers, those that weren't afraid of our dreams of self-determination and control over the factors surrounding our survival is going to die with them, and the generations to come will curse and condemn us for irresponsible cowardice.249

George Jackson

Furthermore, as Panthers and their offices came under intensified attack throughout the country, **Newton issued Executive Mandate No. 3 on March 1, 1969**. It stated:

We draw the line at the threshold of our doors. It is therefore mandated as a general order to all members of the Black Panther Party for Self Defense that all members must acquire the technical equipment to defend their homes and their dependents and shall do so as mandated. The Party urged Blacks to develop armed self-defense groups in the communities from house to house, block to block, community to community throughout the nation. The Panther Party was now under military-style attacks nationwide by COINTELPRO, whose sole intention was to exterminate all Party members. Reminiscent of the Maroons, and of Martin Delaney's "defending your threshold" approach, the Party did not break its stride. Its motto was, *"If I break my stride, a bullet in my head will kill me."*

It was under these most trying times that the Panther Pads in Berkeley formed political coalitions with the UC Berkeley student community and leaders of the

Black community in Berkeley, while engaging in an initiative to put the community control of police initiative on the ballot. Door-to-door organizing would provide the BPP with the power to gain some influence over policy with the Berkeley City Council. This was never accomplished by any other city throughout the country. We had political cover from Ronald Dellums (who would later become one of the original leaders of the Congressional Black Caucus) and D'Army Bailey, who were both members of the Berkeley City Counsel and instrumental in passing the community control of police initiative. With Panther offices under imminent threat of attack, I instructed the Panthers under my command to start tunnel excavation from the Berkeley Chapter Office into the sewer systems, creating an escape route as conditions warranted.

By early 1970, the mounting fatalities and loss of life had produced a numbing effect on the Party's ability to recruit while trying to sustain a viable base in the community. Former East Coast Panther leader and comrade Dhoruba Bin Wahad recounted: *"We achieved a genuine mass base of support for our programs. People became scared. Nobody wanted to go to prison for life or be pop-up targets for the death squads."* And so, just when it had become possible to accomplish what we had set out to do, a lot of people abandoned us, distanced themselves and became cowards!

We were at a crossroad in our struggle for the liberation of black people from the capitalist system of oppression and the racist brutality of white supremacist police officers. Our dream of organizing our black communities into a black nation bound together by community programs and self-determination was in peril. We had developed a sense of belonging to something greater than ourselves, a cause, an idea that the Black Man and Black Woman, our Queen, were willing to arm themselves to fight for the freedom of Black people. It was exciting and intriguing. It was a powerful motivation for those of our generation and future generations. We fought together, died together, went to prison together and gave birth to a new generation of children together. We developed a profound love for each other.

Indeed, many Panther Babies born out of this revolutionary love. My second son, Fedayeen Turner, was one such baby. His mother Deborah Bonito was my other half and second-in-command at the Berkeley Chapter. We laid in each other's arms at night, as did Panther members throughout the country, anxiously awaiting another attack, wondering if we would ever see the light of day, while our armed comrades stood at their post, guarding our lives, awaiting the same commando operations executed by police in Chicago and LA. The beauty of it all. We did it with CONVICTION, for the love of ourselves and the People, the beautiful people in the community, our ancestors in chains, in the bowels of the slave ships, in the slave dungeons throughout the Gold Coast of Africa and for all those faceless ancestors in unmarked graves.

So, when you ask, what was going on at that time? We felt we were engaged in a revolutionary struggle to liberate our black communities from racist police domestic terrorism and violence while servicing the needs of our communities. We were acting in concert with our revolutionary brothers and sisters, fighting to liberate their countries from the yoke of Yankee imperialism on the African continent. When we examine circumstances today, in terms of the number of young black people being killed during our struggle it was twice as many and done with impunity, which is why we chose the path that led us to an armed revolutionary political stance. Police occupied our communities like troops occupying foreign territory. They were there to detain, threaten and brutalize and murder our people, desecrate our black bodies. During that time there were no cell phone cameras, no cop watch, or body or dashboard cameras. There was just the Black Panther Party, who took it upon us to be the original cop watch with guns. We let them know we would be watching and holding them accountable for their actions. And to the best of our abilities, we did and paid the price we knew we would have to pay – the termination of our lives or imprisonment.

Furthermore, to control our own destiny while defining our own space in time, for us to have been engaged in struggle, was a noble act. It was a noble act for any person who would fight for their dignity and inalienable rights as human beings, and the collective rights of the black community. We were the young brothers and sisters who understood the moment when the enslaved revolted, slavery died, the master-slave relationship ended. We refused to pass down this acceptance to another generation. We saw our Panther babies as the start, the new Black Man/Woman emerging from the jaws of defeat. George Jackson saw his young Panthers as the vanguard and urged our people to protect us, nurture us and allow our growth within their midst. Jackson concluded, *"We must learn from them, pick them up when they stumble, walk hand in hand with them, join them and never, never allow their demise."*

Soon however, as the counter insurgency attacks and COINTELPRO disinformation intensified, the Party became split between two factions. Jackson would break with the Party he had grown to love. What Jackson began to see were actions contrary to the theory and actual practical application of armed revolutionary struggle while leading the masses. Jackson's growing relationship with the Party was becoming tenuous at best.. His ideology of armed revolutionary struggle was contrary to the Party's move towards electoral politics as the only viable strategy for black liberation. For a few years Jackson had been recruiting, educating and training members of his Black guerilla family inside and out of prison into an underground apparatus that would become a part of the Black Liberation Army. And in that sense, he felt Newton had betrayed him. The East Coast faction headed by Dhoruba was more akin to Eldridge Cleaver and that of George Jackson.

The East Coast under attack: The Panther 21 and the Disinformation Campaign

THE N.Y. 21

The dominoes were falling, and wedges were being driven even further between Party members, aided and abetted by COINTELPRO raids, arrests and political trials. Consequently the Party was in mass retreat. On April 2, 1969, twenty-one members of the Harlem Chapter of the Black Panther Party were formally indicted and charged with 156 counts of conspiracy to blow up subway and police stations, the Queens Board of Education Office and the Bronx-based New York Botanical Garden.

By the early morning hours of April 2, mass sweeps were conducted citywide by combat squads of armed police. Law enforcement agencies, ranging from the FBI and U.S. Marshals to state and local police who worked simultaneously to coordinate assaults on Panther homes and community-based offices. After the raids, 21 Panther men and two Panther women were formally arrested, processed and quickly jailed. To anyone who supported radical politics in the late 1960s, there was no doubt that the indictment of the Panther New York 21 was a political and racist frame-up to not only "disrupt, discredit and destroy," but utterly dismantle the Black Panther Party from the inside out.

The absurd and excessive nature of such charges was clearly intended as a federal effort to pit chapters and regions against each other in a manner that would paralyze the Panther party leadership. What these charges represented was a form of unprecedented legal repression, created as a structural alternative to break the party's stronghold, reputation and community base of support. For Panthers who fortunately were not murdered or assassinated, exiled or imprisoned, the courts became the fascist ruling class's effective form of legal lynching, a robbery of valuable time and resources. Accordingly, the strategy worked. The community programs were disrupted, and the misinformation had sown internal conflict among Party members. The informant label was placed on David Brothers, Jorge Aponte and Robert Collier, further driving a wedge between our headquarters in Oakland, California and that of the New York Office. The distrust in leadership was now official. The split had intensified.

But the real target was Brother Dhoruba Bin Wahad, head of the NY Chapter of the Black Panther Party who along with Fred Hampton, Chairman of the Chicago Chapter, and Geronimo Pratt, head of the Los Angeles Chapter, had been targeted as the most dangerous and most articulate among the Panther leadership. Dhoruba was in the FBI security index file, and Hoover gave orders to neutralize him and the other Panther leaders by any means necessary. Chairman Fred would be assassinated, Geronimo would be framed for murder and now Dhoruba would be next on their hit list. Consequently, On April 2, 1969, Dhoruba and 20 other Panthers were indicted on charges and conspiracy in the Panther 21 case.

In July 1969, the NYPD sent officers to Oakland, California to monitor the Black Panther Party's nationwide conference calling for community control of police departments. An NYPD memorandum candidly acknowledged that community control of the police, "*may not be in the interests of the department. Community* control of police was a signature program and an organizing tool for the Party nationwide. As the repeated attacks on Panther offices became widespread it was in our best interest to organize around police violence and brutality against the Party and the black community in general. One of the few instances of success was achieved with the Berkeley Chapter. Our collective efforts as students at the UC Berkley, along with the National Committee to Combat Fascism successfully organized the passing of such an initiative in Berkeley city.

Thanks to their warrantless wiretaps of BPP offices and residences, the FBI received confirmation in May 1970 that their disinformation strategy was working and had sown dissatisfaction among New York BPP members, including Dhoruba, with West Coast BPP members. It was a phenomenally successful tactic of COINTELPRO, which used forged letters and documents to pit Panther against Panther while sowing seeds of mistrust. Suddenly everyone was looked upon with a jaundiced eye. Aware of this disillusionment, the FBI disseminated a steady stream of information regarding BPP strife to the media and participated in a plan to either recruit Dhoruba as an informant or have us believe he was an agent for the FBI.

Huey Newton

The shift in the Party's vision was instrumental in heightening internal contradictions. These contradictions were only intensified upon the release of **Brother Huey** from prison in August 1970. After his release we accompanied Party leadership to New Haven, Connecticut where I was working in conjunction with Doug Maranda, head of the Boston Chapter of the BPP, to free Bobby Seale and the New Haven Nine. We were blindsided at a meeting when Huey let it be known that the Party would no longer advocate political power from the barrel of a gun. Electoral politics would now become the Party mantra. A plethora of counterintelligence actions followed, seeking to amplify the division between

Huey's new direction of electoral politics, which ran counter to the East Coast Panthers steadfast belief in revolutionary politics as well as that of Cleaver who was now head of the International office in Algiers and a major proponent of armed struggle in America. This change in strategy was the tipping point in the effort to keep the Party unified. Unfortunately the dye had been cast, and there were now two separate Parties vying for the loyalty of its members.

Conversely, those of us who kept our eye on the prize remained clear-eyed and on-mission. Our purpose was to Free Bobby, to bring our chairman home, as well as Erica Huggins who had been wrongly accused of conspiring to end the life of another human being.

Bobby Seale and The New Haven 9

In 1969 New Haven, Connecticut, attracted national attention when Black Panther Alex Rackley was alleged to have been killed by fellow Panthers Warren Kimbro, Lonnie McLucas, and George Sams Jr. (also an FBI informant) after being held and tortured for two days. Rackley was suspected of being an FBI informant, and the allegations were a part of the disinformation campaign to further divide the ranks of the Party. National party chairman Bobby Seale was visiting New Haven at the time of Rackley's murder, and authorities implicated him in the crime. They also indicted Ericka Huggins, founder of the New Haven Chapter of the Black Panther Party. Investigators heard her voice on a taped recording of the interrogation of Rackley before his murder. In total, the authorities indicted nine people.

One of my early assignments was to fly to New Haven and organize and coordinate the New Haven Nine Defense Committee. I, along with Doug Miranda, the Leader of the Boston Chapter of the Party, bore the responsibility of organizing the defense fund and legal strategy, and to consolidate support in the black community as well as the major college campuses on the East Coast. Of course, Yale University was our primary focus and base of operation, but our travels also took us to the University of Connecticut, Princeton, Harvard, and Columbia, to name a few colleges, in support of the 21. Our purpose was to organize student support, speak at organized rallies and plan a joint march on Yale University the day of the trial.

Capitalizing on the mass support, and to help pay for the defense of the accused Party members, we discussed plans for a three-day fundraising campaign on the New Haven Green, set to commence on May Day. To solicit support, we invited a slate of nationally recognized speakers to appear, including Youth International Party leader Abbie Hoffman and anti-war activist Dr. Benjamin Spock. The plan called for Panther supporters to descend on the Yale Green on May Day weekend to protest the impending trial. Fearing the potential for violence, state and local authorities teamed with federal law enforcement to prepare for what they perceived as an impending assault on the City of New Haven. The following was an article published in the local newspaper:

Yale Faculty Decides to Suspend Academic Activities During Strikes
NO WRITER ATTRIBUTED

April 24, 1970

The Yale faculty yesterday voted to "suspend normal academic activities" during the current student strike and called on those professors holding classes to "take a tolerant attitude" towards students boycotting classes.

But the faculty resolution, which represented almost complete adoption of a list of demands presented at the meeting by a group of black faculty, urged the Yale administration not to close the university officially.

The student strike, now entering its third day, has been about 70 per cent effective so far, according to the Yale Daily News.

The strike was called Tuesday at a mass meeting sponsored by the New Haven Black Panther Party, the Black Student Alliance at Yale, and the Third World Liberation Front to support Panther National Chairman Bobby Seale and the eight New Haven Panthers being tried in New Haven on charges of murder.

Rally

*Earlier yesterday, about 880 Yale students led by **John Turner, a New Haven Black Panther and head of the United Front for Panther Defense**, rallied in Beinecke Plaza and marched to Sprague Hall, where the faculty was meeting.*

Three black students entered the meeting and presented the demands of the Black Student Alliance at Yale (BSAY).

Yale's colleges-residential units like Harvard Houses-held "advisory" votes on the strike Tuesday, and all but one – Saybrook – voted their support. Most of the colleges also voted to open their doors to demonstrators coming to the May 1 rally called by the Conspiracy defendants in support of Bobby Seale.

However, two student groups – BSAY and the Strike Steering Committee, an ad hoc group of white students – have issued demands. BSAY ask that Yale give $500,000 to the Panther defense fund, give financial aid to the Panthers' Free Breakfast program, and rehire two black workers fired earlier this month.

Yale Pres. Wonders If Blacks Can Get Fair Trial

Yale University President Kingman Brewster Jr. says he is skeptical that black revolutionaries in the U. S. can receive a fair trial under the nation's judicial system. Brewster, who was instrumental in achieving a Yale faculty compromise to hold a week-long moratorium on classes to discuss the current trial of 12 Black Panthers, expressed his sentiments at a faculty meeting. "I am appalled and ashamed things should have come to such a point that I am skeptical of the ability of black revolutionaries to achieve a fair trial anywhere in the United States," Brewster told the faculty. "I believe that in large part this atmosphere has been created by police actions and prosecutions of the Panthers across the country."

porting "Apple" cap, Black Panther John Turner urges Yale

Panther leader John Turner orchestrating a rally for the New Haven Nine

In advance of reports that anticipated anywhere from 50,000 to 500,000 demonstrators, Connecticut Governor John Dempsey mobilized the Connecticut National Guard, while U.S. Attorney General John Mitchell in conjunction with Nixon and Hoover asked the Pentagon to deploy 4,000 Marines and Army paratroopers to armories on the outskirts of the city, *The New York Times* reported on April 30, 1970. Yale University President Kingman Brewster publicly expressed reservations that a Black revolutionary could receive a fair trial in the United States and played a role in keeping the state apparatus from provoking violence, while encouraging the University to remain open, provide housing and feed peaceful protestors. Aside from a few minor skirmishes, the protests remained peaceful even as radical students, antiwar protesters, and a variety of other activists swelled our ranks of supporters.

The trials attracted enormous attention. After a swift trial and conviction, Kimbro, McLucas, and Sams all received prison sentences. They only served a portion of their sentence before they were released, but Bobby and Ericka's trials proved more problematic. Jury selection took four months, and after hearing circumstantial evidence, the jury became deadlocked. Judge Harold M. Mulvey, who many expected to call for a retrial, instead dismissed the charges against Bobby and Ericka, and the call to Free Bobby ended with one of our few victories during these most difficult times. Our mission was accomplished, and we were able to bring our chairman home. Unfortunately, what he would encounter would be a sea of discord and disinformation ripping the heart from a Party that he co-founded and loved dearly. I would later have a one-on-one conversation with him and share my observations that would alter my direction and have a profound effect on my future within the Party.

Bobbie's release from New Haven jail

My conversation with Bobby would come on the heels of intensified counter-intelligence efforts by the FBI to sow seeds of distrust, which had become the norm. The West Coast became suspicious of all individual motives of fellow BPP members, particularly those like Dhoruba, who were on the East Coast. By early 1971, the plan bore fruit. On January 28, 1971, we later became aware that FBI director Hoover reported that Huey had become increasingly paranoid and had expelled several loyal BPP members: *According to the FBI Newton responds violently... The Bureau feels that this near hysterical reaction by the egotistical Newton is triggered by any criticism of his activities, policies or leadership qualities, and some of this criticism undoubtedly is the result of our counterintelligence projects now in operation.* This operation was enormously successful, resulting in a split within the BPP with violent repercussions.

In early January 1971, Fred Bennett, a BPP member affiliated with the New York Chapter, was shot and killed, allegedly by Newton supporters. Some claimed it was by a police informant to heighten tensions between the two growing factions. Brother Sam Napier, who headed the Panther newspaper, also became a casualty. Some alleged it was an East Coast retaliation; others said it was an execution by FBI moles to heighten tensions between East and West. I do know there were a lot of confused, and heartbroken Panthers as we watched these events unfold before our tear-filled eyes. We knew not who to trust or what to believe. We on the West coast were warned to be weary of Dhoruba because Huey came to believe that he was plotting to kill him. Allegedly, Dhoruba, in turn, was told by Connie Matthews, Newton's secretary, *that Newton was planning to have Bin*

Wahad and Panther 21 co-defendants Edward Joseph and Michael Tabor killed during Newton's upcoming East Coast speaking tour. As a result of the split and fearing for his life, Dhoruba, along with Tabor and Joseph, were forced to flee during the Panther 21 trial.

During this period, the eye of the storm was swirling. Certain East Coast members of the Party had left the Party and gone underground. On the West Coast we were in preparation for arguably the most significant political trial of the struggle, the Soledad Brothers trial in San Francisco. I had just been released from jail for assault charges on police officers during a courtroom brawl. Guards attacked Comrade Jackson in court during a preliminary hearing and Jimmy Carr and I leaped the railing and came to his defense. Carr had recently been released from prison and was Jackson's point person and conduit for black revolutionaries released from prison into the underground.

On May 13, 1971, the Panther 21, including Dhoruba, were acquitted of all charges in the less-than-one hour of jury deliberations. Even though the acquittals were a defeat and blow to the COINTEIPRO/NYPD coalition, the victory was achieved during the disinformation campaign. The Party was now splintered and most of the East Coast leadership had gone underground.

On May 19, 1971, NYPD Officers Thomas Curry and Nicholas Binetti were shot on Riverside Drive in Manhattan. Two nights later, two other officers, Waverly Jones and Joseph Piagentini, were shot and killed in Harlem. In separate communiqués delivered to the media, the **Black Liberation Army** claimed responsibility for both attacks. Immediately after these shootings, the FBI initiated an investigation of these incidents, called "**Newkill**," as an extension of their long-standing program against the BPP. Before any evidence had been collected, BPP members, in particular those acquitted in the Panther 21 case, were targeted as suspects. However, all would be later acquitted.

With Dhoruba as the main target, the conspiracy to frame him for the police killings began. Although the initial ballistics test on the weapon failed to link it with the Curry-Binetti shooting, the NYPD publicly declared they had seized the weapon used on May 19. The NYPD now had in custody a well-known and vocal Black Panther leader, and the alleged weapon linked to a police shooting. His prosecution and conviction would both neutralize an effective leader and justify the failed Panther 21 case. But there was no direct evidence linking Dhoruba to the May 19th or May 22nd police shootings. The state's star witness recanted an earlier statement fabricated by the DA.. Later that day, she was interviewed by

BSS Detective Edwin Cooper. Joseph repeated that Dhoruba was innocent. Ms. Joseph was arrested and committed as a material witness.

Dhoruba was indicted for the attempted murder of Officers Curry and Binetti on July 30, 1971. After three trials, Dhoruba was convicted of attempted murder and sentenced by Justice Martinez to the maximum penalty of 25 years to life in prison. Years later, in December 1975, after learning of Congressional hearings which disclosed the FBI's covert operations against the BPP, Dhoruba filed a lawsuit in the Federal District Court, charging that he had been the victim of numerous illegal and unconstitutional actions designed to "neutralize" him, including the frame-up in the Curry-Binetti case.

In 1980, after documents with Dhoruba's name on them turned up in the **Fred Hampton** lawsuit against the Chicago Police Department and FBI, the FBI and NYPD were ordered by Federal Judge Mary Johnson Lowe to produce their massive files on Mr. Bin Wahad and the BPP, that they had claimed did not exist (Judge Mary Johnson Lowe was the first Black woman appointed to the Federal Bench, and a former member of the NAACP Legal Defense Fund legal team that won 1954 *Brown v Board of Education* decision that struck down the separate-but-equal standard of segregation).

The FBI and NYPD documents revealed that Dhoruba was indeed a target of FBI/NYPD covert operations. For the first time, the documents depicted the FBI's intimate involvement in the Curry-Binetti investigation. The "Newkill" file, which was finally produced in unredacted form in 1987 after 12 years of litigation, contained numerous reports which should have been provided to Dhoruba during his trial. In a decision announced on December 20, 1992, Justice **Bruce Allen** of the New York State Supreme Court ordered a new trial. The court found that the inconsistencies and omissions in the prior statements contradicted testimony *"crucial to establishing the People's theory of the case."* On January 19, 1995, Brother Dhoruba was released from prison and has since moved to Ghana where he presently resides.

Assata Shakur

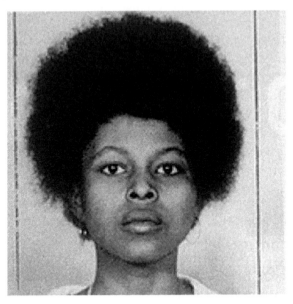

On May 2, 1973, our beloved Panther Sister Assata Shakur (a.k.a. JoAnne Chesimard) lay in a hospital, fighting for her life, handcuffed to her bed, while local, state and federal police interrogated her about the shootout on the New Jersey Turnpike, which ended the life of a white state trooper. Shakur was long a target of J. Edgar Hoover's campaign to defame, infiltrate, and neutralize the Black Panther Party, and to save face following the failed NY 21 trial of which all Panthers, including Dhoruba and Assata Shakur, were acquitted. It was not a secret that the Black Panther Party was targeted by the FBI and the COINTELPRO off-shoot, Newkill, and later "Chesrob" (an FBI acronym named after Assata Shakur, a.k.a. Joanne Chesimard). Members of the Black Panther Party were forced underground by COINTELPRO-instigated violence and were hunted down by local and federal law Police State apparatus. Such was the story of sister Assata Shakur. To understand how she arrived at this particular moment, let us explore the ripples of time.

Only our ancestors could have written a better script, for during her formative years Shakur was raised by her grandmother who lived in Wilmington, North Carolina, descendants of the victims of the Wilmington Massacre of 1898. It is only fitting that a daughter of the Massacre would decades later become a beacon of light for those beleaguered souls who suffered from the knee of domestic white terrorism. She ultimately returned to Queens where Shakur, this beautiful warrior Queen, would grow into one of our most notable figures in the Black Panther

Party, and international hero to those freedom-loving people throughout the Diaspora.

Even though Assata loved the Party dearly, she was disenchanted with the way in which sisters were treated within it. More importantly she was disenchanted with the Party's direction and the lack of recognition given to the African-centered approach to Revolutionary Nationalism. I recall our conversation while in Harlem where I met with her and Afeni Shakur. Both women expressed the same sentiments, and I could see the disenchantment in their eyes. I then knew that they both would follow their hearts and leave the Party. Between April 5, 1971 and January 23, 1973, Assata was accused six times of crimes ranging from kidnapping, armed robbery, attempted murder to murder. On each of the six occasions, Assata Shakur was found not guilty through dismissals, mistrials, acquittals and a hung jury. It later emerged that in 1973 the FBI had two separate task forces (COINTELPRO and CHESROB – which had been an evolution of NEWKILL) attempting to tie Shakur to any and every violent activity on the East Coast of the United States, to discredit the Black Panther Party and the Black Liberation Army.

In 1972, Assata was the subject of a nationwide manhunt by the FBI. It called her the *"revolutionary mother hen"* of the Black Liberation Army cell that had conducted a "series of alleged assassinations of New York City police officers," including Joseph Piagentini and Waverly Jones on May 21, 1971, and Gregory Foster and Rocco Laurie on January 28, 1972. Shakur was alleged to have been directly involved with the Foster and Laurie murders, and involved with the Piagentini and Jones murders. Operation CHESROB went even further, identifying Shakur as the de facto leader and the *"soul of the Black Liberation Army"* after the arrest of the alleged co-founder Dhoruba. Robert Daley, Deputy Commissioner of the New York City Police, for example, described Shakur as *"the final wanted fugitive, the soul of the gang, the mother hen who kept them together, kept them moving, kept them shooting."*

While all the counter-intelligence agencies working together with the criminal injustice system they tried to bury sister Assata with multiple cases and charges. Shakur was found guilty on one occasion: the Turnpike Shootout. Assata was convicted of first-degree murder, second-degree murder, atrocious assault and battery, assault and battery against a police officer, assault with a dangerous weapon, assault with intent to kill, and illegal possession of a weapon. However, evidence shown in her defense proved her innocence, but the words fell on deaf ears; ears that were determined to neutralize this revolutionary, this maroon

215

warrior by any means necessary. The basis of Shakur's evidence demonstrated she had already surrendered before the shooting ensued, making the charges against her invalid. The evidence shown by a medical doctor's evidence proved that Shakur did not handle a gun and, due to her injuries, was unable to fire a weapon even if she had been handling it.

A key element of Assata's defense was medical testimony, which sought to demonstrate that she was shot with her hands up and that she was subsequently unable to fire a weapon. According to the testimony of a neurologist, the second bullet severed the median nerve in Shakur's right arm, leaving her unable to pull a trigger. Accordingly, neurosurgeon Dr. Arthur Turner Davidson, Associate Professor of Surgery at Albert Einstein College of Medicine, testified that the wounds in her upper arms, armpit and chest, and severed median nerve which instantly paralyzed her right arm, would only have been caused if both arms were raised. To sustain such injuries while crouching and firing a weapon (as described in Trooper Harper's testimony) "would be anatomically impossible."

For that reason Davidson based his testimony on an examination of Shakur taken on August 4, 1976, and on X-rays taken immediately after the shootout at Middlesex General Hospital. Prosecutor Barone questioned whether Davidson was qualified to make such a judgment 39 months after the injury. Barone proceeded to suggest (while a female Sheriff's attendant enacted his suggestion) that Shakur was struck in the right arm and collar bone and "then spun around by the impact of the bullet so an immediate second shot entered the fleshy part of her upper left arm" to which Davidson replied, "Impossible."

 Dr. David Spain, a pathologist from Brookdale Community College, testified that her bullet scars and X-rays supported her claim that her arms were raised, and that there was "no conceivable way" the first bullet could have hit Shakur's clavicle if her arms were down.

The presiding Judge Appleby eventually cut off funds for any further expert defense testimony. Shakur, in her autobiography, and defense attorney Evelyn Williams, in *Inadmissible Evidence*, both claim that it was difficult to find expert witnesses for the trial. Not only because of the financial expense, but also because most forensic and ballistic specialists declined on the grounds of a conflict of interest because they routinely performed such work for law enforcement officials.

Furthermore, neutron activation analysis administered after the shootout showed no gunpowder residue on Shakur's fingers. Her fingerprints were not found on any weapon at the scene, according to forensic analysis performed at the Trenton, New Jersey crime lab and the FBI crime labs in Washington, D.C. According to tape recordings and police reports made several hours after the shoot-out, when Harper returned on foot to the administration building 200 yards (183 meters) away, he did not report state trooper Foerster's presence at the scene; no one at headquarters knew of Foerster's involvement in the shoot-out until his body was discovered beside his patrol car, more than an hour later.

Assata was convicted on all eight counts: two murder charges, and six assault charges. The prosecution did not need to prove that Shakur fired the shots that killed either Trooper Foerster or Zayd Shakur: being an accomplice to murder carries an equivalent life sentence under New Jersey law. Upon hearing the verdict, Shakur said—in a "barely audible voice"—that she was "ashamed that I have even taken part in this trial" and that the jury was "racist" and had "convicted a woman with her hands up." Judge Appleby told the court attendants to "remove the prisoner" and Assata replied: "The prisoner will walk away on her own feet."

Assata would spend much of the 1970s in several prisons before her escape in 1979. As a political prisoner considered dangerous, Assata would be fifth on the FBI's Most Wanted list. There were many futile attempts at recapturing Shakur, who, for five years remained a fugitive before fleeing to Cuba under political asylum in 1984. One of the strengths of the underground movement during those times were the numerous underground safe houses. Our history of hiding or being hidden out of sight (and sometimes in plain sight) was a strength during the ripples of time, starting with the Underground Railroad during slavery. The beauty of our struggle was the undying love we had for one another, for those who embraced the cause at all cost, including the risk of losing one's life or freedom for the common cause of freedom. We were of the mindset that when a comrade was in danger the degree of risk was determined by the level of commitment and the value of the comrade worth saving. The decisions were always made not necessarily on sentiment alone, but solely on the value of the person in relation to the revolution. Therefore, it was necessary to weigh the value of the person in question, against the expenditure of the revolutionary force necessary to free him/her.

In Assata's case it was a no brainer. In early 1979, a BLA underground cell later identified as the **Family**, expropriated funds from Bamberger's in Paramus, New Jersey and planned the extraction of sister Assata Shakur from her captors. On November 2nd, Assata was extracted from the Clinton Correctional Facility for

Women in New Jersey. Three members of the Black Liberation Army who were visiting the sister drew concealed weapons (45-caliber pistols) and sticks of dynamite. They seized two correction officers as hostages, commandeered a van and escaped with their precious cargo, leaving the two officers in the parking lot unharmed.

The beauty of success is often predicated on the efficiency of a particular underground cell. Dry runs dictate how much intel is gathered and how to effectively utilize the data. It can be surmised that those who executed the extraction knew visiting procedures were lax, and they probably were not searched during their initial visit. Moreover, according to state correction officials, no identity checks were run on the participants who presented false identification to enter the prison facility.

After her escape, it is alleged that Assata lived in a safe house in Pittsburg until her extraction to Cuba, which may or may not be true. One thing is for certain: wherever the safe house may or may not have been, she was well-protected until the underground connections were able to provide safe passage connecting her to the Bahamas and then to Cuba.

To this day, Assata has remained in Cuba. The FBI has classified her as a domestic terrorist since May 2nd, 2005 and placed her on the Most Wanted Terrorist List in 2013, on the 40th anniversary of Trooper Foerster's death, the FBI placed Shakur on the Most Wanted Terrorists list, conferring upon her the dubious distinction of being the first woman and the second domestic terrorist to appear on the list. It also increased her bounty to $2 million dollars.

Since her escape, her life has been depicted in songs, documentaries and various literary works. Shakur never had a chance of receiving a fair trial at the time she was convicted and sent to prison. Assata is an amazing woman who is celebrated in different parts of the world. She was part of the Black Panther Party; she was also part of the Black Liberation Army. She is our Nzinga, our quintessential African Queen!

The Soledad Brothers

During the course of Assata's early journey, these difficult times had taken me to New York for the Panther 21 trial, Connecticut for the New Haven 9 trial, and back to the Bay Area to prepare for another political trial of great magnitude and proportion: The Soledad Brothers.

In addition, the Soledad Brothers were three Black inmates charged with the murder of John V. Mills, a white prison guard at California's Soledad Prison. On January 16, 1970, George Jackson, Fleeta Drumgo and John Clutchette were alleged to have murdered Mills in retaliation for the execution-style shooting deaths of three black inmates during a fist fight between black and white prisoners in the prison yard three days earlier. Even though white inmates were involved in the melee, only black prisoners were shot and killed by expert marksman and prison guard, Opie G. Miller from a guard tower 13 feet above the yard. No warning shot was fired. W.L. Nolen and Cleveland Edwards died immediately while Alvin Miller died in the prison hospital a few days later.

On January 16,1970, a Monterey County grand jury convened. It did not take long for them to exonerate Miller. According to their verdict it was justifiable homicide. Certainly, a story we have heard through the ripples of time. A white racist police officer 14 feet above the prison yard, life not in jeopardy, assassinates three black inmates. Of course, the white inmate is wounded in the leg. Oh, by the way, no black inmates could testify, even though they were in the yard and witnessed the shootings. When the verdict was announced over the radio, the prisoners responded: thirty minutes later, Officer John V. Mills was beaten and thrown from a third-floor tier in Y Wing (George Jackson's cellblock) and died shortly thereafter.

On February 14, 1970, George Lester Jackson Jr., Fleeta Drumgo and John Clutchette were indicted by the Monterey Grand Jury on first-degree murder charges. George Jackson was crushed by the assassinations of his fellow comrades, especially Nolen, whom he had considered his mentor. Moreover, the Black Guerilla Family, of which they were both co-founders, was a political organization within the walls of Soledad. It was a haven for black inmates who were given cover from the prison guards and their counterparts, the neo-Nazis and Aryan Brotherhood, white supremacist inmates.

Soon thereafter, the Black Panther party would become the infrastructure designated to provide legal cover for the brothers. It would also be around this time that the publication of Jackson's international bestseller *Soledad Brothers* would be released. Jackson's disquieting and eloquent collection of prison letters (reminiscent of the slave narratives, which are voices from the ripples of time) made our comrade an international celebrity. Jean Genet, the famous and fiery French writer and revolutionary, insisted the book "must be read as a manifesto, as a tract, as a call to rebellion."

A national movement arose in defense of the Soledad Brothers, drawing the support of the likes of Marlon Brando, Noam Chomsky, Jane Fonda, Pete Seeger, Allen Ginsberg and many others. In its early phases, Fay Stender and Angela Davis were focal points, and the Congressional Black Caucus attempted to give the Soledad Brothers Defense Committee (SBDC) some legitimacy by conducting an investigative report on the conditions inside Soledad Prison. Ultimately, the Jackson Family became more involved, especially, the fiery and beautiful mother of Jackson, Georgia Jackson, who put complete control of the SBDC in the hands of the Black Panther Party.

Having just returned from the East Coast while working on the New Haven Nine Political Prisoner Project, I got a call from our Chief of Staff, David Hilliard, asking me to meet him at Central Headquarters in West Oakland. On my arrival I was introduced to the Jackson family: Mother Jackson, as we so affectionately called her, George Jackson Sr. and Penny Jackson, George's baby sister, who had the same fire and rage as her brother. It was there I learned that the family was not satisfied with the handling of the SBDC, or its direction. The family had requested for the Party to take the lead and David informed me that it would be my responsibility to assume the role of leadership as long as the family was happy with the direction and Central Headquarters remained in the loop. I informed all parties that it be my honor and privilege, and to add a little levity, I asked, "Why are we still sitting here? Let's get to work."

The bond forged with the family was a close one, we traveled to college campuses in cities where there were Panther Offices. We would provide security in cities where there were no offices, and I would bring in security from my location in Berkley. We utilized the Berkeley Chapter and Community center as the focal point of all SBDC activities, and we obviously utilized the UC, Berkley campus as a staging ground for any local rallies and fund-raising events. We provided shelter and lodging at our secured Panther Pads and Community Center in West Berkeley, and whenever the Jacksons moved they had bodyguards attached to their movements. On many occasions Penny would volunteer her services to stand night watch to relieve the stress from those comrades who may have needed some relief. On other occasions she would volunteer to be put on schedule. I recall other precious moments when she or Mother Jackson sat with those on night duty and shared memorable stories about comrade George while our eyes watched for any suspicious movement on the streets as we sat and peered out the window always anticipating a possible attack.

Later that month the defense team won a motion to have the trial moved to the San Francisco district court. The Soledad Brothers were moved from Soledad prison to the Maximum-Security Unit in San Quentin. Not only was this a plus for the SBDC but for the Jackson family as well. UC, Berkeley was the flash point for the revolutionary movement, and our Panther Chapter had a great deal of influence in the radical white community in the San Francisco Bay Area. Moreover, the Jacksons now had a temporary home with us at the Berkeley locations – no more long drives from LA to Soledad Prison; now they could visit George daily and stay at the Panther Chapter in Berkeley. It was during this time that I met Derrick Maxwell, the younger brother of John Clutchette, one of the Soledad Brothers on trial. Derrick would become a new Panther member, my permanent bodyguard and my brother-in-law after falling head over heels in love with my sister. He would eventually give me two beautiful nieces, Faiza and Mecca Maxwell.

Eventually we piqued Brother George's curiosity and he wanted more in-depth information about these folks who had won over the trust of his family. He sent me a letter through his number one confidant, his sister Penny. I received it, read it and responded to it, and from that day forward we became brothers bonded by the common struggle of the black liberation movement. Our first face-to-face encounter would take place during the Soledad Brothers' first preliminary hearing in San Francisco District Court. In April of 1970, armed guards escorted the Brothers into the packed courtroom. Chained from waist to wrist, and down to the ankles, one of the guards snatched papers out of George's hand. When George complained he was blindsided by another guard. A fight broke out, and as they attacked George, I and ONLY two other spectators jumped over the railing to come to our Brother's defense. For a brief second, we fought hand-to-hand combat, side by side until we were beaten down by additional guards.

I gathered much satisfaction knowing that my first impulse was the correct one and not the impulses that drove countless other so-called revolutionaries fleeing out the courtroom door. I remember seeing the backsides of several of my comrades who later claimed they were simply escorting the sisters out of harm's way. While in the courthouse holding cell, we were beaten again. The strange thing about receiving the blows is that I felt no pain – only satisfaction when I glanced across the way and saw the wry smile on George's face as he gave a nod of approval. An approval which said, *Thank you for coming to my defense*. From that day forward our brotherhood had been forged. Shortly afterwards, he sent a message via his sister Penny, asking me to participate in the research for his next book project.

The notoriety catapulted the Soledad Brothers and George Jackson to international prominence. The California Department of Corrections (CDC) and the California Intelligence Division (CID) were growing weary of his influence among prisoners throughout the California prison system and the country. At the behest of Jackson and the Black Guerilla Family, prisoners were becoming politicized and began organizing strikes to protest the racism and prisoner abuse inside the prison systems nationwide. With Jackson now holding the title of General Field Marshall of the Black Panther Party, his influence grew, as did the prison movement. Outside, prison support groups exploded. Prisoner legal defense funds grew with the mounting briefs filed in courtrooms throughout the country in general and California in particular. The prison movement was now an integral part of the revolutionary movement in the streets.

As Jackson's notoriety and influence rose, he told his sister Penny about the growing threats on his life. The prison hierarchy was beginning to perceive Jackson as a threat inside, especially when it became known that prisoners who were politically educated and trained when paroled were being funneled into the revolutionary movement and underground apparatus on the streets. As the Party became increasingly under attack by COINTELPRO, and as more and more political prisoners filled up the nation's prison facilities, Jackson became as apprehensive about Panthers losing their lives as he was of his. These matters overlapped up to a point, with Jackson wanting to escalate the resistance movement in the streets. After the assassination of Chairman Fred and military-style assault on the Los Angeles Chapter, Jackson became firmly convinced that America's black underclass was a colonized people; that the country's institutions depended on their continued enslavement and subjugation; and that this situation could only be reversed by an armed, revolution.

It was during these times that Jackson began to believe that Panthers were straying away from their and his central core political beliefs. With the rise of the liberation struggles of oppressed peoples here in the United States and throughout the world, a new consciousness and level of struggle had arisen in the prisons. It was reflected in the letters from prisoners, printed in radical papers throughout the country; and in George Jackson's "Soledad Brother", poems and articles in *The Black Scholar* journal, etc.

The struggles taking place outside prison walls for jobs, for good wages, lower prices, and unity of all peoples—white and all national minorities in our common fight for a better life—all these struggles on the outside have their counterpart on the inside of the prison walls. The U.S. prison system has always reflected the corruption and institutionalized racism of the world outside it. The country saw massive tax cuts for the rich as Nixon called for "law and order". He tightened our belts and approved cuts in domestic programs and wage controls. Inflation was wild. The men and women in prison are not only victims of these policies but are most often the direct result of these policies.

On August 7, 1970, George's baby brother, the 17-year-old man-child, Jonathan Jackson, was killed in a failed attempt to take a judge and DA hostage as a bargaining tool for the release of his brother and three other prisoners. At the same time, Huey was released from prison and changed the Party's direction from armed struggle to ballot box liberal politics. Jackson, embittered was hardened by this change in policy, and the loss and betrayal of his brother became more committed than ever to revolutionary struggle.

He now gave himself a punishing daily push-up routine. He taught himself karate and slept, he claims, for three hours a night. "I have completely restrained myself and my thinking to the point now that I think and dream of one thing only, "I have no habits, no ego, no name, no face. I feel no love, no tenderness, for anyone who does not think as I do." This is the tone of Jackson's thinking as he began to see the rising tide of fascism in the form of a corporate state as domestic terrorism inflicted pain on its victims. Losing his brother was a blow from which he never recovered. To George, armed struggle was the only way out and he now felt betrayed by the very Party whom he loved dearly.

During these times George became more fearful of his life. After the guards told him he was next, that they were going to take him out, Jackson aspired to lead nothing less than an armed revolution against America's white ruling class. *"Pure nonviolence as a political ideal ... is absurd,"* he wrote to Stender, his lawyer in 1970. *"If this agitation that we term as nonviolent is to have any meaning at all we must force the fascist to taste the bitterness of our wrath."* His letters were vigilance exercises; didactic monologues; purification rituals; preparations for the violent emergence of a new order. Unfortunately, during this period in his life, Jackson aroused the "sincere moral indignation" of white supporters and the false pretenses of pseudo-revolutionaries who, he surmised, never had honest intentions to wage war on a growing corporative fascist terrorist state.

Later I received word through his sister Penny Jackson that George had requested that I assist him in writing and editing his second book, *Blood In My Eye*. He wanted to create a blueprint for the black liberation struggle in America. His political analysis on the rise of corporative fascism in America has since been proven by today's political climate. He felt it would form the basis for arguing for the continuation of armed struggle and not electoral politics as advocated by Newton. On August 21, 1971, Jackson was assassinated in San Quentin during an alleged escape attempt. His second book was completed a few days afterwards. With Jackson's death the heart and the soul of the revolution died inside the walls of San Quentin and throughout the country. One week before, George had warned me that J. Edgar Hoover and the prison authorities had targeted him for assassination. He had become a symbol of resistance and he was eliminated especially when it was determined that he was the General Field Marshal of the Party and that freedom fighters of the Party were being trained within the prison walls, to be funneled onto the Party's underground apparatus. In many ways, the death of George Jackson coincided with the moment at which the BPP entered the trajectory of its final decline.

Before his death he had explored the possibility of connecting with the underground movement or connecting to what some may call the Black Liberation Army. Whether it was an existing infrastructure or not, a Panther offshoot of which members were encouraged to join as part of the underground apparatus is irrelevant and will remain in the shadows. When James Carr, who was Jackson's point person, was paroled, it was his responsibility to assess Newton's intentions and the Panthers, and advise Jackson going forward.

Jackson had given Carr the responsibility to push his concept of a professionally trained warrior cast of trained guerrilla freedom fighters to lead the revolution. Instead, what Carr found and what he shared with Jackson was as follows, coming out of jail, '*I was expecting to find a guerrilla army ready for war instead I saw Panthers posing and lending street credibility in luxury high rise apartments and high-end fundraising with the rich left leaning white folk*'. Carr began to surmise that what seemed feasible while behind prison walls as presented by the revolutionary left was contradictory to the conditions on the streets.'

What was important was the idea or concept that was embraced by those who refused to back pedal, who refused to turn their backs on those fallen soldiers, those political prisoners and principles that were established during the struggle were maintained.

As the Party grew in stature and in prominence, we all became targets for assassination. J. Edgar Hoover hated African Americans, especially black militants. He already had his fingerprints on the assassinations of Malcolm X, Martin Luther King Jr. and Fred Hampton, and now he turned all his firepower on the Black Panther Party.

The COINTELPRO wanted to identify "all potential black messiahs or leaders and neutralize them by any means necessary." Their strategy was to assassinate, imprison and sow the seeds of disinformation, thus creating a rift between Party members. Panther's leadership had been attacked all over the country; both Huey and Bobby had been falsely imprisoned and since released. Fred Hampton and Mark Clark were assassinated in their sleep by FBI agents; Sam Napier was burned to death in New York by the FBI, or their plants. Revolutionary political prisoners received the same treatment. Some were placed in isolation and received regular beatings. My comrade and friend, George Jackson, was assassinated on August 21, 1971.

I remember receiving an overseas phone call from Algiers in August of 1971. It was Eldridge Cleaver, wanting to know what position I had taken on the divide within the Party. Knowing that the phones were tapped, and the Feds were listening, I told him that our actions would give him the answers he was seeking. When Bobby was released, I had a few meetings with him and raised the question of the betrayal of revolutionary principles within the movement, as I did with other Party members. He was solemn in his response and demeanor, but always honest, and I could tell in his absence the Party had become completely under the control of Huey. It became apparent that I was becoming a target of reprisal for my objections to the change in the Party line, and I was warned by some comrades in Central Headquarters that my safety may be in peril. I valued the Parties revolutionary principles of criticism and self-criticism. When contradictions surfaced it was the leadership that decided on the resolution and not the collective membership who may have raised internal contradictions. Purges became commonplace and many good people were expelled because of disagreement with leadership on violations of the principles of the Party and its intended direction.

I was later instructed to come to Central Headquarters where I spent the night. For my safety I brought three of my male bodyguards with me. I will not reveal the conversation or who it was with, but I will say I was asked to take a retreat to the Santa Cruz mountains at a cabin location which had a dubious history, and I will leave it at that. At that moment in time the entire Berkeley Chapter, except for one individual, would leave the Party and go underground. Those of us who were loyal to the Black Liberation Movement decided to go underground while continuing to wage revolutionary warfare against the system of oppression with the state police apparatus.

We felt strongly, as comrade Jackson had felt, that the corporative fascists and their institutions that reflected the social, racial economic injustices were too harsh to compromise on principles. These principal elements of armed revolutionary struggle as defined by a clear Marxist analysis were at one time important to the Party. Consequently, their deviation from the original principles of our Marxist analysis, despite our proclaimed revolutionary thinking, caused many fundamental errors of judgement while leaving many members disillusioned, imprisoned or dead.

The Aftermath of a Failed Revolution

In the late 1960s, the historical conditions and its contradictions were ripe for an ultra-leftist movement. Such contradictions were vital to allow the masses to go through the political experience that would lead them to revolutionary consciousness and therefore revolutionary actions. A political and social crisis was paralyzing the country. The antiwar movement brought millions onto the streets. The fight against racial and social injustice was front and center and it brought hundreds of thousands onto the streets. Police violence and assassinations of people of color and their prominent leaders while suffering economic hardship sparked protest from inside the slave colonies. We had a pre-revolutionary set of conditions and a political crisis ripe for revolution. This multitude of conditions created a crisis within the ruling elite. At that moment we needed to boost confidence among the masses and build a united front to address the history unfolding in front of us. We failed in our obligation. We miscalculated the sheer brutality of our enemies (the police state apparatus) and underestimated our ability to organize our political base and move them to the left.

Instead, we allowed Nixon to unite the ultra-right and create a counterinsurgency movement called COINTELPRO. Most importantly, most Americans, while they could have been swayed toward revolutionary politics by a wise political program, were not interested in "revolutionary violence" in the streets. They wanted change and rallied to the anti-Vietnam War movement, which fulfilled their desire for an end to the war through peaceful and legal means. Our miscalculation was that we didn't marshal that energy from the antiwar movement towards the fight against institutionalized racism and the rise of American-style fascism.

In other words, ultimately it became a disparate movement with no effective leadership. BLA cells expropriated monies and engaged in commando-style operations before being finally extinguished in the early 1980s, around the same time that the Black Panther Party closed its last office. While the BLA was engaging in shootouts with police officers, and expropriating money to fund their operations, the BPP was trying to get back to basic political organizing while engaging in night club ownership and other nefarious activities violating revolutionary principles. The internal contradictions within the Party and the eroding support in the community stifled efforts to restart the momentum gained during the previous years. The hierarchical cult of leadership plus the reformist social and political program of electoral politics brought home the realization this would be an obstacle to any ongoing movement. The purely military resolution of power ultimately for the BLA became suicidal and futile as we watched our revolutionary struggle go up in flames.

Indeed, the personal degeneration of some remaining Party leaders and the changed political atmosphere stifled any attempts to maintain a wide base of support. This is not a recrimination against those individuals, but their actions. Without input, chapters nationwide canceled any possibility of a sustained movement of social justice and revolutionary change. Consequently, as the Party moved toward electoral politics in the Oakland bay area most Panthers were shipped to Oakland which only facilitated demise of the Party while closing most offices nationwide.

Jackson's fears had become a reality. Panthers were avoided, were not protected; we were not nurtured, and we were not allowed to grow. In many ways, we were abandoned by our own community, comrades, friends and relatives. On the one hand, the BPP in America died in a hail of police and army gunfire. And on the other hand there was a glut of misinformation, mistrust, a lack of clear analysis, and abandonment by suspicious party members and the communities we served. WE made serious errors of judgement, which carried a heavy cost. It is the result of a revolutionary thrust that was weak and miscarried – a consciousness that was compromised.

COINTELPRO had successfully destroyed the Party in its most revolutionary form. We had challenged the inequality and brutality of the American socioeconomic and justice system along with the rule of law and law enforcement. Moreover we questioned the imposed divisions of class, race and gender on society. But in the final analysis, we violated the very principles that had been so vital in our initial push for revolutionary change. But we were no longer outraged or surprised to discover further reason to oppose that government. Many errors were made because the BPP was a young organization and was under intense attack by the state. I do not want to imply that these internal errors were the primary contradiction which destroyed the BPP, the police attacks on it did that, but if it were better and more democratically organized, it may have weathered the storm. So, this is no mindless criticism or attack: I loved the Party. And neither myself nor anyone else who critiqued the Party with hindsight, will ever take away from the tremendous role that the BPP played in the Black Liberation movement of the 1960's. But we must look at the total history of the organization as it unfolded, so that others may learn from our mistakes. In retrospect the inexperience of our leadership and the overwhelming youthfulness of our membership served to prevent the Party from the appropriate response to our dilemma.

We were hit with a tsunami of violence never experienced with such intensity, speed and brutality by the police state apparatus. The massive scale of repression to which we were subjected would undoubtedly destroy any professional revolutionary activist:

According to Ward Church, in Disrupt, Discredit and Destroy *it should come as no surprise that the Panthers were destroyed. Instead, as imprisoned BLA soldier Herman Bell has observed, we should find it "remarkable...that the Party lasted as long as it did."628 And, as Dhoruba Bin Wahad has pointed out, "What's most amazing is how much was accomplished in so short a time. The growth of the Party, its programs and resiliency, the support it was able to command from the community, all that was put together in just two years, really. Had it not been for COINTELPRO, one can readily imagine what might have been achieved."629 Both Bell and Bin Wahad believe there are important lessons to be learned from the experience of the BPP.*

Although an entity bearing its name would continue to exist in Oakland, California for another decade, as would several offshoots situated elsewhere, the Black Panther Party in the sense that it was originally conceived was effectively destroyed by the end of 1971I am more outraged and surprised we made ourselves and our Party even more vulnerable to the state with the internal bickering, false accusations, and the rumors invented by the FBI and COINTELPRO. We should have been stronger in our resolve but as I reflect, we were children with ideals and aspirations beyond our ability to bring forth a new world order. At least we tried and by doing so, we paid a very heavy price.

It was a campaign of disinformation which ultimately led to the destruction of the Party as an effective national vanguard party. I may feel outrage because as far as the Panther Party was concerned, we were the vanguard of our revolution and the pressures we faced were overwhelming. Our enemies tapped our phones, kicked in our doors, corrupted our comrades, and shot us down with the law on its side. The mistakes the Panthers made under those pressures, are mistakes we and future generations may learn from, as we continue down the path of liberation from this monstrosity called institutionalized racism and neo-slavery. Never forget our struggles throughout the ripples of time. No matter the time space continuum, the success of our struggles will always depend on unity of purpose with a clearly defined agenda, and the willingness to change selfish behavior from leadership at the top, of which I was also guilty. Let it be understood – any criticism I had about the Party was never personal. The Party taught me that we must always admit to our mistakes and succumb to self-criticism while taking that criticism to a higher level of understanding. Those of us who put our lives in harm's way, knowing we might never see the light of day must always be held in the highest regard by the court of history.

The legacy of the Panthers must be viewed not only for its failures but for the positive values, ideas, analyses and love for the people, which propelled our Party so rapidly to a position of prominence, and which lent our members their astonishing valor, courage and tenacity. To do so can elevate the understanding embodied in the Party's programmatic successes in community organizing around community-based programs servicing the needs of the community. No matter the abbreviated duration, the intrinsic value is to learn from the successes which tendered our organization skills to accomplish program development under such perilous conditions. To assess and reclaim the potential for those successes is necessary for no other reason than nobody has been able to equal our accomplishments or equal in any Post-Panther era.

Indeed, only in this way may we discern a proper understanding of the Party's strengths and weaknesses, embracing the strengths while correcting the deficiencies. The BLM today must understand the dynamic unfolding and place the struggle within history unfolding. What accelerated our demise was the unwillingness of leadership to retain internal discipline for the collective wellbeing of the organization without despotism exemplified by a personality cult which ultimately violated the collective wellbeing of the community one pledged to serve.

We must always remember that our adversaries are watching and will seize the moment to exploit our weakness and destroy our efforts to create equal justice for the social common. One of the more valuable lessons learned from the Panther experience is the nature of the corporative fascist arrangement which, no matter the oppositional forces in their varying differences in ideology and political stances, if threatened, will unleash the wrath of the state upon its victims. This state apparatus will not allow itself to become subject to moral suasion or other such manifestations of policy servicing or benefiting the social common to the detriment of the corporative fascist elites. We know what happened to Dr. King when he began to attach his politics to organized labor and the corporate state war machinery and military industrial complex.

The state will always have a police apparatus fine-tuned to coerce, manage and control its black citizenry as displayed with such brutality evident in the destruction of the BPP. Any attempts to compel fundamental changes in the social order, i.e. economic and political equality, as well as complete restructuring of policing will be suppressed with similar systematic and sustained efforts of lethal force demonstrated against the BPP. Those committed to achieving fundamental change rather than window dressing must consider the realities of state violence as an integral part of their calculus. Massive community organizing sustained by massive community infrastructure servicing those communities are the buffer to blunt such displays of aggressive behavior on the part of the fascist arrangement.

Black America, we are and have been in a war since we were shackled and chained, whether we wish to be or not, the only question before us being how to go about winning. We must remember and never forget that for us to win we must break the cycle of a captured people, contained and controlled. Unity of purpose and an organized collective effort is our weapon. Here too, the legacy bequeathed by the Black Panther Party provides invaluable lessons. By studying the techniques with which the counterinsurgency war against the Party was waged, we can, collectively, begin to devise the ways and means by which to counter them, offsetting and eventually neutralizing their effectiveness.

We owe it to all those millions of fallen victims since slavery and to Panthers who sacrificed before BLM to fulfill the destiny all have embraced. Most of all, we owe it to tomorrow's generations to break the cycle of the containment and control of black bodies. We owe it to ourselves, to history, today and tomorrow through the ripples of time, enduring whatever sacrifice we may have to make.

We, the Black Panther Party, have left you many tools and an indelible blueprint with which you may at last continue the completion of the task.

San Quentin Six and George Jackson and his Legacy

In order to understand the significance of, and reasoning behind, the Soledad Trial, and the San Quentin Six (the six inmates accused of murdering prison guards during Jackson's alleged escape attempt), it is important to investigate the legal and political dynamics of these cases. This is important because they did not develop in a historical vacuum. Its roots are to be found in the long history of prisoner resistance, the rise of the prison support movement, and the efforts of the state to smash and co-opt this struggle. To summarize the lessons to be drawn from these cases, then, it is necessary to place it in a much broader political and historical context.

As the Black Liberation Movement and the upsurge in radical left-wing consciousness developed during the 1960s on college campuses, the anti-war movement and the African Liberation Movements fomented a growing social consciousness across the country. The impact of this growing consciousness was being felt inside the prisons nationwide, in part because of the influx of prisoners who were already politicized from the struggle in the streets. Initially, Muslim organizations inside the institutions had the greatest effect on blacks. Even those that did not join were impressed with their collective discipline and wall of protection. Many other black prisoners were deeply affected by the civil rights struggle and new forms of cultural nationalism.

The legacy of George Jackson

In addition, civil rights organizers and Black Panthers entering the prison system found a new audience. From 1968 to 1971, as the COINTELPRO imprisoned more of my comrades (Panthers) we began to have some impact on the California prison population. Our activities outside the prison had even more effect. Even those black prisoners who did not understand or agree with the Panthers' ideology admired our attitude and practice of armed self-defense in the streets of the black neo-colonies.

Enter the Black Guerrilla Family, founded by W.L. Nolen who mentored George Jackson and become a leader of the prison movement.

The prison movement was accelerated by Jackson's organizational skills. His razor-sharp political analysis clarified the contradictions between the prison hierarchy and the prisoner population. Indeed, the formula for success for prisoner activists was organization and unity. Earlier, The Wolf Pack, the forerunner of The Black Guerilla Family, had become the early focal point of the prison movement, while transforming into The Black Guerilla Family. These founding freedom fighters, Jimmy Carr, George Big Jake Lewis, W.L.Nolan, Bill Christmas, Terry Gipson and Jackson himself, conducted political education classes, and from their ranks grew strong revolutionaries who challenged the racial injustice inside prison. According to Jackson, "we attempted to transform the black criminal mind into a black revolutionary mentality. As a result, each of us became targeted and subjected for years to the most vicious reactionary violence by the prison slave master."

Because these revolutionary prisoners had challenged and undermined the states authority, the CID unit (Criminal Investigation Division), who was working together with the COINTELPRO, began to neutralize the prison movement. Certainly, the governor's office was involved, but the primary direction came from the Nixon/Hoover tandem, the same cast of characters that orchestrated the assassination of Brother Fred Hampton.

Theses coordinated attacks unleashed more physical attacks on the prison leadership while guards recruited Hitler's Helpers (white supremacist neo-Nazis) to carry out assassination attempts on black leaders. Jackson described the growing suppression of the black revolutionary inmates; they never allow us to leave our cells without first handcuffing us and belting our chained cuffs to our waist down to our ankles. This is preceded by a very thorough skin search. A force of a dozen or more Pigs will converge on us at one time destroying personal property at the same time. Their attitude is defensive and hostile. This brutality will continue to escalate."

The impact of social upheaval on the white prison population was not at all progressive. The growing revolutionary consciousness among people of color saw a rise on neo-Nazi white supremacism, a growing reactionary militancy on the part of whites frightened by the gains being made by blacks and other nonwhites, which they saw occurring at their expense. Neo-Nazi organizations helped perpetuate the racial division of the outside society within the prisons. Prison administrators and guards counted on this racial antagonism as an instrument of control.

Those who ran prisons were frightened of the "new type" of prisoner, who was primarily black and had a political consciousness. They were not prepared to bend down and lick the boots of their captors to seek an early parole date or in-prison favors. Race-baiting, therefore, became the modus operandi throughout the prison system, in which black was pitted against brown and against white in a never-ending circle. Race-baiting was not, of course, the only means of control employed by administrators and guards. The penal institutions have an array of rewards (bribes) and punishments (threats) that have generally served the purpose.

The "rewards" ranged from the amenities of daily living (showers, canteens, mail, TV and movie "privileges"; out-of-cell work and study activities) to parole. What made George Jackson and the BGF so lethal is that they would challenge the norm: when out of cells they would control the TV room. Previously, blacks had been forced to sit in the rear. That practice ended, and black prisoners organized themselves against reprisals by guards or Nazis inmates. They controlled their study activity by conducting their own political education classes. You break the cycle by becoming a self-contained unit within the prison system. Jackson's influence spread throughout the nation's prison system. Where there was mistreatment of inmates, he would call for a strike and the prison would shut down.

The new normal for the new breed of political prisoner were punishments which included loss of these "privileges", placement in strip cells (the "hole") or other forms of isolation; denial of parole, unofficial punishments such as beatings, gassings; and, often, the destruction of personal property during cell searches. We had to protect ourselves from indirect killings that occurred when guards set prisoners against each other but often provided weapons to favored white inmates. In many cases, guards specifically solicit inmates to get rid of a progressive prisoner. Direct killings of political prisoners occurred when guards beat inmates, gassed the cells, prevented inmates from getting medical care in an emergency, faked "suicides" and shot prisoners on some pretext of escape.

During the 1960s, the prisoners chosen for assassination were those involved in organizing within the prisons, which was why George Jackson became a target.

The selective assassination of prison leaders was bound to have some effect on prisoners. But the initial response was the opposite of suppression.

Revolutionary prisoners – strongly influenced by resistance struggles in Africa, Asia, and Latin America, as well as the growing movement in the revolutionary stateside – added a new element to the unwritten Convict Code: general retaliation against guards who killed or injured inmates. Initially, the Convict Code was a pact between prisoners protecting themselves against snitches. You did not report activities of other inmates to guards, under any circumstances. An offense by one prisoner against another was to be handled by that prisoner and his friends (or members of his gang, ethnic group or, eventually, political organization). If an inmate were brought to trial for an in-prison offense, the Convict Code meant that you did not testify against him. George Jackson was instrumental in changing the code in Soledad and other California prisons. The Convict Code came to be a measure of self-defense against attacks by guards. The prisoners were to regard themselves as one "class", the guards and administrators as another.

If a member of your "class" were injured or killed, you had the right and responsibility to strike out against any member of the opposing "class." In practical terms, it meant that if a guard shot down or gassed a prisoner to death, then every other prisoner should take on the responsibility of avenging the prisoner's death. It was the Martin Delaney threshold theory: we draw a line you cannot cross. If the guilty party were out of reach, any other guard would do. George Jackson explained the reasoning behind this: *"Prisoners are defenseless to prevent guards from killing any member of the prison population. They have all the weapons. We've got to make them stop and think that if they kill one of us, their own lives might be in danger."* This kind of retributory justice is necessary because of the impunity with which guards have been able to kill prisoners in the past.

This was the Legacy of George Jackson,The Soledad Brothers and the San Quentin Six. They politicised a forgotten segment of American Citizens, taught them their fundamental value as human beings, and their civil rights according to the rule of law as prisoners. They created the unwritten law to at least ensure that their bodies would be shielded from the wanton brutality inflicted by fascist and racist goons behind those walls.

Life as a Political Prisoner

Soon I would taste the bitterness of what it was like to live the life of a political prisoner. Six months after leaving the Party and going underground, I was captured on December 31, 1971, for armed robbery and assault as we attempted to expropriate money to fund a community-based school, which saw its funding cut by the federal government. I was immediately remanded to solitary confinement in the Marin County Facility, the same facility where the man-child Jonathon Jackson had been gunned down on August 7, 1970

No longer a member of the BPP, but part of a secret underground cell, we were called upon to fund various community action programs. In this instance, it was to fund a school that had recently been defunded by the local government. Of course, in any fund cuts, the black community was the first to feel the effects. Our goal was to expropriate funds and funnel the money into a private school which had been defunded. The morning of my captivity the FBI showed up with a briefcase containing $250,000 and stated it was mine to have if I shared with them the information they were seeking on Party members. I refused and they guaranteed they would make my life miserable. And they did. Those of us who had left the BPP with broken hearts had felt betrayed by those who had violated the principles of revolution. We had continued the struggle on a different level and by any means necessary.

So, there I sat, a caged prisoner of war who had refused to abandon the revolutionary struggle and those brothers and sisters who were either still engaged in the struggle, imprisoned, hiding underground or had died, making the ultimate sacrifice for the freedom of our people. I felt the pain and grief of mothers like Mother Jackson who I had accompanied when picking up their sons' bodies, standing at their side during funerals and burial processions. Could I turn my back on the fallen? I did not, and now I sat awaiting an unknown fate.

Our trial was held in a courtroom that was specially made for revolutionaries at that time. A wall of Plexiglas from ceiling to floor formed a barrier between us and the spectators. One year earlier in a packed courtroom in San Francisco, I had jumped over a railing and gone toe to toe with guards who had jumped my mentor, George Jackson. From that day forward, barriers were placed between revolutionary defendants and spectators. My comrades and I were convicted and sentenced to life imprisonment. Truthfully, it was then, and only then, that I realized how much some white men feared this black body. The following morning, chained from neck to waist to ankles, I felt a sense of power and respect. In a weird sort of way I knew how my ancestors felt. As I was escorted to the prison medical facility in Vacaville, a two-hour drive away, there were two cars in front of us and two behind, both occupied by armed guards brandishing AR-15 rifles. Overhead, a helicopter patrolled the airspace until we reached our destination.

After the Medical Facility in Vacaville, San Quentin became my permanent place of residence. The Q was a cold and desolate place located in Marin County Bay. The mental preparation for a life of captivity was the first order of business. I did so by instructing my sister whom I loved dearly to return to our parents' home in Indiana. When I last saw her and my two-year-old son (who was born a Panther baby), he tried to climb up the Plexiglas separating us from the warmth of human touch that exists between father and son. When he could not do so he took his fingers and clawed his face, drawing blood. It was the first time we had been separated and I knew then I had to cut ties. With a life sentence hanging over my head I knew if I were going to confront my circumstances, a certain mental preparation would be necessary to exist in isolation. It would require some heavy psychic adjustments. Deep inside I addressed some innate fears of having been captured. Much like our ancestors, it must have been an acquired characteristic built up over centuries of bondage. It is something I believe we run from all our lives. Captivity was like dying, and then having to reinvent the self. Even today, that is the fear of every black man. Deep in the subconscious is always the lingering fear of jail, the possibility of captivity and even death.

The world, which awaited me, I could have never imagined. The harsh and brutal conditions of prison life, the frightening diffusion of physical violence and mental terror was constant. Especially those targeted as political prisoners. Solitary can destroy the logical processes of the mind, with the intended purpose of completely deprogramming any rational thought. I recall the many letters exchanged with my mentor. He would point out the things then that I was now experiencing firsthand. The sounds were continuous, the madness streaming from every throat; frustrated sounds, metallic cups banging on the bars, screams of pain and desperation, continuing throughout the night. The same suffering, I imagined during the middle passage or the slaves being captured and packed into the holding cells of Elmina slave castle. Our ancestors must have similarly experienced the smell, the human waste thrown at you, the unwashed bodies lying in their own excrements, and death waiting patiently. I was living in Ripples Of Time.

Surely, this experience also gave me firsthand experience of what it may have been like as a slave and having to deal with prison guards who were of the same racist mentality as their police officer counterparts on the streets. Both had the mentality of the slave patroller and overseer during slavery. The racist mentality of these guards was unimaginable. To paraphrase Brother Jackson, *"Is there any way to isolate or classify generally, who can be trusted with a gun and absolute discretion as to who he can kill? Most of them are KKK members, or KKK types. The rest of them are so stupid that they should not even be allowed to run their own bath water."* My encounters with these guards were not the normal encounter a prisoner would have. Our overseers were ex-green beret, Special Forces types, hired specifically to contend with the growing ranks of political prisoners. We called them the goon squad.

A typical week would consist of being woken up during the night for a search and destroy mission. Your cell would be ransacked, and what personal belongings you may have had would be destroyed. You were physically assaulted at times, and other times your cell teargassed. My toilet became my best friend. Flushing the toilet would create oxygen flow and my head often would be in the toilet bowel as water and tear gas fumes made their exit. Living under such horrific conditions tests your strength, your will to survive. More importantly, it forces you to dig deep into your soul and examine who you are and how to survive.

It forces you to ask critical questions about how you got here and how you survive day to day. The two most important answers I produced were forging and maintaining bonds of comradeship, while drawing from the vast well of knowledge from your ancestral past. In doing so, however, it was paramount that you seized control of your mental faculties, and never surrendered your mind to your captors. From a mental perspective, however, there were two occurrences from outside forces that made it difficult and made me determined to never allow anyone to control my mind. If nothing else, I had to always remain in firm control.

The first occurrence was a second visit from the same FBI agents who visited me while in the county jail. This time, according to their words, they were happy to inform me that my first-born son Anthony Turner had been adopted by his mother's mother and was given the last name Caudle. But of course, they could fix that if I cooperated with their inquiries. I again told them absolutely not, and they again reminded me that they will always make life miserable for me until such time I decided to befriend them. To this day I have never gotten over such betrayal from another, my first love. The second devastating moment was receiving the heartbreaking news that my beloved first cousin, Robbie Mayes, had been ruthlessly murdered by her boyfriend. She was leaving him, and he followed her out the door, shot and killed her and watched her die in her sister's arms. Needless to say, my comrades and I waited patiently for his arrival.

As a result of both occurrences my heart was broken. My mind began to buckle with grief, even though my body was captured and locked down in a fixed physical place and always threatened with harm, mind was still free to roam. While grieving I became vulnerable to attack. I had to seize the moment and take charge. With the help of my comrades, we developed a regimen of daily physical workouts, chess matches and study time, examining the BPP's mistakes and the history of our ancestral past.

 I began to practice yoga and meditation, learning how to detach my body from the moment, understanding that there was such a thing called the multi-verse where the past and present exist simultaneously. The ripples of time took me back to the beginning. Slavery in the past became the present. My birth into this world was simply on the time stream, down river which all yesterdays became my todays, reliving multiple choices taken and lived and relived. I was witnessing a revolution and a Party die before my very eyes and was saddened as I assessed the choices made and the possibilities lost.

When we were let out to exercise or shower, we were prime targets for those white Neo Nazi or Aryan Brotherhood inmates who wanted our life, our black bodies for their trophy case. Their reward for their efforts was an early parole date. Often, the neo-Nazi inmates worked hand in hand with the guards to control the black inmate population. The guards would give them knives from the street to use as weapons or give them drugs in order to control the drug ring inside prison.

On the lighter side, I continued my UC Berkeley Independent Studies Program, where Dr. Leon Litwack, the chairperson at UC Berkeley history department, continued to be my mentor. Since I was an Independent Studies Honors Student, classes were not necessary, and we continued our research. I had become a revolutionary and a scholar of the History of the Revolutionary movement of our times. I lived it, I researched it and I wrote about it. With time on my hands, I now turned to the most difficult task at hand, the Reconciliation of African civilization and authentic African history with that of slavery and its Enlightenment thinkers. I was always an avid reader, but when I was not dodging knives, clubs and tear gas, my reading became prolific: Hubert Henry Harrison our black Socrates and leader of the Harlem Renaissance Movement, John G. Jackson; author Alfonso Schomburg, Joel Augustus Rogers, Dr. Nathaniel Huggins who mentored the fabulous John Henrik Clarke; and of course the founder of The Blyden Society, Edward Wilmot Blyden.

I also became more committed to my faith. At first I was bitter because I had been entombed in the dungeons of one of the most notorious prisons in the world. Languishing in a cacophony of cement insanity and steel where cowards brutalized men handcuffed from their wrist to waist to ankles. The only sanity or sanctuary we found was in the strength and determination of every man in that dungeon. We watched each other's back. That is how we survived. We took turns sleeping, while entrusted comrades stayed awake to guard our lives from cowardly attacks by prison guards.

Spiritually, I became stronger as my ancestors gave me vision and understanding. I began to understand that they put me in a position in which I was able to feed hundreds of thousands, provide free medical and dental for hundreds of thousands, provide a forum for African American studies, and the countless influences of millions of lives. Our ancestors had chosen us to draw a line in the sand and say never again will we allow our people to be gunned down in the streets. For we knew better than anyone that the KKK had abandoned their hood and robes and infiltrated the northern police departments. As a strategy, the gun and badge became their legitimate way of killing African Americans; after all, they were policemen just doing their job – killing young black men. They were the modern-day slave patrollers, the patty rollers keeping black folk in their place.

During our frequent, heartfelt conversations, the brothers inside these walls felt that we had been abandoned by our own people, especially those who had not had the guts or heart to draw that line. We were the misunderstood; our people were afraid to associate with us for fear of reprisals. I had two uncles by marriage who had fit that cowardly description. On the other hand, I was blessed. I constantly had groups of people outside focusing on my plight; there were two sisters I will never forget, both TV anchor women in the Bay Area: Valerie Williams from the ABC affiliate KGO in San Francisco, and the other sister who did the evening news from Channel 2 in Oakland. Her name escapes me now, but both kept lines of communication open and kept my name out there and kept eyes open, which afforded me some degree of protection inside.

Time and entombment equal the resurrection of the spirit. To experience resurrection, one has to bear the cross and we certainly did. One also has to be entombed and we certainly were. That entombment has to be followed by the resurrection inside the tomb. Only the Spirit, the presence of ancestral past, can resurrect your being. He will not free you from your physical bondage, but as you grow stronger in the spirit he will send his angels to remove that boulder blocking the entrance. There must be an angel that was God-sent to release your presence from that entombment. In my case it was Governor Jerry Brown. In 1975 Brown had married Linda Ronstadt, the famous pop singer and ardent supporter of the revolutionary movement. One year later, in 1976 he had reviewed the sentencing procedures that affected how political prisoners and the indeterminate practices affected how people were being sentenced. There were adjustments made in the process and it affected how we were sentenced. Six months later my boulder was removed, and I walked out a free man.

PART THREE

CHAPTER 13
THE PHOENIX REBORN

The Great Pyramids of Giza-My Grandson

A different man, a different world. For over a decade I spent my young adult life fighting for the ideals and principles I embraced as a student activist, grounded in the belief that all persons on this earth had the right to a productive life and the pursuit of happiness. I paid a heavy price for those beliefs. I lost ten years of my life, I lost the right to see my first-born son and, most importantly, I lost those years without the love of my family whom I loved with all my heart. When I walked out of prison, I took my shoes off, wanting to feel the grass caressing the bottom of my feet. I remember being taken to a disco for celebration and realized I had never been inside a nightclub-disco what was that ?. The music, the sounds, the flashing lights and the beautiful women were a bit overwhelming. I became paranoid and had to leave – too many people – and there was nowhere I could press my back against the wall for protection. My space was being violated. Inside the prison walls we had a standing rule that no one was allowed within five feet of your space without a show of their hands. All that I knew was being violated. It took me a few years before I was comfortable being in that position again.

This world I did not know. The comrades I had known were either dead, still imprisoned or hiding underground. My mental stability was fragile. There was no structure, nor were there any revolutionary guidelines to follow. I had to start from scratch. The FBI kept their word. They continued to make life miserable. At times I was followed, and every time I applied for employment they would make sure I was blackballed. I re-enrolled at UC, Berkeley, received my degree and left California in 1980.

When I returned to the Mid-West and I visited certain family members, doors were shut in my face. Some cousins and uncles by marriage looked upon me as an outlier, a renegade Blackman who bucked the system. I tried for years to re-connect with my first-born, my first love, but her mother had her under lock and key and would always threaten to call the Feds if I did not disappear. I loathed that woman because she was a tyrant and had succeeded in stealing my first born simply because I chose to become a Panther. The blow that could have destroyed my will to live was the execution-style murder of my beloved Panther son Fedayeen Turner in 1991. He was tied up, placed on the floor and shot in the back of the head by a white man. For a while I turned to drugs and alcohol to numb the pain. I still have horrible dreams of his execution, of me being recaptured and remanded back to San Quentin; or dreams of life-threatening confrontations with the police while in the Party.

In 2002 I came to Charlotte, NC, along with my youngest son Brandon Turner, whom I raised and has always been at my side since his birth in 1983. Accompanying me to Charlotte were all those memories created along the ripples of time, a past fraught with heartbreak, joy and pain in life's sometimes seemingly cruel hoax. I moved to Charlotte from Chicago after having spent the previous two years in Indianapolis caring for my dearly beloved mother who was terminally ill. With the collective efforts of my two wonderful sisters Marlonna and Rochelle, we made sure that she had all the love, attention and care that made her life as comfortable as possible under the circumstances.

Those were the most difficult days of my life, watching the person you love more than life itself slowly slipping from your grasp. I recall certain nights while I was sleeping in her hospital room. She would awaken, as if to ensure herself that I was present. On seeing me, she would smile and return to her slumber. Those smiles and those moments I still hold dear to my heart and I am so thankful that I was able to give comfort to her during those moments in time.

She was released from the hospital. Two weeks later her conditioned worsened. One evening I heard her call me, I ran upstairs. She said, "It's time." I immediately wrapped her in a blanket and picked her up. My mother looked at me and said, *"I'm in good hands, my big chief got me."* And I looked at her and said, *"I got you Mother."* But I knew in my heart it would be the last time she would ever see the inside of her house that she loved, the sanctuary given to us as a family. After losing my mother and my father two years earlier, I was a lost and lonely soul, filled with an unimaginable emptiness. Sometimes in life, fate or destiny conceals and then reveals strange illuminations of the life visited on us so unexpectedly. In 2001, a few days after Christmas, having buried my mother earlier, I heard a knock on the door, and there stood my first-born son, Anthony, my beautiful daughter-in-law Nina, and two little angels, my granddaughter Krystin and grandson Tony whom I had never laid eyes on. We embraced and sobbed without shame. My grandchildren, one on each side, vowed never to leave me alone in life. Until this day they have never broken their promise and have always remained at my side.

The experience and compassion I gained led me down yet another path. I opened a Home Health Agency dedicated to people in the community who had AIDS and HIV in Charlotte. The success of that endeavor could not have happened without the involvement of my beloved sister and family. Thanks to her strong leadership and professionalism, HHC became a success. It afforded me the opportunity to take care of unfinished business, the pursuit of post-graduate education, which would allow me to complete the mission, to leave an indelible imprint on the minds of generations of African American youth going forward. I would fulfill my dream and my continued obligation to the plight of my people as I continued my quest to be an instrument of change and service during this lifetime.. I vowed to use this instrument as a weapon to educate students about the true history of African people throughout the Diaspora.

The experience, the wisdom, the spiritual love and the never-ending commitment to my brothers and sisters during and after the struggle, have led me to many parts of the country and world. One year after being released I received my degree in history from the University of California at Berkeley and went on to receive postgraduate degree from North Carolina State A&T University. As a professor of African American Literature and the Humanities at North Carolina State A&T, I was committed to introducing my students to a wide variety of texts while providing a learning environment that enabled them to think critically about the textual relationship of literature/voice as representative of our historical past, as it unfolds into the present. My students' engagement was within our history unfolding as a captured and enslaved people. African and African American Literature and the Humanities was their guide. The purpose of the engagement was to demonstrate how deconstruction can be used as a tool to expose the multiple textual interpretations of what is deemed knowledge. Through writing exercises, small group discussions and singular and creative presentations, my students had the opportunity, not only to think critically but to communicate their ideas effectively and put their faces to their own voice. I taught them how to trace the footprints of our ancestors throughout the ripples of time.

Moreover, as an activist scholar interested in the various nuances of African American Literature and the Humanities, I challenged my students to question the canon and how it has been developed in a particular discipline. I assigned traditional canonical texts alongside less recognized and familiar texts to demonstrate both the constraints of the canon and the range of writings and knowledge that transcends it boundaries. I demanded the students understood the maxim 'existence precedes essence'; that what appears to have validity may only be a fleeting illusion called truth. We placed particular emphasis on European Enlightenment thinkers, while deconstructing their falsehoods and illusions of African inferiority. I wanted them to understand the falsehoods created by our captors, the ghost, these strange apparitions called civilized and enlightened European men.

A prime example of Enlightenment thought can be seen in Johann Friedrich Blumenbach's, 1776 volume, *On the Natural Varieties of Mankind*. He alleges biological differences between the races in which universal freedoms and individual liberties are based on the power of reasoning. Race seen by the Enlightenment thinkers was a socio-political order based on a permanent hierarchy of race, which turns physical differences into relationships of dominance, therefore white supremacy. I wanted to ensure my students understood the illusions of Enlightenment thinking while tracing the footprint of white supremacy.

Finally, for me, teaching was synonymous with life's experience. I had the incredibly unique experience of being an agent of history and its advocate. An active participant in the Black Liberation Freedom Struggle in America in the '60s and '70s, while working with and in the presence of Bobby Seale, Huey Newton, Dr. King, George Jackson and others. It has left an indelible imprint on my life and has shaped my worldview. This worldview motivated me to implement Free Health clinics while with the Black Panther Party in Berkeley, California, and contribute to the establishment of mobile health clinics in Swaziland and other parts of Southern Africa, while working with former ANC freedom fighters to set up programs to address the AIDS epidemic in Soweto and Johannesburg, South Africa.

This worldview allowed me to attend conferences and lectures at the University of Accra in Ghana, at the University of Calabar in Nigeria, as well as the University of Nigeria, Nsukka. I have studied and researched Kemetic history in Cairo, Egypt and to the Fourth cataract in Nubia now known as the Sudan. I have sat at the foot of W.E.B Du Bois at his tomb in Ghana and gazed upon the tomb of Khufu inside the great pyramids of Giza. Moreover, I gazed upon the face of Ramses and Hatshepsut in the Valley of the Kings. I have sailed the Nile to the port of the ancient city of Luxor and there I gazed upon the face of Thutmose III in the Great Temple of Luxor while looking in wonder as I walked the Avenue of Sphinxes. I have been greatly influenced by my overseas experiences. I hear the whispers of our distant past, and I strive to impart this unique life experience to those who may listen... resolutely and unequivocally. I humbly thank my ancestors for their blessings!

Our journey started in the Holy Land, an experience I did not know what to expect. Questions were abounding. How much of what we know is myth and how much was reality? Compounding the problem was the Israeli-Palestinian conflict. In my diary I wrote: "*Thus far my stay in Israel was mixed. I find the Israeli people to be in many respects hostile and rude to those of us with the darkest skin.*" Of course, this did not include all Israelis. There were some smiles and a sense of hospitality from the younger crowd. Perhaps the older Israelis suffered psychosis from the Holocaust, or maybe it is the deep-rooted fear of recognizing the kinship that we share and refusing to accept its origins. Tel Aviv is a beautiful city on the Mediterranean, but you feel the tension in the air, a city constantly on alert, a city under siege. The military is quite visible and ready to take you down at a moment's notice.

Today, our journey takes us to Jerusalem, the most glaring contradiction. It separates the souls of men and women; hatred is manifested in the horrific wall which separates Palestinians from Jews. Will it ever end, this madness? We proceeded to the birthplace, the resurrection tomb and the trans configuration of Christ. My Lord, we just left the birthplace of the Christ child. To be able to touch the alleged birthplace of Christ released an adrenalin and emotion that can never be explained. I wished my entire family could have borne witness and experienced such an historical and precious moment. If there is such a thing as dying a spiritual death and transforming the inner spirit to a higher state of being, I may have achieved that euphoric state of being.

Unfortunately, our euphoria was short-lived. We are now sitting at a checkpoint outside Bethlehem and are staring at this horrendous and ugly wall caging in the Palestinian people in land unfit for human beings. This wall is so symbolic of the apartheid system imposed on the Palestinian people by the Israeli government, right here in Bethlehem, the birthplace of the Prince of Peace. Israeli soldiers armed with AK 47s and M15s, barbed wire everywhere. Such Hypocrisy!

It is rather ironic that the Ethiopian Coptic church, the original church of Christianity, sits in a small corner of the Holy City. This beacon of light during the early days of the Christian era has now been reduced to an afterthought. After visiting the Church of the Holy Sepulchre, where Christ was allegedly crucified, we proceeded to the Garden of Gethsemane, the place where Jesus spent days of contemplation before he was betrayed and arrested by the Roman legions in this very garden. As we stroll through history it was eerily strange how the face of Christianity changed from blackish/brown to white. When we visited the shops in Israel and especially Palestine, all biblical figures were black/brown, hmmm.

After leaving the Holy City we headed to Egypt, we took a detour and stopped at a kibbutz in Dimona a black Jewish settlement of African Americans who left America at the height of the liberation movement in 1968. From Chicago, Brother Ben Amin took 200 African Americans to Israel during the liberation struggle and was ridiculed by the movement as a traitor. Unfortunately, they also took sharp attacks from both the Israeli and American governments which tried to deny them sanctuary on the grounds that they were black and not Jewish – a prerequisite for Israeli citizenship. Ultimately, the governments' attempts failed, and the self-proclaimed Black Israelites claimed their rights of citizenship. Israel has on occasions been accused of being a racist state, and their attempt to deny citizenship rights was only an example of the racism that the Palestinians have felt throughout their most recent history.

The Kibbutz now has a population of 4,000 and they have developed green energy, solar cooking and farming, replete with an irrigation system in the middle of desert country. Moreover, they produce plant-based beauty and health products, and have created an educational institution that rivals anything in Israel. Our time spent with these African American brothers and sisters was spiritually rewarding. As we sang and worshipped, I was brought to tears by their warm embrace and generous spirit.

One of my greatest take-aways from our seminar and conference was how Kemetic history and what we called Israel are irreversibly intertwined. It is amazing when you read books that are not written by Western scholars. You receive a different perspective on life, people and their humanity. Indeed, when you read translated versions of indigenous writings, their true history and culture comes to life.

Furthermore, it is amazing how the study of linguistics, culture and history can cast a brilliant ray of light on a subject. Take for instance, Biblical history. Most names, places and events are from principally an African experience. The Jewish experience was an African experience; they did not become Jews until they migrated to Europe, having been driven out of Rome by Constantine in 300AD. Before that, they were Afrim people who were part of the Akan tribe who were part of the Exodus out of Egypt. The word 'Israel' is a transposed Greek word from the Akan word Asrae, which was the home of David, from the Akan word Daed. Moreover, Solomon, is transposed form the Akan word Solome. All Akan words are from the Affirm tribe who would later become the Jews of Europe. Lastly, the word Hebrew is a French word Heabrus, which was introduced into the world around 400-700 AD, long after the Afrim had inhabited the earth. The conference was enlightening and certainly shed light on a historicity alien to the Western World.

Driving into Cairo, it became apparent that the mood of the group had changed drastically. The warmth shown by the Egyptians was heartfelt. When you were greeted the initial gesture is hand over heart followed by the embrace. Such warmth after the cold and indifferent reception we received in Israel. There were so many memorable moments, discussions and lectures, but most of all I remember the walking debates and information-gathering as we viewed the antiquities of the past.

What a wondrous sight to see the Pyramids of Giza for the first time. To imagine the tremendous effort and genius put into these accomplishments are beyond measure. Each individual block measures roughly 36 square feet and weighs over one ton. They are huge, and to ascend into the burial chamber was a spiritual journey, the sounds of strange melodies whispering into the ears. Imagine ascending at a 45° angle equal to the height of a 40-story building, then entering a chamber that was at least 60x60x120 feet. What a magnificent structure. One can only wonder what secrets this chamber holds, what marvels were revealed and what spiritual heights our people accomplished in such a holy place. It is unimaginable. And then the echoes of the past could be heard in the deafening silence laced with a slight melodic whisper of the wind – or their voices: Kufu, Menes Ramses, Thotmose III, Tahariq, all came rushing forth in a melody of song. And their voices manifested themselves in the body of my granddaughter as she sang, like a sparrow, the words of Amazing Grace.

From Cairo, we sailed the Nile River to Luxor. It was a journey to behold. Imagine the grandeur of our ancestors, who with pomp and ceremony sailed this glorious river, 4,120 miles in length from the mouth of the Mediterranean, snaking its way through the heart of Northern and Central Africa, forking south of the Sudan (then known as Nubia) west into Uganda and Lake Victoria and east to Ethiopia. Once we disembarked in Luxor we were totally overwhelmed with the majesty of such a place.

The modern town of Luxor is the site of the famous city Thebes (Waset, in ancient Egyptian), known as the City of a Hundred Gates. It was the capital of Egypt from the twelfth dynasty on (1991 BC) and reached its zenith during the New Kingdom. Imagine disembarking and strolling down the Avenue of Sphinxes as seen in the picture below, and eventually entering the Great Temple of the Gods.

It was from here that Thutmose III planned his campaigns, Akhenaten first contemplated the nature of god, and Ramses II set out his ambitious building program. Only Memphis could compare in size and splendor but today there is nothing left of Memphis: it was pillaged for its masonry to build new cities, and little of it remains. However, Luxor has left an indelible footprint as a reminder of the splendor and majesty of the accomplishments of this once great African empire, the epicenter of civilization.

Although the mud-brick houses and palaces of Thebes have disappeared, its stone temples have survived. The most beautiful of these is the temple of Luxor. It is close to the Nile and laid out parallel to the riverbank; the same riverbank from which we disembarked and then strolled down the Avenue of Sphinxes to Royal Temple. The temple was built by Amenhotep III (1390-52 BC) but completed by Tutankhamun (1336-27 BC) and Horemheb (1323-1295 BC) and then added to by Ramses II (1279-13 BC).

The temple has been in almost continuous use as a place of worship right up to the present day. During the Christian era, the temple's hypostyle hall was converted into a Christian church, and the remains of another Coptic church can be seen to the west. Then for thousands of years, the temple was buried beneath the streets and houses of Luxor. What was utterly amazing was the excavation process was still uncovering carefully preserved buildings and artifacts as we were attending our conference and exploring the city. We watched with excitement as the past was uncovered before our very eyes. Those ripples of time, those yesterdays became our todays, and the corridor to the past stood naked before our very eyes.

The building works by Ramses II at the northern end of the court were originally the entrance to the temple. It was an enclosed colonnade of seven pairs of 52-foot (16m) high open-flower papyrus columns. It was begun by Amenhotep III and completed by Tutankhamen and still support its huge architrave blocks. The Court leads into a Hypostyle Hall, which has 32 columns and what wonders these structures represented. Indeed they truly represented such engineering genius and milestones.

After we held our seminars and scheduled topical discussions, we mingled with the people. Street life and nightlife was thoroughly enjoyed. The smoke shops and restaurants were full of people, and the streets were packed. It is much cooler at night and during the day crowds are not seen in such abundance. Having to deal with temperatures above 100°F would certainly keep one inside. One thing which was quite noticeable and obvious to all was the intentional destruction of the nose and lips of most of the artifacts. The curator explained how the Europeans tried to cover up the African origins of the Egyptian people.

Today our conference, discussion and presentations centered around the intersection between Nubia and Egypt. We learned that the original Egyptians were called the Anu who traveled from the Sudan to Egypt. As they continued to populate the Nile river basins over time, Nubians and Egyptians were of the same family tree. When we visited the Nubian Museum, unlike the Cairo museum where a portion of the artifacts had been stolen and removed to London and Paris and Moscow, the artifacts there represented the Nubian presence as part of Egypt. We saw the think lips, the broad or flat noses and the black skin of the people, the Queens and Kings who left their footprint on African history. Conversely, we could only marvel as we witnessed the extraordinary artifacts that gave witness to the greatness of African history. We marveled at what was left of the rape and pillage of this great land. I am only reminded of the audacity of the Enlightenment thinkers who claimed Africans were without a history and lacked rational thought. Any mathematician or engineer will tell that the Pyramids are a perfect 45-degree angle representing a perfect right triangle.

If I may take a moment and remind my students these marvels of history, structures which are built on superb mathematical formulas of a perfect right triangle extending some 40-45 stories in height, were structures built by black hands some 4500-6000 before there was ever a Europe or a thing called the Enlightenment period.

Correspondingly, according to our host's lectures, the ancient Greek historian Herodotus and the Roman historian Diodorus thought otherwise and claimed that this land, from Ethops to the Indus Valley, was called Ethops (Ethiopia) and were all occupied by burnt-faced people (blacks) who had created civilization thousands of years before in those regions and had maintained family relations dating back many generations. Their race was called the Anu, the great tribes of Ethops. Anamin represented the greatest leader, and they founded the first cities on the north, Heliopolis and in the south, known as Hermonthis in prehistoric times. According to our host's presentation, they continued down the Nile and founded the cities Esneh and Erment. Our host's legends say the Anu taught their black races all the characteristics of civilization. They created the agricultural techniques of irrigation and flood control with dams. Accordingly, it would be this technique of flood control that would ultimately allow the Kemetic civilizations to flourish along the Nile.

Our host said their ancestors were an agricultural people, raising cattle along the Nile River and shutting themselves within walls for defensive purposes. They were familiar with metals and its technical application. According to the Griot, they were the first to master writing, attributing the art to the great Toth, the great Hermes, and the Anu like Osiris, who is called the Onian in Chapter XV of the *Book of the Dead* and in the Pyramid Text. We concluded that their people already knew the principles of art and architecture. The proof lies in the construction of the Mastabas (forerunners of the pyramids) and hieroglyphs bearing the unmistakable stamp of their origins. It was they, who along with the Akans, wrote the Egyptian Book of the Dead and the Sumerian epic poem Gilgamesh. Indeed, they were the forerunners who, in the ripples of time, were responsible for science, art, writing and the calendar, for the cosmology of those moments on that time stream. Our guide took us to those moments on the time stream and introduced us to Mantheo, the last student at the Ancient Mystery School of Anu at Alexandria before the invasion of Alexander the Great in 330 BCE. He explained that this civilization called Egypt began to develop a long time ago, roughly 10,000 years ago. It is common knowledge that by 4245 BCE the Egyptians had already invented the calendar but, according to the calendar uncovered, its cycle is thousands of years long.

After the conference ended, there was much to consider, most of which was the need to reconcile the edited version of Western scholarship with that of indigenous scholars of The Motherland who left us breathless with the flow of information from ancient texts. It shed an entirely different light on the influence that ancient African cultures, i.e. civilization, had on the way we see the world today.

I thought about the transformation of human civilizations and the role played in its development by persons/spirits who occupied black bodies. Then I thought about how Europeans eventually invaded the Motherland, expropriated the land, enslaved its people, dehumanized their value and then **wrote them out of history**. With clarity, my mission was becoming even more apparent – to continue to unearth the truth, to expose the big lies, of which there were many.

The last conference on the African continent to sharpen my vision was the ALA, African Literary Association, held at the W.E.B. Du Bois Convocation Center in Accra, Ghana. There I met some of the most articulate scholars and activists on the continent, whose literary talents and historical contributions to the freedom struggles on the continent were beyond reproach. Some of the most intense conversations were with brothers including former members of Frelimo, the Mozambican nationalist liberation, members of the ANC who were fighting the Apartheid regime in South Africa, and brothers from the secessionist Biafran Movement out of Nigeria. It was the voice of Africa on all aspects of Africa and the African Diaspora. Its interdisciplinary approach examined, with a critical eye, the socio-economic, political and cultural life of Africans and those of African descent spread throughout the diaspora. There was an emphasis on the history, literature, politics of revolutionary struggle and the culture and folklore of the Diaspora. The exchange of ideas gave me a different historical perspective of my involvement with the Black Panther Party and its place in history.

Upon returning to America, I was asked to publish a paper for OFO-Journal of Trans-Atlantic Studies placing the Black Panther Party in the historical context of freedom struggles through the Diaspora and its impact. Later I was given the honor to Present the premier of the Marvel Movie Black Panther in the Chicagoland Area. The following summer we held the first Black Panther Wakanda International Conference at the Hilton Hotel in Chicago. The headline was the intersection of the movie Black Panther and the history of the Black Panther Party.

Fred Hampton Jr. and I share a moment with his dad

Fred Hampton Jr. and my son Anthony at Wakanda Conference

CHAPTER 14
THE EVOLUTION OF CORPORATIVE
FASCISM AMERICAN STYLE

In America, only the gullible, lunatics, the blindered, the deluded, the inattentive, the over-medicated, the too-easily propagandized, those too impoverished and/or too busy to find the time to think rationally *The American fascist would prefer to poison the channels of public information.* *"With a Fascist the problem is never how best to present the truth to the public but how best to use the news to deceive the public into giving the fascist and his group more money or more power."* Carl Sagan

The Rising Tide of Trumpism

The events unfolding during the last four years in the Trump administration must be placed in proper historical perspective. The rise of populism and white nativism and the rise of American-style Trumpian fascism, has had a profound negative effect on the body politic. In the past few decades, the correlation between fascism, capitalism and imperialism – and now racism – has begun to receive close critical analysis, especially during the age of Trump. Are these -isms antithetical to the concept of moral economy as it applies to the social common of equality and social justice for all the people? While a member of the Black Panther Party, I had the honor and privilege of collaborating with our General Field Marshall, George Jackson (Soledad Brother) in writing his bestselling book *Blood Is My Eye*. We argued that the psychosocial dimensions of American-style fascism had evolved into corporative fascism and racism, and its confluences could be felt worldwide, more importantly on American soil. Moreover, it was determined that fascism is not one definition nor is it static but an ever-evolving phenomenon that changes its shape and colors like a chameleon.

The question I raised was in relation to Jackson's *Blood Is My Eye*. The confluences and its history especially pertaining to race and socio-economic injustice will always have its roots in racism and the brutal history of slavery. The ownership of the black body as a commodity along with the 100 percent profit margin produced for the slave owner always created a wealth gap between the races. The capital exploitation of labor based on race and class after slavery created the seeds of populism where poor whites always felt threatened by the entry of black bodies into the arena of the labor market and political office. Therefore white grievance and white populism were born during and after slavery and have always existed throughout the ripples of time.

From the end of post-Reconstruction to the black codes and grandfather clauses, to Jim Crow and now James Esquire Junior (a new form of voter suppression has come front and center), the issue is always the same. The continued denial of social and economic justice for black people as institutionalized racism continues to dominate the political landscape of America. The rise of Trumpism is a continued subversion and perversion of indefensible race prejudice, which makes me feel personally insulted and ashamed for what goodness there is in this country. From the coup staged in Wilmington in 1898 to the Elaine, Arkansas massacre and the total destruction of the socio-economic structure of Tulsa,

Oklahoma in 1921, white localized power structures have exercised their will over a Black majority denied equal treatment under the rule of law.

To better understand this process we must correlate Jackson's writing with the rise of corporative fascism American-style as it evolves into what we know today as Trumpism. I argue that the sheer nature of this form of capitalism is antithetical to a moral economy for people in general but even more so for people of color. The birth of this particular form of capitalism (trafficking in human flesh as a commodity to profit from slave labor, and the forced removal of indigenous people from their homeland while laying claim to all natural resources which created the basis of wealth for the ruling minority), has created a social matrix of white supremacist violence, racism, class and gender discrimination, fomented by the hollowing out of the democratic institutions that were to act as safeguards to protect the rights of its citizens. The perpetration of this systematic exclusion of the majority, especially people of color, is justified through the demonization of its victims while exclusive control of most of the wealth remains in the hands of an exclusive class of minority white males who gained and maintained their wealth through acts of genocide and exploitation.

Let us begin by examining George Jackson's basic premise, that the economic and political restraints of corporative fascism are essentially the same as slavery. Jackson's position is that the system of slavery is ever changing, shifting, and adapting to camouflage the oppression of the original slave, who is now a neo-slave. The question is what new strategies need we explore to stop the shape shifter in his tracks.

Jackson explains his philosophy of neo-slavery in the following passage

According to Jackson (1970), "*ever since the end of slavery our principal enemy must be isolated and identified as capitalism. The new slaver was and is the factory owner, the businessman of capitalist America, the man responsible for employment wages, price control of the nation's infrastructure of Europe and the U.S. This was responsible for the rape of Africa and Asia. The Europeans would not have wasted the ball and powder were it not for the profit motive*" (p. 236).

As Jackson continues to expose the element of this new form of slavery, he says, "*It was capitalism that armed the ships, free enterprise that launched them, and private ownership of property that fed the troops. Neo-slavery and imperialism took up where the slave trade left off (p. 236).* It is Jackson's contention that "It was not until after the slave trade ended that America, France, England and the

Netherlands settled Africa and Asia in earnest. *The transformation of slavery to neo-slavery occurred as the industrial revolution took hold, and as new economic attractions replaced the older one: chattel slavery was replaced by neo-slavery (p. 236).*

From these conditions, the socio-economic life of the slave changed from slavery to neo-slavery. Greed from profit built the tenement houses, and these city projects became the neo-slave colonies. Jackson (1971) explains further in the following quote: *Profit and loss prevent repairs and maintenance. Free enterprise brought the monopolistic chain stores into the neo-colony (neighborhoods). The concept of private ownership of facilities that the people need to exist brought the legions of hip-shooting brainless pigs (slave patrollers/police) down upon our heads, our homes, our streets."*

According to Jackson the Slave Patrollers/Police are there to "protect the property of the entrepreneur, his chain stores, and his businesses, his banks" as they were there to protect the property of the slave owner by keeping them confined to the plantation. In a letter to his lawyer, Jackson's biting description of neo-slavery and the meager wages in the 1970s is clearly linked to chattel slavery. An excerpt:

Dear Faye,

Slavery is an economic condition. Today's neo-slavery must be defined in terms of economics. The chattel is a property, one man exercising the property rights of his established economic order, the other man as that property. The owner can move that property or hold it in one square yard of the earth's surface; he can let it breed other slaves, he can sell it, beat it, work it, harm it? fuck it or kill it. But, if he wants to keep and enjoy all the benefits that property of this kind can render, he must feed it sometimes, he must clothe it against the elements, and he must provide a modicum of shelter. Chattel slavery is an economic condition which manifests itself in the total loss or absence of self-determination. The new slavery, the modern variety of chatted slavery updated to disguise itself, places the victim in a factory or in the case of most blacks in support roles inside and around the factory (service trades) as well as the service industry, working for meager wages. Today's neo-slavery does not even allow enough wages for a modicum of food and shelter. You are free to starve. The sense of neo-slavery comes through as a result of our ties to the "meager wage". If you do not make any more in wages than you need to live, you are a neo-slave. If you are held in one spot on this earth because of your economic status, it is the same as being held on the plantation by the slave master. (Jackson, 1970, p. 251)

Indeed, Jackson's narrative is an uncompromising antithesis to the proposition that slavery has ended, and the African American is free from bondage. Today, African American men working full time year around have 68 percent of the average earning of comparable white men. The net worth of a typical white family is 117,000.00 ten times that of a black family (17,000.00) The transformation from slavery to neo-slavery and from capitalism to corporatism is the ebb and flow of the many faces of capitalism, always working to the disadvantage of the slave/neo-slave.

According to Jackson, corporatism is the ebb and flow of capitalism grown from the slave economy to bourgeois capitalism to monopoly capital, from national to international markets, and hence the birth of corporative fascism. As one force emerges, the opposite force must retreat. "I contend that fascist corporatism emerged and advanced in the U.S. At the same time, it was making its advances, it caused by its very nature, an advance in the worldwide socialist consciousness. When U.S. capitalism reached the stage of imperialism, Western great powers had already divided among themselves almost all the important markets in the world. After WWII, the U.S. became the most powerful and the richest imperialist power." (1971, p.131)

Indeed, if we consider the historical events of the last 60 years, Jackson's predictions ring true. The countless wars and interventions in Africa, Asia and the Middle East bear witness to this process unfolding. The very nature of its fundamental elements, and its economic, social, political and military mobilization distinguish it as the prototype of the corporatism fascist state. Jackson (1971) continues: "The U.S. is the Korean problem, the Vietnamese problem, the problem in the Congo, the Middle East? It is the grease in the British and Latin American guns that operate against the masses of common people." (p.131) Lest we forget Naomi Klein's *Shock Doctrine* (2007), Pinochet and the Freidman School of Economics unleashing the reign of terror against the people's movement in Chile during the Reagan years.

Let us examine more closely this evolving face of international corporative fascism American-style. According to Jackson (1971) *"The nature of fascism, its characteristics and properties have been in dispute ever since it was first identified as a distinct phenomenon growing out of Italy's state supported industries in 1922. There have been a hundred party lines on exactly what fascism is. But both Marxist and non-Marxists agree on at least two of its general factors: its capitalist orientation and its anti-labor, anti-class nature. These two factors almost by themselves identify the U.S. as a focused corporative fascist state."* (p.134). In 1983, 20.1 percent of working Americans were union members. Today that percentage is 10.1 and fewer than 8 percent in the private sector (U.S Department of Labor, Labor Statistics, 2018). Fewer workers are receiving the benefits of collective bargaining, and even if a worker is a union member, the wage advantage has diminished.

Jackson's uncanny intellect discerned that there was no exact definition of fascism. The final definition of fascism is still open, simply because it is still a developing movement, snaking its way through time. We have already discussed the defects of trying to analyze a movement outside of its process and its essential relationships. One thing is for certain, according to Jackson: the true face of corporative fascism has been disguised. "Fascism was the product of class struggle. It is an obvious extension of capitalism, a higher form of the old struggle-capitalism versus socialism and labor. I think our failure to clearly isolate and define it may have something to do with our insistence on a full definition – in other words, looking for identical symptoms from nation to nation." (Jackson, 197 1, p.136) Jackson's interpretation of corporative fascism is its evolution from nationalistic trappings to becoming international in the truest sense of the word. Jackson makes the point succinctly: *"We have failed to understand its basically international character. In fact, it has followed international socialism all around the globe. One of the most definite characteristics of fascism is its international quality"* (p.136). The European Union as an example of its international quality today.

Jackson's book was researched from 1967 to 1969 and published in 1971. His prophetic words were realized from 1973 to the present. During that time, South America, Africa and Asia experienced strong nationalist movements with socialism knocking at its door. And in most cases, strong labor movements were of particular concern to the state department which feared possible incursions of socialism into capital markets. The CIA-sponsored coup d'état in Chile was an example of international corporative fascism following socialism around the globe. On September 11, 1973, General Pinochet and his supporters ended the reign of Salvador Allende. All the gains made by the Chilean masses – land reform, strong labor unions, rising living wages and healthcare were nullified by the implementation of the Friedman School of Economics or corporative fascism. The privatization of land, free trade, deregulation, destruction of the labor unions and the drastic cuts to social spending ushered in the beginning of the new face of American-style fascism. Pinochet appointed Sergio de Castro to become the finance minister. He stacked the government with Friedman's Chicago Boys a group of economists who were trained at the University of Chicago's Friedman School of Economics, appointing one of them to head the central bank.

In a letter written to me on 6/22/1971, Jackson explained the events unfolding in Chile and throughout the world:

'The trends toward monopoly capitol began effectively just after the close of the civil war in America. Prior to its emergence, bourgeois democratic rule could be said to have been the predominant political force inside American society. As monopoly capital matured, the role of the old bourgeois democracy failed. As monopoly capital forced out the small, dispersed factory setup, the new corporatism assumed political supremacy. Monopoly capital can in no way be interpreted as an extension of old bourgeois democracy. The forces of monopoly capital swept across the Western world in the first half of this century. But they did not exist alone. Their opposite force was also at work, i.e. 'international socialism' – Lenin's and Fanon's – national wars of liberation, guided not by the national bourgeois but by the people, the ordinary-working class people.

At its core, fascism is an economic rearrangement. It is international capitalism's response to the challenge of international scientific socialism. It developed from nation to nation out of differing levels of decline in traditionalist capitalism. The common feature of all instances of fascism is the opposition of a weak socialist revolution. When the fascist arrangement begins to emerge in any of the independent nation states, it does so by default. It is simply an arrangement of an established capitalist economy, an attempt to renew, perpetuate and legitimize that economy's rulers by circumflexing and weighing down, diffusing a revolutionary consciousness pushing from below. Fascism must be an episodically logical state in the socio-economic development of capitalism in a state of crisis. It is the result of a revolutionary thrust that was weak and miscarried – a consciousness that was compromised. "*When revolution fails ... it's the fault of the vanguard parties. Class struggle is an ingredient of fascism it follows that where fascism emerges and develops, the anti-capitalist forces were weaker than the traditionalist forces. This weakness will become even more pronounced as fascism develops! The aim of fascism is the complete destruction of all revolutionary consciousness.*" (Jackson, 1971, p.137)

Let us travel back through the ripples of time to get a true measure of the seeds of American-style fascism. At the beginning of the Civil War, America was ranked fourth in the world among industrial states, behind the British, German and French empires. By 1970, the U.S. had doubled the value of its products. The number of factory workers drawn out of other sectors of the economy caused the industrial workforce to nearly double during the same period. Improvement in the technology of agricultural production drew some workers from the countryside and sent others westward toward the expanding frontiers. The craftsman lost his privileged economic position with the appearance of newly invented mass production machinery. This new machinery, and the factory setup up in general, made individual workers more expendable and made it possible to reduce their share of the profit. By the mid-1890s the U.S. was producing one-third of the world's manufactured goods and was on its way to becoming a world power. Hello world, here comes the storm!

The Founders of American-Style Corporatism Fascism

Andrew Carnegie, J.P. Morgan, John D. Rockefeller

The expansion of American industry out of the demands of the Civil War involved a complex concentration of several violent and predictable capital mandates. The old traditional sector of the landed aristocracy was broken. Machinery, transportation networks and methods and sources, and communication technology boomed (the framework of the industrial state, and of course the emergence of an industrial elite). The growing demand for new raw material, coal, iron and other ores, boosted the industrial complex. The value of labor shrank, and the drive for monopoly accumulation was firmly established. One of the contributing factors of increased monopoly capitol was the rise to prominence of the chain gangs (forced labor) the continued exploitation of black bodies and a new style of policing victims. This form of slave labor would result in the building of Birmingham, Ala as the main industrial (steel and iron ore mined by convict labor) city during the early 20th,century.

This period of capital accumulation, inventions of new machinery used in the factory setups, and the new mining industry all created a closed economy setup by the Republican Party legislation. Capital investment through government contracts were in part the beginning of a new chapter in the authoritarian process in American history. Monopoly capitol was seeded during this period, while not stopping there, Morgan helped reorganize several railroads, and in 1885, he facilitated the agreement between the New York Central Railroad and the

Pennsylvania Railroad (the two largest railroads in the country at the time). The restructuring dissipated tensions with competition between the two powerhouses. And, following the panic of 1893, the banker helped rehabilitate several more railroads including the Southern Railroad, the Erie Railroad and Northern Pacific Railway. According to Britannica, by 1902, the mogul controlled over 5,000 miles of American railroads due to his influential status.

Perhaps most notably, Morgan created a syndicate to help resupply the U.S. government's dwindling gold reserve to the tune of $62 million. By providing the government with the gold, Morgan was critical in aiding the treasury crisis and the Depression. Still, only a few years later, he ventured into financing industrial consolidations, including his 1891 financing of the merger of Edison General Electric and Thomson-Houston Electric Company to form General Electric, one of the most enduring industries in the country. Not finished with groundbreaking corporations, Morgan charged on to finance the merging of the Carnegie Steel Company with the Federal Steel Company and others in 1901, to create the United States Steel Corporation, which was reportedly the world's first corporation worth $1 billion.

Moreover, in 1907, Morgan convinced fellow bankers to help bail out several failing financial institutions during the financial panic to save markets. It was this other action that led to Morgan being called to testify before a congressional committee led by Arsene Pujo (D) of Louisiana, which reportedly investigated some of the Wall Street heavy hitters (known as the "money trust") who, as the concern went, had accumulated too much power. The Pujo Committee influenced both the creation of the Federal Reserve System in 1913 and even the Clayton Antitrust Act in 1914 to help regulate markets and power.

The bank's first major act was selling New York Central Railroad stock while keeping the stock price stable. It was a smash success. The bank then became a go-to for financing mergers, consolidations, and the founding of mega industry titans in the railroad, electric and steel industries. By 1904, J.P. Morgan & Co. helped finance projects such as the Panama Canal, raising $40 million for the United States to help purchase the land rights from the cash-poor French Panama Canal Co. And, notably, J.P. Morgan & Co. played an influential role in financing the Allied victory during World War I, reportedly arranging a $500 million Anglo-French loan, the largest foreign loan in Wall Street history at the time. Monopoly capital was now controlling a large share of the nation's GDP.

Indeed, the owners of the largest share of the nation's GDP will always control the political agenda and the government. Monopoly capital is one face of corporatist fascism. By 1889, with the growth of the steel industry, U.S. output of steel exceeded that of the UK and all of Europe. Andrew Carnegie became the leading industrialist as he dominated the steel industry, and monopolies were on the rise. Carnegie's empire grew as he began to buy out all his competitors, such as Braddock steel, owned by Carnegie's former boss and president of the Pennsylvania Railroad. He then proceeded to buy Pittsburgh Bessemer Steel Works, the Lucy Furnaces, the Union Iron Mills, the Union Mill (Wilson, Walker & County), the Keystone Bridge Works, the Hartman Steel Works, the Frick Coke Company, and the Scotia Ore Mine.

John d. Rockefeller

The sectors of industry and finance were now at the hub of growing fascist corporative arrangement. To continue growing, Rockefeller would finance and go on a buying spree, buying two dozen refineries in 60 days. To finance everything, he reinvested the profits and begged banks for more money. Before this series of acquisitions, few businessmen understood how monopolies worked. Rockefeller was the first to focus on aggressive growth by buying smaller companies, a move that pioneered modern American capitalism. John D. Rockefeller would now become one of the major players in this new fascist arrangement. The contrapositive shift would augment and facilitate the strengthening of the rise of monopoly capital and corporative fascism, and interlocking industry and trust would become antithetical to the concept of the moral economy and labor.

In the essay *The Moral Economy of the English Crowd in the Eighteenth Century* (1971 author E.P. Thompson, comments on the making of the English working class: "It is possible to detect in almost every 18th century crowd action some legitimizing notion. By the notion of legitimating, *"I mean that the men and women in the crowd were informed by the belief that they were defending traditional rights or customs, and, in general, that they were supported by the wider consensus of the community. The implementation of the social contract for the common good of the community is the obligation of the institutions of governance."* (p.188)

Indeed, the concept of moral economy will always suffer at the hands of corporativist fascism. In order to understand that statement one must comprehend the foundation on which capitalism was built and how it evolved from a slave economy to unfettered capitalism fueled by racism and class distinctions, which only benefited the white male ruling elite. The motive to maximize profit for the ruling elite at the expense of cheap labor was the only concern. By masking this strategy with the dehumanization and demoralization of its victims, a system of corporative fascism has grown exponentially, and the sheer weight of its dominance can only be measured by the destruction of any semblance of profit sharing with the masses, while rendering labor unions ineffective.

A moral economy is based on goodness, fairness and justice. In *Human Nature and the Moral Economy* (2013) Michael Johnson argues, "*Fairness and cooperation are intrinsic features of the human species. So why is it that corporations that are too big to fail don't seem bound by the moral economy as the rest.*" The answer is simple: we are witnessing the transformation of capitalism into a particular form of corporative fascism, which has absolutely no regard for the wellbeing of the masses. There is no morality in greed and the maximization of profit over its people. We do not have to look any further than the predatory lending practices of the financial institutions or the terms of the payday loans/title loans. The belief that markets can regulate themselves in the interest of people and for the common good went up in flames during the housing bust and the Wall Street debacle in 2008. Corporative fascism is irrevocably antithetical to the moral economy and must be exposed.

Clearly, limitless profit-seeking has always been the mantra of the corporativist ideology which is grounded in the Friedman School of thought, which is the demand for radical **privatization, massive deregulation**, and the **war on labor unions, minimal taxes** on corporations, **free trade,** and the **removal of the safety net (cuts on social spending)**. All of these wage war on the moral economy. Within the walls of their think tanks such as The American Enterprise Institute, Heritage, Cato and Americans for Prosperity are the brain trust and bankrollers of the corporate fascist elite, i.e. the Tea Party and Trumpism movement. They will continue to be antithetical to the moral economy. We have witnessed the full brunt of this fascist mentality in the policies of Donald Trump.

The Friedman doctrine (i.e., tax cuts, privatized services, deregulation, cuts in social spending, and union busting) all became known as the **Chicago School Revolution**. What started with the Republicans' war on President Lyndon Johnson's War on Poverty (Social Programs) mushroomed into Reaganomics. Once a Republican (Ronald Reagan) became president, all federal programs to aid the poor and unions became fair game. The war on the moral economy and the rise of corporative fascism accelerated. Friedman economics led the charge and Ronald Reagan carried its banner with his dog whistles on race, calling women of color 'the *Welfare Queens*"-hence the beginning of the war on food stamps and all social programs that would aid the poor and disposed people of color.

In fact, it was Ronald Reagan, who inherited America's unique tapestry of racism woven into the fabric of corporative fascism in America. John Ehrlichman, Reagan's Chief of Staff said: "our strategy was to associate the niggers with heroin and then criminalize them heavily which could disrupt those communities. We could arrest their leader, raid their homes, break up their meetings, and vilify them night after night on the evening news. Did we know we were lying about the drugs, Of course we did?" Disinformation has always been an effective tool of fascist propaganda. It was used by the Nixon administration to wage war on the Black Liberation movement, and by Reagan on the Black communities of the '60s and '70s. To criminalize the black man and community, the war on drugs became the watchword and the prison population began to increase.

What Reagan did was to take it to another level. His fascist arrangement cut $6.8 billion from social programs. It busted the unions and militarized the police by declaring a War On Drugs. He gave tax cuts to the rich, shifted federal dollars from the cut in social programs while funneling the money to the various states to purchase the most advanced military style weaponry to fight this so-called War on Drugs. Mass incarceration of black bodies ensued. Black communities were decimated as well as black families. The prison population exploded from 350,000 in 1975 to 759,100 in 1985, under Reagan's watchful eye. Essentially a highly militarized police state was now emerging under the pretext of the war on drugs.

Young African American bodies had once again been demonized, this time under the label of the 'super predator'. By 1990, the prison population had grown to 1,179,200. The privatization of prisons were sprawling private facilities, which were built; and white males made billions off the body count of its victims. And I know some don't want to hear it, but President Clinton and his $30 billion crime bill was a major player in the abuse and demonization of black lives. Mandatory minimums and the three-strike syndrome were a part of his watch and he certainly bore responsibility for this fascist arrangement of building and maintaining the militarized police force we see on the streets today. Remember the words of the brilliant Cheikh Anta Diop," it is by design the colonizers' will always maintain a policy to neutralize at least forty percent of the captive male population in order to maintain control of its victims".

Corporative Fascism became a shapeshifter, forever changing its name and switching identities. According to Naomi Klein's *Shock Doctrine*, "Friedman called himself a liberal, but his U.S. followers, who associated liberals with high taxes and government intervention, tend to identify as conservatives, 'classical economist, free marketers and later, as believers in 'Reaganomics' or 'Laissez-faire'." In present day shift shaping they are the neocons, the Tea Party, the Party of Donald Trump. The corporative fascism first identified by George Jackson had morphed from the '80s into the intellectual movement, which is always a **key part** of the fascist arrangement, led by the right-wing think tanks with which Friedman had a long association: the Heritage Foundation, Cato Institute and the American Enterprise Institute.

According to Klein's *Shock Doctrine* (2007), "All these incarnations share a commitment to the policy trinity – the elimination of the public sphere, total liberation for corporations and skeletal social spending, total deregulation and union busting." (p. 18). What has occurred over the last 30 years, according to Klein, and the last 50, according to Jackson, corporative fascism has harnessed the full force of a seedy alliance between large corporations and a class of extremely wealthy politicians in the service of a corporative state agenda.

Indeed, in Jackson's *Blood In My Eye*, he describes a system that erases the boundaries between big business and big government. Once these boundaries disappear, we have a corporative fascist arrangement. Its main characteristics are huge transfers of public wealth to private hands, often accompanied by an exploding debt, an ever-widening chasm between the dazzling rich and the disposable poor, and massive tax cuts for the rich.

We only need to look at the recent Trump tax cuts that transferred trillions of dollars into the hands of corporations and into the pockets of the one percent who control the U.S. economy. In the last 20 years the rich have enjoyed a 298 percent increase in their earnings but just 4 percent for the disposable poor. Moreover, 10 percent of Americans account for 87 percent of stock ownership while the richest one percent own or collect 35 percent of household income. (Bill Domhoff, 2013) It appears that in the corporatist state it is impossible to integrate our moral and economic values to benefit the masses. How ironic, that those politicians who represent the people blocked legislation to raise the minimum wage to $15 per hr. The morality of moral economics so often appears to be at odds with corporative fascism. The rise of Trumpism has only exacerbated the lack of empathy for the common good, especially when applied to people of color.

I argue the perversion of the idea of freedom democracy and capitalism is nothing but a smoke screen for the corporatist state to exploit workers through the meager wage. This rampant exploitation can be measured by the astronomical rise of corporate profits and the stagnation of middle-class and working-class wages. According to a sociology study at the University of California at Santa Cruz, the top 200 corporate CEOs saw a 16 percent increase or $200,000 in their salaries while working class wages were flat and bottomed out at $27,519.00 the lowest since 1998. Furthermore, the mean household financial (non-home) wealth of the top 1 percent was $15,171,600 while the bottom 4 percent is $14,800 (Domhoff, 2016). Lastly 46.5 percent of African Americans are living at or below the poverty line, and at 12.2 percent, the black unemployment rate is double the national average of 6.6 percent (Black Demographics, 2018).

Clearly, I challenge the central and most cherished claim in this perversion of the idea of freedom – that the triumph of deregulated capitalism has been born of freedom, that unfettered free markets go hand in hand with democracy. Behind this illusion of freedom is the rise of corporative fascism. In fact, it was during the Bush-Cheney administration, which stood for the violent and creative accumulation of a 50-year campaign, that we witnessed the total corporative fascist takeover, which extended into the age of Trumpism.

The Koch Brothers and the Tea Party

Any attempts to hold ideologies accountable for the committed transgression against its citizens can only be understood by stripping away the illusion, the perversion of the idea. Ideologies or -isms became dangerous to the public when they are perverted, and they need to be identified to the public as such. Those fundamentalists who believe that freedom is a free-market economy unfettered by any form of government intervention is simply a smokescreen for the total negation of moral economics. Supporters of the Friedman School and its anti-labor, anti-regulation, anti-social spending are the right-wing conservatives, Tea Party (now the Freedom Caucus), and the Trumpists who demand an absolute hand to implement their perfectly unfettered market system which demonizes people of color and looks upon white privilege and grievance as the cornerstone of their base of support.

Clearly, these white power elites and their white supremacist diehards, these right-wing evangelical Christians, must remake the world by erasing all things that do not fit their model, their idea of freedom for the white aggrieved. Klein makes the point succinctly: *"Rooted in biblical fantasies of great floods and great fires, it is logical that it leads to violence. The ideologies that long for that impossible clean slate, which can only be reached through some kind of cataclysm, are the dangerous ones."* (p.27). We had only to wait for a short period of time. On January 6th,2021 we all watched as this cataclysmic event unfolded.

The Freidman School or the Chicago School of Economics offers no social justice in the moral economy. The needs of the citizens are bypassed, and the only justice and gain is for the tiny corporate elite. Let us examine the socio-economic landscape of the last 20 years.

Citizens United Strengthens Corporativist Fascism

The passing into law of Citizens United opened the door for corporative fascism to firmly entrench itself within the American political system. Citizens United was/is that thin line between the corporate elite and the political elite and has been erased. It gave corporations the green light to spend unlimited sums on political ads and buy elections. Concisely, the Supreme Court decided 5-4 that it is ok for corporations to spend as much as they want to convince people to vote for or against a candidate. (Dunbar, 2012) Because of the wealth possessed by the Koch Brothers, they could outspend and outmatch any adversaries. They persuaded candidates to support their views on taxation, business, deregulation in return for funding. With the passing of Citizens United by the Supreme Ct., they created the legal foundation for the corporation to act with the same rights, privileges, and protections accorded to individuals, thus sanctifying the role of disproportionate power within in a mythical construct of a corporate entity. The Koch Brothers and their corporate dollars could now act as individual donors masking their intentions as an act of free speech and freedom of expression. My people, look closely so that you see how the game is played. It's called deception. There are no longer any boundaries between the corporate elite and the politicians who are in their pockets. Corporative Fascism rules the American landscape!

By law, the corporativist state can now create shadow political parties with unlimited funds from billionaires to buy and influence elections. Not only can they prop up their candidates, but they can also set the political and economic agenda with dark money and with dark intentions. Moreover, thanks to Trump's election to the White House, Mitchell McConnell has been able to stack the Supreme Court with three conservative appointees. By circumventing the concept of the three branches of government, and with the Senate having been controlled by Republicans for the last three confirmations, McConnell evoked the simple majority vote for the first time since 1917 and gave Trump three appointees. Making the false claim that no nominee can be appointed during an election year, McConnell robbed Obama of his nominee, Merrick Garland, following the death of Anthony Scalia in 2016, and did the same thing after the death of Ruth Bader Ginsberg in 2020.

For our purpose, we will use the state of North Carolina as example of how the rise of the Tea Party morphed into Trumpism and the entrenchment of corporative fascism in America. I saw and experienced this phenomenon firsthand while I was a professor at North Carolina State AT&T University. In 2012, Pat McCrory, the newly-elected Republican governor of North Carolina, was heavily financed by the billionaire Koch Brothers, the power behind the corporative fascist movement.

Their think tank and shadow political organization, <u>America for Prosperity,</u> was headed by Art Polk who was budget director for the McCrory machine and the state of North Carolina. In Margret Newkirk's article <u>A Tea Partier Takes Charge of North Carolina</u>, she makes the point succinctly: "North, Carolina is about to find out what happens when a Tea Party die-hard gets his hands on the levers of government." Consequently, Art Polk, an original board member of America for Prosperity, became the state's budget director in January. He was once dubbed the "Knight of the Right" by Raleigh's *News & Observer*. In real time, Polk was given the opportunity to push through tax and spending cuts he had long championed. His think tank favors a repeal of North Carolina's income tax, privatizing Medicaid and reducing the state workforce. In order to get a better understanding of these persons called the Koch Brothers, let us go back through the ripples of time.

The Koch Brothers: The Fascist Arrangement Their Beginning

Charles Koch (the only living Koch brother)

The Koch Brothers are descendants of right-wing billionaire Fred Koch, who rose to prominence when his company Winkler-Koch built oil refineries for the Nazis, producing high-grade octane gasoline for the German Luftwaffe during World War II. Fred was a staunch supporter of Germany, Japan and Italy during that conflict. Twenty years later, this right wing neo-fascist mentality was evident in Fred's membership as one of the founders of the John Birch Society, an ultra-right-wing organization that opposed civil rights, any form of redistribution of wealth and no government intervention in the matters of business. Fred supported the Jim Crow South and his attacks on people of color. In 1960, Koch wrote: *"The colored man looms large in the Communist plan to take over America."* He strongly supported the movement to impeach chief justice Earl Warren, after the Supreme Court voted to desegregate public schools in Brown v Board of Education. His sons became Birchers, embracing libertarian politics and the exclusion of people of color from the seat at any table.

The exposure of the Koch Brothers to right wing politics at an early age entrenched their belief system. They have always been ultra conservative and became more invested in the extreme libertarian wing, which promotes an unfettered free market economy. They had a strong belief in minimal government regulation and policies that maximize personal wealth at the expense of the body common. It would be the Koch Brothers who would master the blueprint for the corporative fascist movement in America.

The pendulum swung to the extreme right after the social upheaval in the sixties and seventies. Much of what the American right has accomplished was the antithesis to the civil rights movement, the black liberation movement and, "where the college campus, the pulpit, the media, the intellectual and literary journals, the arts and sciences", and "politicians" to neutralize all educational, political and social gains. The Social upheavals had changed the landscape of American society. In 1971, corporate lawyer (and future supreme court justice) Lewis Powell wrote a 5,000-word memo that was a blueprint for a broad attack on the liberal establishment and their gains – the "real" enemies, Powell wrote.

But those of us who were involved in transforming the political landscape in the '60s and '70s knew we had to deconstruct the world of false narratives and create alternative Third World and Africana Studies departments to level the playing field. Because we succeeded in establishing these departments in institutions of higher learning, we were able to produce a whole generation of scholars, textbooks and political thinkers that changed the narrative, that exposed those peddlers of falsehoods. We were their antithesis, a thorn in their side and now they had regrouped, fortified their war chest and came back with a vengeance. Koch's think tanks were now on full blast, arguing that conservatives should control the political debate at its source by demanding "balance" in textbooks, television shows, news coverage and college campuses – themes that were echoed in inflammatory speeches by Richard Nixon's vice-president, Spiro Agnew, Ronald Reagan, and Donald Trump.

In order to create an alternate universe to combat ethical social and political revolution of the '60s and '70s, the AEI was one of dozens of new think tanks being bankrolled in the hundreds of millions by the Kochs and their allies. Sold to the public as quasi-scholarly organizations, their real function was to legitimize the right to pollute for oil, gas and coal companies, and to argue for ever more tax cuts for the people who created them. Richard Scaife, an heir to the Mellon fortune, gave $23m over 23 years to the Heritage Foundation, having been the largest single donor to AEI.

Next, the right turned its sights on American campuses. John M Olin founded the John M. Olin Foundation, and spent nearly $200m promoting "free-market ideology and other conservative ideas on the country's campuses." He bankrolled a whole new approach to jurisprudence called "law and economics", and quietly Law and Order, another dog whistle to reign in the black progressives on HBCU campuses. Olin gave $10m to Harvard, $7m to Yale and Chicago, and over $2m to Columbia, Cornell, Georgetown and the University of Virginia. The effects it had on historically black colleges (HBCUs) were controversial. Where I was teaching, those of us who considered straying away from the canon were asked to stick to the standard text and the standard syllabus. We obviously did not comply and of course our contracts were not renewed the following year. We later discovered that Koch brother monies found their way onto campus with the understanding that textbooks and syllabuses had to meet a new standard.

Another point of contention with the Koch brothers' policy during those ripples of time, is that the billionaire brothers pressed Art Polk's agenda to reflect that of the Kochs' national agenda: deregulation, no corporate taxes, cuts to Medicaid and social spending; privatization, and the merger of the political agenda with the corporate agenda. If we fast-forward in time, these are the same policies supported and further extended by the Trump administration. We need look no further than the Duke Energy/Pat McCrory relationship during his administration. During his 28 years as an executive for Duke Energy, McCrory relaxed state regulations on Environmental Protection Agency (EPA) standards, which allowed Duke Energy to release toxic waste into the North Carolina public water system, creating the second largest coal and ash spill in the state's history. (Rmuse, 2014)

The Koch Brothers were now the face of corporative fascism. An article in the Los Angeles Times on Feb. 6, 2011 reads as follows: *The billionaire brothers David and Charles Koch no longer sit outside Washington's political establishment, isolated by their uncompromising conservatism. Instead, they are now at the center of Republican power, a change most evident in the new makeup of the House Energy and Commerce Committee.* It was those members who joined with the Trump administration and removed all environmental restrictions implemented by the Obama administration to undo all restrictions on greenhouse gases. The Wichita based Koch industries formed the largest oil and gas special interest group that lobbied members of the committee. (Hamburger, Hennessey & Banerjee, 2011)

The article continues to expose the marriage between big business and government, and how corporations buy and set the agenda in their interests. *"Perhaps Koch's most surprising and important ally on the committee was the new chairman, Fred Upton. The Republican from Michigan, who was once criticized for his middle-of-the road approach to environmental issues, is now leading the effort to rein in the EPA aligning himself with the Koch backed advocacy group calling for the. End to the "EPA choke holds." (Hamburger, Hennessey&Banerjee,2011)*

Upton introduced a bill that would strip the EPA of its ability to curb carbon emissions. The legislation was in line with the Kochs' long-standing advocacy of deregulation of all private industry. The Koch's oil refineries and chemical plants stand to pay millions to reduce air pollution under currently proposed EPA regulations. *"Koch industries are the country's second largest privately run company, and a conglomerate of refineries, pipelines, chemical and paper business* (Forbes Magazine: 2012" listed the two brothers as the nation's fourth richest people, each worth $36 billion.

It has become increasingly clear that the Koch brothers stand for the forces that refuse to achieve the proper balance between social needs and economic freedom. The thirst for more profit and selfish greed makes it virtually impossible to integrate moral economy and free market economics. Indeed, the human spirit has always been blessed with a sense of fairness and cooperation, let us not forget that we hold the power – it's called people power.

The Ugly Face of Fascism Wearing An Orange Tupee

The CEOs and owners in the corporate community, along with the top executives at the foundations, think tanks, and policy-discussion groups, work together as a leadership group that I call the power elite.

- Domhoff

Fascism is always a threat to the principles of democracy and the rule of law. Any anti-democratic actions taken by the strictly shadow political arm of a fascist arrangement are attempts to centralize or upstage the principles of democratic rule. It is significant to note that no emerging fascist regime has advocated the abolition of the corporative economic order. Their objective is to hollow out all the institutions that allow democratic rule while centralizing power in the hands of an authoritarian personality. The objective is to usurp power while merging the control of the political apparatus with that of the dictator to control policy and the corporative economic state. Trump's fascist arrangement was dangerous because he attempted to hollow out the institutions of democracy, create a cult-like, mass conservative base, revolving around meaningless electoral politics, spectator sports, military parades and anthems, especially in his bid to influence the beer-drinking crowds of sports enthusiasts.

Let us not forget that the shock troops of fascism on the mass political level are drawn from a Trumpian style base, which often are drawn from the lower to middle class. These classes feel that any change in the present economy resulting in the upward thrust of the "Other" will affect their economic status. This has always been the root of white grievance politics. They are joined by a sector of the working class who are backward enough to be affected by nationalistic trappings or what we call today 'identity politics', or the rising tide of populism. This is essentially what some sociologist would call the loyalty syndrome or, better yet, white privilege, or to us down home folk- sheer white racism.

One primary aim of this fascist arrangement, Trump-style, is to create the loyalty syndrome among those who have drunk the Kool-Aid while diffusing working-class consciousness between the races with a psycho-social appeal to white privilege. Never mind that gutting Obama Care would affect all people. Never mind that $15 per hour minimum wage would benefit all people. Development and exploitation of the authoritarian syndrome is at the center of corporative fascism. It feeds on a false sense of class and race consciousness and the need to vilify the other. The collective spirit in fascism is a morbid phenomenon and a need that grows out of the psychopathology of mob behavior.

With each development in the fascist arrangement, the marriage between the political elite and the economic elite becomes more apparent. The first phase of a fascist takeover is to render the labor movement ineffective, by either infiltration or passing government policy that strikes down union participation in business and industry. It behooves the corporative state to have the tools to maximize profit at its disposal.

The contrapositive mobilization of corporative fascism is to strike a balance between forces while inflating capital interest and deflating the interest of the working class. Easy credit, inflationary financing keeps the working class tied to the corporative state forever in debt, much like the sharecroppers in the ripples of time. Minimal increases in annual purchasing power are always negated by the subtle but strictly regulated rise in the cost of living. With no discernable rise in wages, the exploited worker will be tied to the fascist arrangement in perpetuity. The heads of any labor organization in a corporative state are an elite tied to the interest of the regime and consequently tied to the interest of the economic status quo. Labor is a part of this arrangement and will often strike a balance for the state as opposed for the working class.

Trumpist corporative fascism has injected the demons of racism into America's peculiar form of fascism. The form of a fascist state will always need the Other. Germany had the Jewish People. Trump played the race card, beginning with Birtherism (skepticism over whether Barack Obama was born in the United States). Trump played on the inherent racism against blacks, and then the Muslim ban, the Mexican "rapists" crossing America's borders illegally; the desire to inflict pain on brown bodies by snatching their babies while placing them in cages. Those who dared to compete in the industrial sectors, in the American way of life pose a threat to white privilege. White grievance and the fascist demagogue play to the crowd that feels threatened by the Other. The resentment and seedbed of fear was already embedded in the American psyche. Trump called on their demons of racism and his based answered his call.

Their white grievance has its historical roots during and after slavery and Trump weaponized those fears. Those fears of the 'Other' were exacerbated by the insecurities and insignificance inculcated into poor white working-class people by the socio-economic conditions of their lives since slavery and post-Reconstruction. All the while, the ruling elites have actively fomented and instigated racism against blacks and people of color. This programed racism has always been used to distract the people who suffer from the same exploitation of capitalism and labor. Racism has always served in the U.S. as a pressure release for the psychopathic destructiveness evinced by a people who were made to feel fearful and insecure by a way of life they never understood and resented from the day of their birth.

Through It All Obama Stood Tall

This tactic utilized by the ruling class has always been a tactic of division, to sow confusion between poor whites and people of color. It is the contextual structure of the fascist/white supremacist class hierarchy. It was never more evident during the Obama years. There was that assumption that we could now put race behind us, now that change had come to America. No one knew better than First Lady

Michelle Obama, as she watched attentively during his First State of the Union Address. She saw the stoic look on the faces of all the old white men, arms folded, refusing to stand and give her husband the ovation due every incoming president. She saw the resentment, the racial overtones, the Mitch McConnells and John Boehner the Lindsey Grahams and the likes. It was apparent the ebb and flow of change, coming closer to calculation, and then receding. That night our majestic First Lady saw that change had come to that point but was quickly receding in the cold, ugly faces she witnessed piercing the air of retreat, subsiding from that moment in time, the forces of racism would regroup. As the President laid out his vision for America, they had already met in secret and planned to utilize the fascist arrangement to stonewall his agenda for the people, for all times.

The demons of racism were summoned during Obama's tenure in the White House. Revived by Sarah Palin's hateful and racist rhetoric during the campaign, the Tea Party of the Koch Brothers rose to power on the mantra of white grievance and hatred. The history of President Obama's birth certificate became the clarion call for racism to fly. During those ripples of time the Birther movement, spawned by Donald Duck, the evangelical Christians and the far right were given sanction by Fox News. These forces could localize their fears, which were a smokescreen for their inability to accept that an African American was President of the United States and his black body and those of his family were occupying 'their' **White House**. The birth certificate gave them the false narrative to justify non-acceptance and to delegitimize Barack Obama as their sitting President. Donald Duck had orchestrated this charade and his attack on truth, just as he did so in his attempts to delegitimize the Presidency of Joe Biden.

The growing fascist/white supremacist arrangement was taking shape. The reactionary forces against Obama's election were taking shape. The fact that Mitch McConnell and John Boehner led congress during his second term did nothing to further governance. Their arrangement utilized the process to stop policy in its tracts. The vicious attacks from Tea Party loyalists during town hall meetings were ugly. Obama was labeled a Hitler and should be dealt with as such. An entry into my diary date 08/12/2009 makes the point succinctly: "The wolves are gathering, the birthers, the deathers, right wing militias, evangelical Christians – all on the attack in their attempts to destroy our president. The death threats are mounting. According to the secret service, 400 a day. Posters with the N… word, faces of monkeys (remember the Enlightenment Thinkers), the putrid face of racism has reared its ugly head once again. From this cesspool of hate would emerge the M.A.G.A crowds which would become Trump's base."

Fueled by the right-wing Fox News, and commentators like Shaun Hannity and Rush Limbaugh and Glenn Becks, the mob mentality had returned to the forefront of American politics as the race card once again becomes a part of the fascist arrangement. They used the attacks on Obama's healthcare reform to torpedo his entire political agenda. The white politicians played on the fears and insecurities of a segment of the white population in their attempts at delegitimizing Obama as President, his policies and whose black face was stamped with that of an American President. How repugnant they felt.

On 8/24/2009, I wrote an entry into my diary: "the right-wing politicians are creating spurious and illogical arguments to defeat Obama politically, while playing on the fears of gullible and shallow right wing, midlife evangelical Christians who march to the beat of a growing racialized fascist arrangement. Fascism takes root when state sponsored media types begins to inculcate its following with disinformation, and the vilification of the Other!"

Certainly, Fox News played the role of a state-sponsored voice of a growing fascist arrangement. Let us not forget that it was Neal Boortz and Glenn Beck on Fox News who gave the call for white America to arm themselves and train their sights on young urban thugs (a code word identifying young black Americans). The same day Glenn Beck, while calling on white Americans to arm themselves for the impending war, he is pointing at the picture of a sitting president, Barack Obama. For those of you who thought change had come, it was a stark reminder that black people had always had a target on their back, if a sitting president could be threatened then certainly our lives, our black bodies were still objects of scorn to be removed from this earth without notice and at any given time.

It will be this fear, this stupidity, this arrogance of white identity politics that would bring Donald Trump to power. And while these fears were a part of Obama's opposition it was never so obvious than within the white, so-called 'Christian' evangelical base. Traversing the ripples of time, I wrote on 8/30/2010: "The evangelical Christian extremists are continuing to beat the drums of assassination of our President Obama. They are now circulating T-shirts and bumper stickers quoting Psalms: 109:8: *"May God remove the corrupt King and replace him with another, may his children become fatherless and his wife a widow."*

Why was there not a national outcry among the public and among politicians against this call for the assassination of a sitting President, Barack Obama? Why were there no indictments against these pseudo-Christians, wearing these shirts so proudly? Are they not just as guilty as the extremists who adhere to the Muslim faith and misquote the Koran? It is alright for you to condemn them in their thirst for blood, but when you call to quench your own thirst, you look stupid and confused as to why we look at you in pity and disbelief. We know you. These strange apparitions, or demons called men. The ripples of the time stream exposed your thirst for Native American blood at Wounded Knee, Sand Creek, and the Trail of Tears; for black blood at Tulsa, Oklahoma; Elaine, Arkansas; all the black bodies swinging from the limbs of white oak trees. The watery graves at the bottom of the Atlantic give testimony to your thirst for blood, you hypocrite. How dare you insult our intelligence. Ooops, I forgot – according to your Enlightenment thinkers, we do not possess the power of reasoning.

Despite it all, the accomplishments of the first sitting African American President, whose Black body represented those black bodies who had been dehumanized, desecrated and tortured throughout the ripples of time, would be the sitting President responsible for saving the American financial empire from collapse after the economic crash of 2008. Yes, a man clothed in black flesh to the rescue of the colonizer's empire. What poetic justice. It would be his stimulus bill, The American Recovery and Reimbursement Act of 2009 that spurred economic growth during the depression of 2009, the greatest depression since the Great Depression of the 1930s. Weeks after the bill went into effect, unemployment claims began to subside, and employment began to slowly rise. Twelve months later the private sector began to produce more jobs than it was losing, and it continued to do so for 23 straight months and into the Trump Presidency. By the end of his term Obama had created 12.2 million jobs, the third highest of any sitting President. And yet some had the gall to be indignant simply because his skin is of a darker hue. But he didn't stop there – he began to address the needs of the common people at the expense of the corporative fascist elite. Other Obama accomplishments include:

Passed and signed the Dodd-Frank Wall Street Reform Consumer Protection Act (2010) to re-regulate the financial sector. New laws tightening capital requirements on large banks and other financial institutions. Limit banks from trading customers money for their own profit. Created the Consumer Protection Bureau to crack down on faulty lending practices and products from companies.

1. **Passed Health Care Reform:** After five presidents, over a century, failed to create universal health insurance, Obama signed the Affordable Care Act (2010). It would cover 32 million uninsured Americans,

beginning in 2014 and mandated a suite of experimental measures to cut health care cost growth, the number one cause of America's long-term fiscal problems.

2. **Turned Around the U.S. Auto Industry:** In 2009, Obama injected $62 billion in federal money (on top of $13.4 billion in loans from the Bush administration) into ailing GM and Chrysler in return for equity stakes and agreements for massive restructuring. Since bottoming out in 2009, the auto industry has added more than 100,000 jobs. In 2011, the Big Three automakers all gained market share for the first time in two decades. The government expects to lose $16 billion of its investment, less if the price of the GM stock it still owns increases.

3. **Repealed "Don't Ask, Don't Tell":** Ended 1990s-era restriction and formalized new policy allowing gays and lesbians to serve openly in the military for the first time.

4. **Kicked Banks out of the Federal Student Loan Program, Expanded Pell Grant Spending:** As part of the 2010 health care reform bill, Obama signed a measure to end the wasteful decades-old practice of subsidizing banks to provide college loans. Starting in July 2010, all students began getting their student loans directly from the federal government. The treasury hoped to save $67 billion over ten years, $36 billion of which would go to expanding Pell Grants to lower-income students.

5. **Created Race to the Top:** With funds from the stimulus, Obama started a $4.35 billion program of competitive grants to encourage and reward states for education reform.

6. **Boosted Fuel Efficiency Standards:** Released new fuel efficiency standards in 2011 that will nearly double the fuel economy for cars and trucks by 2025.

7. **Coordinated International Response to Financial Crisis:** To keep the world economy out of recession in 2009 and 2010, Obama helped secure from G-20 nations more than $500 billion for the IMF to provide lines of credit and other support to emerging market countries, which kept them liquid and avoided currency crises with their currencies.

8. **Passed Mini Stimuli:** To help families hurt by the recession and spur the economy as stimulus spending declined, Obama signed a series of

measures (July 22, 2010; December 17, 2010; December 23, 2011) to extend unemployment insurance and cut payroll taxes.

9. **Created Conditions to Begin Closing Dirtiest Power Plants:** New EPA restrictions on mercury and toxic pollution, issued in December 2011, are likely to lead to the closing of between 68 and 231 of the nation's oldest and dirtiest coal-fired power plants. Estimated cost to utilities was at least $11 billion by 2016. Estimated health benefits: $59 billion to $140 billion. It also aimed to significantly reduce carbon emissions and, with other regulations, comprised what was called Obama's "stealth climate policy."

10. **Eliminated Catch-22 in Pay Equality Laws:** Signed Lilly Ledbetter Fair Pay Act in 2009, giving women who are paid less than men for the same work the right to sue their employers after they find out about the discrimination, even if that discrimination happened years ago. Under the previous law, as interpreted by the Supreme Court in *Ledbetter v. Goodyear Tire & Rubber Co.*, the statute of limitations on such suits ran out 180 days after the alleged discrimination occurred, even if the victims never knew about it.

11. **Improved Food Safety System:** In 2011, Obama signed the FDA Food Safety Modernization Act, which boosts the Food and Drug Administration's budget by $1.4 billion and expands its regulatory responsibilities to include an increasing number of food inspections, issuing direct food recalls, and reviewing the current food safety practices of countries importing products into America.

12. **Expanded Wilderness and Watershed Protection:** Signed Omnibus Public Lands Management Act (2009), which designated more than 2 million acres as wilderness. It created thousands of miles of recreational and historic trails and protected more than 1,000 miles of rivers.

13. **Gave the FDA Power to Regulate Tobacco:** Signed the Family Smoking Prevention and Tobacco Control Act (2009). Nine years in the making and long resisted by the tobacco industry, the law mandates that tobacco manufacturers disclose all ingredients, obtain FDA approval for new tobacco products, and expand the size and prominence of cigarette warning labels, and bans the sale of misleadingly labeled "light" cigarette brands and tobacco sponsorship of entertainment events.

14. **Pushed Federal Agencies to Be Green Leaders:** Issued executive order in 2009 requiring all federal agencies to make plans to soften their environmental impacts by 2020. Goals include 30 percent reduction in fleet gasoline use, 26 percent boost in water efficiency, and sustainability requirements for 95 percent of all federal contracts. Because federal government is the country's single biggest purchaser of goods and services, likely to have ripple effects throughout the economy for years to come.

15. **Passed Fair Sentencing Act:** Signed 2010 legislation that reduced sentencing disparity between crack versus powder cocaine possession from 100 to 1 down to 18 to 1.

16. **Invested Heavily in Renewable Technology:** As part of the 2009 stimulus, Obama invested $90 billion, more than any previous administration, in research on smart grids, energy efficiency, electric cars, renewable electricity generation, cleaner coal, and biofuels.

17. **Crafting Next-Generation School Tests:** Devoted $330 million in stimulus money to pay two consortia of states and universities to create competing versions of new K-12 student performance tests based on latest psychometric research. New tests aimed to transform the learning environment in the vast majority of public-school classrooms, beginning in 2014.

18. **Cracked Down on Bad For-Profit Colleges:** In an effort to fight predatory practices of some for-profit colleges, the Department of Education issued "gainful employment" regulations in 2011, cutting off commercially focused schools from federal student aid funding if more than 35 percent of former students aren't paying off their loans and/or if the average former student spends more than 12 percent of his or her total earnings servicing student loans.

19. **Improved School Nutrition:** Obama, in coordination with Michelle Obama, signed the Healthy Hunger-Free Kids Act in 2010 mandating a $4.5 billion spending boost and higher nutritional and health standards for school lunches. New rules based on the law, released in January, doubled the number of fruits and vegetables and required only whole grains in food be served to students.

20. **Expanded Hate Crimes Protections:** Signed Hate Crimes Prevention Act (2009), which expanded existing hate crime protections to include crimes based on a victim's sexual orientation, gender, or disability, in addition to race, color, religion, or national origin.

21. **Brokered Agreement for Speedy Compensation to Victims of Gulf Oil Spill:** Though lacking statutory power to compel British Petroleum to act, Obama used the moral authority of his office to convince the oil company to agree in 2010 to a $20 billion fund to compensate victims of the Deepwater Horizon oil spill in the Gulf of Mexico; $6.5 billion had already been paid out without lawsuits. By comparison, it took nearly two decades for plaintiffs in the *Exxon Valdez* Alaska oil spill case to receive $1.3 billion.

22. **Pushed Broadband Coverage:** Proposed and obtained in 2011 Federal Communications Commission approval for a shift of $8 billion in subsidies away from landlines and toward broadband internet for lower-income rural families.

23. **Expanded Health Coverage for Children:** Signed 2009 Children's Health Insurance Authorization Act, which allows the Children's Health Insurance Program (CHIP) to cover health care for 4 million more children, paid for by a tax increase on tobacco products.

24. **Recognized the Dangers of Carbon Dioxide:** In 2009, the EPA declared carbon dioxide a pollutant, allowing the agency to regulate its production.

25. **Provided Payment to Wronged Minority Farmers:** In 2009, Obama signed the Claims Resolution Act, which provided $4.6 billion in funding for a legal settlement with black and Native American farmers who the government cheated out of loans and natural resource royalties in years past.

The Hope and Change era of the Obama Administration was one that addressed as best he could policies that were favorable for the common good of its citizenry while reducing the policies that maximized corporate greed at the expense of the people. What he was able to accomplish under the circumstances were astounding, given all the obstacles he had to face. What was not mentioned was the violent backlash bubbling below the surface, the racism, the resentment, the aggrieved white privilege and populism that was looking for a place to vent their anger and frustration at a Black family occupying "their" White House. Imagine, Melania Trump refused to move into the White House until the toilets used by the Obamas were replaced. Such toxicity, such a shallow and hollow shell of woman.

The Social Common Vs The Corporative Fascist Elite

The unraveling of the Obama Administration Policies

With Trump's election defeat in 2020 the equilibrium between a pending fascist arrangement and the social common is at play. General equilibrium is distorted when the political system's liberal wing attempts to implement policy for the people while the corporate elite puts pressure on the system to maximize profitability at the expense of common society. During this particular time, the sectors of the economy that hold a large portion of the GDP, when in crisis, will successfully influence policy which has a greater influence on the direction of the economy to the detriment of the working class. In the corporative fascist arrangement, it is always this higher degree of centralization which alters the preexisting equilibrium in its favor. One has only to examine the Trump presidency to understand how he has sacrificed the common good for the welfare of the corporative arrangement.

Indeed, Trump's dismantling of the Obama environmental regulations are an example of how disturbing this equilibrium can be. Trump measured his success in terms of unraveling many Obama-era climate policies, including the Clean Power Plan, fuel economy standards for passenger vehicles, and efforts to curb potential greenhouse gases, from refrigerants and air conditioning. The One of the greatest beneficiaries was Koch Industries. Trump administration eased regulations preventing methane leakage from oil and gas facilities. Following these rollbacks, the Rhodium Group has analyzed implications of each of these regulatory roll backs on USGHG emissions. Previous research shows that Trumps major climate policy rollbacks have the potential to add 1.8 gigatons of carbon monoxide to the atmosphere by 2035. This cumulative impact is equivalent to nearly one-third of all U.S emissions in 2019. Moreover, all of Trump's EPA reversals came on top of a rollback in 2018 to the Bureau of Land Management (BLM), which limited oil and gas methane emissions on public land. A federal court ruling in July 2020 vacated the roll back and required the BLM to reinstate the original ruling.

Another example of Trump's policies was to restrict criminal prosecution for industries responsible for the deaths of the nation's migratory birds. Hawks and other birds that migrate through the central U.S. to nesting grounds on the Great Plains navigate deadly threats, from electrocution on power lines, to wind turbines that knock them from the air and oil field waste pits where landing birds perish in toxic waste in water. As of now, the Migratory Bird Treaty Act of 1918 is a vital tool for the protection of more than 1,000 species of birds, including hawks and other birds of prey. Federal prosecutors used the act to recover damages, including $100 million from BP for its 2010 oil rig spill into the Gulf of Mexico, which killed more than 100,000 seabirds.

To put it more simply, it is private interest over public interest, maximization of profit over the maximization of health and the common good of the people. For the oil and gas industry the opening of the Arctic refuge to drilling and the Trump administration cared less if it meant to sacrifice all wildlife and any living thing in its path to push the agenda of corporative fascism.

If we are to escape the evolution of capitalism to corporative fascism, which promotes maximum profiteering at the expense of the environment and the destruction of the social moral economy, we must take a long look at the bottom-up reshaping of our economic culture. I suggest that we reeducate ourselves to the concept of gift societies where the 'engagements of its members are dedicated to the common good. They made sure that what wealth was produced was shared amongst its members like the kibbutz of Israel, the communal societies of Africa before slavery, and the mixed economies of the Scandinavian countries where market economy and moral economy find common ground. In England, France, Canada and Scandinavian countries healthcare is nationalized, Gross Domestic Product is based on fair distribution and not pure profit squeezed by the maximization of corporate profits. Academicians, scholars and intellectuals of all disciplines must become excavators of truth to expose the dangers of corporative fascism and how it is destroying the social common.

What does this mean for different business models today? It means corporate culture imposes uniformity, which is mandated from the top down throughout the organization. But the cooperative or the group model in which a group of members owns a business and makes group decisions about how to run it is a modem institution that has much in common with the collective tribal values of our species. Worker-owned cooperatives are regionally distinct and organized around their constituent members. They promote a shared identity, resulting in greater trust and collaboration without the need for centralized control.

In conclusion, we must continue to author papers, sponsor symposiums, teach in the classrooms and expose corporativist fascism. On a local, regional, and national level we must organize support for those political candidates and policies that will fight the Tea Party-turned freedom party-turned-Trumpism and any Koch-backed politicians who are the face of corporate fascism. Lastly, we must support those who put forth an alternative to a corporativist takeover of the social common. Serious-minded individuals must find a way to integrate knowledge to create a flexible economy that integrates and stands for both our human diversity and our shared morality. We must take Jackson's words to heart and realize that corporative fascism created the oppressive contract and cannot be broken as long as any sort of hierarchy exists to perpetuate the sensitized relationships of American tribalism, racism and classism in society. An unequal society is impossible without that arrangement. Clearly, according to Jackson, the "oppressed contract must be altered because classic economics were based on the very principle of avarice and economic exploitation." With an economic system reaching epic and unprecedented levels of inequality, it would be immoral not to consider alternatives. For the sake of our survival, we simply cannot afford another Donald Trump.

CHAPTER 15

THE THREAT TO AMERICAN DEMOCRACY: DONALD TRUMP'S FAILED COUP

 Donald J. Trump ✔ •••
@realDonaldTrump

Mike Pence didn't have the courage to do what should have been done to protect our Country and our Constitution, giving States a chance to certify a corrected set of facts, not the fraudulent or inaccurate ones which they were asked to previously certify. USA demands the truth!

2:24 PM • Jan 6, 2021

Trump, Donald J. (@realdonaldtrump). Jan. 6, 2021, 2:24 PM; https://www.gettyimages.com/detail/video/pro-trump-supporters-storm-the-u-s-capitol-following-a-news-footage?295258877?adjpopup=true; Groeger, Lena V., et al. "What Parler Saw During the Attack on the Capitol," January 17, 2021; YouTube Post, "Lawmakers Evacuate Congress as Trump Supporters Storm Capitol Building," VOA News, January 6, 2021.

Phase 1: Fascist Disinformation Campaign

On January 6, 2021, we watched with disbelief as the MA.G.A. Marchers received their marching orders from Donald Trump as he continued to inflame the crowd with the **Big Lie**. Urging them to descend on the capitol to **stop the certification** of an election that had been 'stolen' from him. As he stood at the podium wearing a black coat with black leather gloves flailing hands like the dictator he imagined himself to be, he told the crowd to *"be forceful. You won't accomplish anything by showing weakness."* Later the crowd descended on the Capitol with an anger and rage stoked by their dictator-in-chief. As the crowd rushed the capitol, they could be heard repeating Trump's Big Lie, *"Stop the Steal"* as Trump flags and those of the Confederacy rippled in the breeze. Urged on by a brazen lie these mindless persons used their flagpoles to beat down and terrorize the Capitol Police officers who stood in their way.

Stupidity is not unknown to demagogues and authoritarian personalities, nor is to political policymakers. Participation in electoral politics by the masses in a democratic society is based on transparent information as it relates to competing parties' platforms and how these platforms and policies serve the body common. When the fascist arrangement is represented by a demagogue, the plethora of disinformation serves to discredit the opponent. The whole democratic process must be discredited; it is a tactic for the ultra-right. Trump's attempt to delegitimize the election, to render it rigged, is one more step toward the fascist takeover of the democratic process. When authoritarian personalities exploit the stupidity of the masses, they understand the value of mass psychology, and are familiar with its use, and hold all the necessary implements of its effective control – what to think and how to think, then you understand the debacle that has become Trumpism and its feeble attempts at usurping American democracy.

Donald Trump is the quintessential reality T.V. salesman, the Grifter in Chief, the snake oil salesman who has used Twitter and Facebook to peddle his lies, his demagoguery, his disinformation to destabilize America's institutions and the people's confidence in the democratic process. He has mastered the use of mind manipulation through social media to ravage the minds of his base. The alpha rhythms emanating from Facebook and other social media platforms have created this shared false reality and taken the minds of its victims through a paper shredder while creating a micro reality where they are right and other people are wrong.

These alpha rhythms, which bombard the brain from the computer, dangle this false imagery or ideas into their brain. These false images create the alternate reality of disinformation, while polarizing society and fracturing not only the individual against himself but more importantly against society. This polarization becomes a part of the fascist arrangement and the principal tool of the demagogue.

The masses then, and now, have become susceptible to the Snake Oil Salesman, the demagogue. The social media platform has downgraded the brain. The victims' attention spans are shortened. They do not read books anymore. The art of critical thinking is lost, and disinformation seeps in. They become addicted to the number of likes and followers; that is how they receive their marching orders, so shallow they have become to the demagogue. They believed Trump was going to march with them to the Capitol. These were the new storm troopers of the carnival barker. This was never more evident in Trump's false claims that the presidential election was rigged and was stolen from him by the deep state. "Stop the Steal" had become the new hashtag on Facebook, drawing 2.5 million likes. The dissemination of false information and tweets have created a world of 'alternative facts' and now we have the attempted overthrow of a legitimate election victory by Biden/Harris who have now become the enemies of the Trumpian base.

Trump's four-year war on the legitimacy of elections was his tactic from day one. If he won, it was legitimate. If he lost, it was rigged. He started programing the masses the day he rode down his gold-plated escalators in Trump Tower. Populism i.e., white identity and white grievance, was his base. The seeds of fascism and racism were sown in the Birther movement, the Muslim ban and the total shutdown of Muslims entering the country; the supporting of white supremacy and the "good people on both sides" of the Charlottesville debacle; building the wall to keep murders and drug dealers out; mistreating thugs when you throw them into squad cars; Hispanic judges aren't qualified; shit hole countries of color; brown babies ripped from their mothers and thrown into cages. Anyone who has any doubts about this racist bigot is just as guilty as he is of his transgressions against humanity.

Why were we surprised when the then Attorney General, Jeff Beauregard Sessions, great-great grandson of General Beauregard Sessions, a Confederate General, implemented the zero-tolerance immigration policy which allowed Trump to take brown babies from their mothers? We have witnessed the dark side of America, Trump is an inhuman being who represents the 40 per cent of

American citizens – 72 million – who voted for him, and who still wallow in the mud, their spirit still reflective of the vile residue of slavery. America is replete with Neo Nazis, white nationalists, The Proud Boys, the Boogaloo movement, the Oath Keepers, white militias who are only concerned with the preservation of a white nationalist homeland to the exclusion of people of color. Trump has played to his base by initiating immigration policy that is nativist and nationalistic, a populist form of fascism. Brown people became the new Vernon, the undesirables. Black Lives Do Not Matter, never did nor ever will in the Trumpian world. The continued police killing of young black bodies and the injustice in the criminal justice system is a form of ethnic cleansing, another form of fascism Trumpian style.

America, you have been forced to take a cold, hard look at what your history is about. You need to look in the mirror because what you will see is not pretty. The forced removal of children from their parents is not un-American it *is* American. It is what you do. From the forced removal of millions of slave children from their families and placed on auction blocks to be sold like cattle, to the land stolen from millions of Native Americans with the passing of the 1830 Land Act, and their forced march from those lands on the Trail of Tears. The forced removal of hundreds of thousands of Native American children from their parents to be re-programmed in your religious institutions – it is what you do… nothing to see here, you have become the enemy of humanity.

Fascism has come to America with an orange toupee a flag draped around its shoulders and a cross hanging from his neck, and the head of the Statue of Liberty crumbled in his hand. With the beheading of the statue of liberty why America are some of you now surprised at the mistreatment of people of color and their denial of fundamental human rights? You never heard black voices when we screamed for our liberties, our fundamental rights as human beings. We have always seen the head of the statue of liberty in the hands of tyrants; we have always seen the American flag draped around the shoulders of white men. We have always told you the history of this country is the history of slavery and a slave society, but you ignored us.

The history of slavery IS the dominant factor in the history of this country. It is still an open history, still a developing phenomenon. We told you that you cannot analyze a movement outside of itself, its processes and its sequential relationship to history unfolding-yesterday is today and today is now.. By doing so you only gain a discorded glimpse of a sordid past without understanding that the final definition is still open, still in process. Indeed, we are the faces of that sordid past, morphed into the here and now through the ripples of time, through an incessant struggle against the egregious acts of barbarity committed against our forefathers. You, with that orange toupee, we know you and your kind very well.

Ever since slavery we have had our eyes on you. Our bowed heads was a camouflage, our eyes photographed your ways, your motives and your movements. We always held you under scrutiny. It became a way of knowing our enemy, observations passed on from the big house to the slave quarters throughout the ripples of time. The psychoanalytic readings gave us the detailed and brutal facts about *the ghost, the barbarian, these strange apparitions we were forced to serve.*

We stand before you survivors of this historical experience rooted not only in slavery, but if you factor in post-Reconstruction, the so-called Jim Crow era, slavery was in existence from 1619 to the present. The math speaks for itself, so why are you surprised when we tell you racism is not a word, but a system born out of slavery that has taken firm root in all of your institutions, particularly your criminal injustice system? Mass incarceration and police brutality are not just symptoms, they are in fact the end all ...the tool of negating containing while controlling black bodies. At this particular moment in time, racism has grown exponentially and does not adequately describe our dilemma. We need a new definition to describe the dynamics at play... deconstruct and reconstruct terminology. If we calculate earth time, we have from 1619 to the present 146,365 days of sheer brutality and mental trauma, notwithstanding the 146,365 nights of horror and uncertainty.

Phase 2: Fascist Attempted Coup – When Party in Power Loses Power and Reorganizes

The 2020 presidential election was over. Donald Trump was defeated and yet his attempt at seizing power continued. He continued to claim victory even though the states had certified the vote count, the electoral committees in each state had certified the vote count, and the electoral college had certified Biden and Harris as the victors. Yet Trump still claimed victory, even after his 60-plus lawsuits were thrown out of state and federal courts, including the ruling by the US Supreme court which refused to even hear the case. The blatant attempt to cast out votes in the predominantly black cities of Atlanta, Milwaukee, Philadelphia, and Detroit, was only a mirror reflection of the long-standing practice of attempted suppression of the Black vote.

"Stop the Steal!" became the rallying cry and the new machinery created by the Trump political machine. Roger Stone, Donald Trump Jr, Allie Alexander, Amy Cramer and Alex Jones are the faces behind the scenes. They have raised $250 million on top of the $600 million raised during the election. This gives them a sizable war chest going forward. Any fascist attempt to retain power and usurp the democratic process always regroups, creates a political front organization and resurfaces later.

Phase 3: Low Grade Insurgency, Political Para-Military Forces

Trump's attempt to seize power escalated to threats of violence. Ann Jacobs, the Wisconsin chair of the election committee alerted police and neighbors about threats to her family and kids because she recognized the legitimacy of the electoral votes cast in her state. The Arizona Republican party asked their followers to give their life to the cause and prevent the 'election steal'. The Michigan Secretary of State had her house surrounded by so-called armed patriots demanding the election be overturned. The Vermont Secretary of State, James Condos, received recorded threats that he should be executed by firing squad. The vilest threat was lodged against Cynthia Johnson, a black woman and state representative for Michigan. The message was recorded. "I hope you like burning crosses in your front yard because I am sure before this is all over there will be several and maybe a noose or two hanging from your tree, you dumb fuckin commie bitch, rot in hell."

On Saturday, December 15, 2020, after a Trump rally in Washington, the far-right Boogaloo movement and the Proud Boys were unleashed on the streets of Washington, D.C. They attacked innocent protestors, stabbing some of them, then proceeded to the black church where Frederick Douglass is buried and vandalized the premises.

The paramilitary forces were now emboldened by Trump's endorsement. They have resurfaced believing in the Alpha rhythms created by social media and the Fox news spin machine. They call themselves the "Sons of Liberty," "The Oath Keepers." They are the racist demons conjured up from the past Sons of the Confederacy. They are moving from the legal world to the illegal world, defending Trumpism and believing the illusionary world created by Trump and his disinformation machinery.

Consequently, on America, January 6, 2021, he told you he was coming, he told you he was going to sabotage the electoral certification of the vote in Congress, and the insurrection began. January 6th was a total disgrace to American democracy and the rule of law. Trump held a rally on the Washington Mall, and he marched 20,000 thugs to the halls of Congress. They invaded and ransacked the offices, held Congressional members hostage, and vandalized the premises. And yet a few Capitol Police treated them with kid gloves. Yes, white insurrectionists were greeted by some white police with open arms, taking selfies, opening doors, allowing them to invade the Capitol and ransack the people's houses while laying siege on the United States Capitol. Better yet, these insurrectionists planted the Confederate flag inside the Capitol – something they were never able to do during the Civil War.

You heard the words of Rudy Giuliani at the rally: *"Lets fight, let's give them combat justice."* You heard the words of Donald Trump Jr.: *"Let's take back what is ours, stop the steal!"*. My grandson asks me, "Why are some police nice to them, they're breaking the law? If they were black protestors they would have been beaten." This is a 13-year-old young black male who was witnessing the racial disparity as well as an insurrection taking place in this country on January 6, 2020. His observations were correct. The intelligence reports said this was coming. Hell, even Donald Trump told you they were coming. Hmmm, an inside job?

The pro-Trump insurrectionists stormed the capitol and laid siege to the edifice for the first time since the British 1812. They held people hostage for several hours. This was a coordinated attack with paramilitary cells with specific intent to kidnap and hold hostage Nancy Pelosi, Mike Pence and Chuck Schumer. They were aided by insiders from the White House and from sympathetic Capitol Police officers. Some turned away and allowed entry or provided information on where Jim Clyburn and Nancy Pelosi's offices were located. They knew the location of Clyburn's inner office, and the location of his chair and private computer, which was removed from his office. From the evidence, there is reason to believe that people inside the White House may have been involved.

It is evident that the security of the capitol was breached by insiders who were complicit with the insurrectionists. The Capitol Police, Homeland Security and National Guard were stifled by the White House in their deployment. This allowed the insurrectionists to fight their way through the front door having overrun the police who did stand their ground gallantly. What was witnessed on this fateful day in January were white domestic terrorists engaging in a Seditious Act of insurrection. According to Title 18 of the U.S. Code, when two or more people conspire to employ force to prevent, hinder, or delay execution of any law of the United States, or to forcibly seize, take, or possess U.S. property, they are in violation of the Constitution of the United States.

If these protesters had been Black Lives Matter activists, they would have been shot dead and yet these white insurrectionists were treated differently. Moreover, had it been a Black Lives Matter protest, you would have had state police, National Guard and federal deputy marshals deployed as they have done at all BLM protests. Because these protesters were white they were openly embraced by some, with only a handful of officers awaiting them, some with peace signs while others fought gallantly. Had it been BLM protesters, they would have greeted them with armored vehicles, heavily armed police in body armor and helicopters hovering above.

The ugly face of white privilege was on full display, as these insurrectionists pranced around the halls of congress wearing M.A.G.A. hats, swastikas and waving the confederate flag. Then some officials had the audacity to say, *"We did not want to militarize the moment, it would be bad optics."* Give me a break – you had no problem militarizing Baltimore after you killed Freddie Grey; you had no problem militarizing Ferguson after you killed Michael Brown; you had no problem militarizing Minneapolis after killing George Floyd; and you certainly had no problem militarizing Louisville and Kenosha when you killed beautiful Breonna Taylor while she lay sleeping.

But you know, we were not surprised. We know you, your hypocrisy, your double standards. We remember you buying Dylann Roof lunch at Burger King. Yeah, remember that? After capturing this white supremacist KKK follower who had murdered nine black souls while worshipping in Mother Emmanuel Church in Charleston, S.C. Just recently we recall you giving bottles of water to the man who killed two protestors during the BLM demonstrations in Kenosha, Wisconsin. So, we were not surprised, but we were highly insulted as we watched you treat white bodies with tender love and care. We watched you with disdain and disappointment. Our hearts pained as we watched you open some doors and allowed them into the capital, and as they exited, we watched as you gently walked some down the stairs so that they would not fall and hurt their precious white bodies. We watched with utter amazement as you poured water over their stinging eyes giving them comfort from the teargas still lingering in the air.

We are headed into dangerous times. The savagery witnessed, as these white domestic terrorists beat police officers with a vengeance; they were armed with guns, metal pipes, explosives while hanging up a noose. Who were they going to kidnap, who were they going to hang, Mike Pence? Their vitriol mirrored the blood lust of the lynching mobs during the infamous Red Summers in American history. In early chapters, I addressed the lynching parties that were thrown when blacks were hung, and such events were advertised in the newspapers, attracting crowds who would show from hundreds of miles away. There were organized picnics, carnivals, all treats so the family and the kids could enjoy while watching the spectacle of death taking place. The family outings included pictures taken and souvenirs cut from the burnt or hung bodies. America, we have seen this movie before. Welcome to our world. These perpetrators who have been arrested are for the most part from southern states and the mid-west, or have Southern heritage, the great and great-great grandchildren of the old Confederacy and The Redeemers, who were the forerunners of the KKK during post-Reconstruction. Some are the same fiends in ripples of time and in white bodies.

Phase 4: The Rise of Clandistine Domestic Terrorist Cells

A fascist takeover is an ever-evolving phenomenon. Just because Trump conceded the election and has left office does not mean Trumpism is dead. It is still evolving, still developing in this place and time. You cannot analyze a movement outside its process and its sequential relationship to history unfolding. Do so, and you only gain a glimpse of a dead past that is evolving before your very eyes. The election was lost, it is in the past. But how Trump takes back POWER is still an open process unfolding into the future. Watch out – Trumpism is regrouping. He has a $600 million war chest and 70 million followers. He will be able to conduct both his above-ground movement and those clandestine terrorist cells operating in the shadows. Make no mistake about it, Trumpism has fused with a white supremacist, white nationalist movement that has been in the weeds since the early 1980s. This coalition of skin heads, neo-Nazis, Klansmen, militia men and others like the Boogaloo movement, the Oath Keepers and Proud Boys now have a charismatic figure, a famous reality TV host and former President to give them legitimacy.

When Trump left office there was a call to arms by those who have drunk his Kool Aid and believe he was illegally removed from power. And they will be joined by those who have always wanted a white nationalist revolution in America. Its members are not only the rank and file but also highly trained ex-military soldiers whose terrorist cells are well-equipped. They are highly trained and motivated by a coherent world view of white supremacy at the expense of a multi-racial democratic society. Since the 1980s, these cells have operated with discipline and focus, undertaking acts of expropriation, counterfeiting, weapons trafficking and assassinations. The Oklahoma City bombing was their crown jewel of success.

I draw on my experiences and knowledge gained from my involvement in the Black Panther Party and the underground movement during the 1960s and '70s to understand the dynamics at work. What makes this movement even more dangerous is these groups who operate as a close but loosely connected force now have a central figure who could conceivably funnel millions of dollars into their military operations. No longer having the need to commit acts of expropriation of funds, and risk capture and exposure of other operating cells, there may be a money conduit from Trump as he finances those who would help him seize power. As they continue to broker alliances and white grievances intensify, violence becomes the logical course of action to establish their white nation. They will operate as clandestine cells carrying out the mission, their attack on political targets will include people of color. I speak not as an arm-chair theoretician but as an active participant in the involvement of this type of history unfolding. White Domestic Terrorism is the most dangerous threat to America and its citizens of color.

The bible of the far right is called *The Turner Diaries*, which among other things advocated and imagined a successful coup, an attack on the Capitol. The point of the attack is not to cause mass casualties but to show you have the power to pull it off. And they did. Another tactic is called 'the day of the rope'. In the diary, instructions are given to build gallows in which traitors would be tried and publicly hanged. Its victims would be congressmen and journalists and those engaged in interracial relationships. Indeed, according to the Diaries, the insurrectionists accomplished two of their goals: they laid siege to the capital and held Congress for almost four hours. They succeeded in building the gallows, replete with the hangman's noose, while failing in their attempts to capture specific politicians and executing them as planned.

On the other hand, the white nationalist movement could seek to identify a younger, more willing, Trump-type leader, such as Missouri senator Josh Hawley, because some of Trump's base felt abandoned and betrayed by the former president's belated condemnation of the Capitol rioters. For years Trump's supporters have adored and worshipped him like a god. His base has grown into a cult-like following of which half of his campaign donations are from small donors. His polling numbers from that group are well over 85 percent. Through it all, M.A.G.A. world has stood like a rock at his side, adding $250 million in donations to fund his 'Stop The Steal Campaign'. After losing the Presidential election, Trump turned on some allies who had propped him up during his desperate attempt to overturn the election. First he turned on Fox News after they accurately called the election in favor of Biden. Then he turned on some of his Republican allies, including Mitch McConnell, who acknowledged Biden's victory as legitimate and not rigged, and disputed claims of voter fraud. Following those rejections of Trump's fantasies, Vice President Mike Pence refused Trump's demands to declare the certification unconstitutional and decertify the election. Consequently, Trump tweeted that Mike Pence lacked the courage to do what should have been done "to protect our country."

Now that Trump has left office, some question the legitimacy of his Stop the Steal Movement. Was it a hoax or a money grift scheme? Whatever the case, there exists a potential void left by some of his supporters. What is apparent, after his mass radicalization campaign over the last four years, is that the disinformation claims of voter fraud and stolen election cannot douse the dangerous flames instilled in his believers nationwide. The genie is out of the bottle. Even the FBI warned that white domestic terrorism was the greatest threat to national security in 2021.

All things considered; Trump's departure has left America's democratic institutions in a delicate state. He has denigrated the rule of law, hollowed out the Departments that administer policy, created so many lies that tried to delegitimize the incoming Biden Administration to the extent that only 61 percent of the country recognizes his election victory. Trump has stoked so much divisiveness and polarized the country so badly that even amongst his own ranks, there is a shift. According to the *Huffington Post*, *"Alarmingly, many of those who are irate about Biden's supposed electoral theft are still plotting to forcibly remove him from office."*

American democracy escaped a bullet…. this time. The next four years are going to crucial for America's fragile democracy. Even though Trump has been defeated, a shadow looms ominously over the American political landscape. Remember, he did receive 70 million votes. He came within 50,000-plus votes of winning the electoral college and thus the presidency. His narrow electoral defeats in states like Arizona, Nevada, Georgia and Wisconsin should not be overlooked. Moreover, 143 members of Congress voted to overturn a legitimate presidential election, and now in 43 states they have introduced 253 bills to suppress the vote, and in several of these states have recently passed these bills to suppress the vote which would aid Trump or his chosen successor to regain power. He still has a firm grip on the Republican Party and could come back in 2024. If he does and he is re-elected, American democracy will no longer exist. He will finish the job he did not complete in his first term. Remember, Hitler lost his political power and credibility and served 10 months of a five-year prison sentence for high treason but started his ascent to power in 1927, culminating in his election as Chancellor in 1933. We must remain vigilant and never allow this tyrant and racist named Donald Trump to ever occupy the White House again. We only have history to remind us how catastrophic the outcome was when Hitler was given a second chance.

CONCLUSION
GRASS ROOTS COMMUNITY ORGANIZING

Memories of these past defeats and victories have been all but forgotten and choked off in the passive consumption of fashion, video games, iPads and social media, though the latter functions at times as an increasingly social tranquilizer in post-revolutionary America. We must never lose sight of the historical significance and the contributions of the BPP. Lessons learned from the BPP's community organizing skills and application can easily be noted today in the two organizational infrastructures of the two political parties.

When then senate candidate Barack Obama built his grass roots organization in Chicago, he went door to door in Altgeld Gardens, the housing projects on the West Side of Chicago (the same doors we knocked on in the 1960s) to feel the pulse beat of the community and determine the needs of the people. He then translated his findings into a strategy for community organizing. Combing historical knowledge with contemporary social data is critical in developing informed consciousness and political action. This was the strategy of the BPP, and it is heartening to see this blueprint of grassroots political strategy being adopted as one of the electoral political strategies of the 21st century. The superiority of Barack Obama's grassroots strategy gave him a significant edge in his victories in both elections.

The brilliance of Stacey Abrams and other grassroots organizations in delivering the state of Georgia to the Democrats, as well as the two senate seats, was quintessential community organizing at its best. In order to complete the task and prevent Trump's return, Abrams's formula must be merged with Jaime Harrison the new DNC Chairperson with a national plan so that we ensure the Republicans are defeated in 2022 and 2024. Forging relationships with Black professional athletes and utilizing the power of their platform is a necessity. For that to be accomplished we must continue to take a page from the legacy of the Black Panther Party, a legacy that must be understood in a historical context. Even though our blueprint for community organizing is on display today, we are still the only political party founded on the principles of grassroots political organization with viable community programs reflected in the Ten Point Program. In the process we were willing to defend the programs and the community from the racist policing polices.

Knocking on doors only during election cycles is not enough. To leave a permanent footprint in the community one must take a page from our masterpiece. In the communities and or states where your victory margins were slim, you must anchor your offices in the community with community-based programs that serve the needs of the people daily: perhaps it is a community-based healthcare center, perhaps it is a daycare and preschool program. Or it could be a food bank and nutritional center for health and wellness, or a legal aid and re-entry programs for those released from incarceration and the criminal injustice system. You can set-up non-profit organizations to run these programs while providing employment for our people in the community. We did it with far less resources and your cupboard is overflowing with resources. The idea is to establish an ongoing relationship with the community 24/7. That way, you win their loyalty and put in place the political machinery that will continuously allow you to win local, state and federal elections.

Indeed, there must be a national strategy that will allow you to control the state legislature, city council, the police and sheriff departments, the funding for education, locally and statewide. You then control the state legislature and voting rights for the states, the state's Attorney General, and funding. More importantly you can begin to, if you win local and state elections, make structural changes in policing. On the federal level, you control the congressional and senate seats and kill the gerrymandering of congressional districts. Your will to power starts on the ground in the communities where your community-based programs would exist in conjunction with your victories at the ballot box. That will ensure the needs of your people on all levels of governance. This is where the de-centralized Black Lives Matter organization with boots on the ground could collaborate with you in building infrastructure while creating jobs for those in the community. The BLM must move beyond nicely orchestrated TV interviews and policy wonks raking in millions. Your work and accomplishments have been invaluable. The hard work are boots on the ground and day-to-day community organizing while building serviceable infrastructure. Learn from our mistakes, but also emulate our successes and not repeat our mistakes. If you are to succeed you must take it to the next level.

Contrary to the demonization of the BPP by the state and its media, the BPP only demanded for what was right for its black citizenry. Everyone born in an American city should have access to those things that are necessary to sustain life: meaningful education, medical care, food with substance and nutritional value, decent housing, a living – not meager wage, equal protection under the law and total respect as a human being. We were willing to sacrifice everything, including our lives. These basic needs have been a part of all civilized human societies. If we cannot make these claims to civilization, we can stop recognizing the power of governance and it will always be in our power to organize from the grassroots within the framework of democratic principles and infrastructure to seek redress any meaningful change by any means necessary. That was the story of the Black Panther Party. Don't hate the players, hate the game – especially when you know the game is rigged.

EPILOGUE
IN MEMORY OF DUANTE WRIGHT:
ANOTHER MOTHER'S HEARTFELT PAIN

From the murder of yet another black son
at the hands of a white police officer

REFERENCES

1. html: l/black demographics.com/households/ African-American-income/

2. Retrieved from George Jackson, Soledad Brother: The Prison Letters of George Jackson (Chicago: Lawrence Hill Press, 1970)

3. https://public integrity.org/inside-piblici/citizens-united-explained/ The Citizens United decision and why it mattered.

4. G W. (2013). Wealth. income. and power. html):2.ucsc.edu/whorulesamerica/powe r/wealth.html Domhoff

5. Hamburger T. Hennessey, K. Banerjee. N. (2011). Koch brothers now at heart of GOP power.

6. Retrieved from http://articlcs.latimes.com/2011/feb/06/nation/la-na-koch-brothers-21/feb/02/06

7. Jackson. G. (1971) Soledad Brother) The prison letters of George Jackson. New York: Coward- George Jackson, Soledad Brother: The Prison Letters of George Jackson (Chicago: Lawrence Hill Press, 1970)

8. Jackson, G. (19T). Blood in my Eye. New York: Bantam Books.

9. Johnson F. (2012 Human Nature and the Moral Economy. Retrieved from http://scientificamerican.com/primate-diaries/2013/09/23/human-nature-and-the-moral-economy

10. Klein, N. (2007): The Shock Doctrine: The rise of disaster capitalism. New York: Metropolitan Books.

11. https://www.forbes.com/sites/forbespr/2012/09/19/08/forbes release 39th Annual Forbes 400 Ranking of the Richest Americans

12. Newkirk, V (2013). A Tea Partier Takes Charge of North Carolina's budget. https://www.bloomberg.com/news/articles/2013-01-24/a-tea-partier-takes-charge-of-north-carolinas-budget

13. <u>Rmuse</u>. (2014) Republican hypocrites force NC taxpayers to pay for Duke Energy's toxic coal ash dumping. https://www.politicususa.com/2014/03/14/republican-hypocrites-force-nc-taxpayers-pay-duke-energys-toxic-coal-ash-dumping.html

14. <u>Smith, A.</u> (1776). Wealth of nations, edited by C. J. Bullock. Vol. X. The Harvard Classics. New York, P.F, Collier & Son

15. <u>Thompson, F.P</u> (1893) Customs in common: Studies in traditional popular customs. New York: New York Press

16. <u>U.S Department of Labor Statistics</u> (2014) Union members 2013. Retrieved fromhttps://www.bls.gov/news.release/pdf/union2.pdf

17. OFO: Journal of Transatlantic Studies Vol 3, Nos.1&2 (JUNE/Dec2013), 81-96

18. Mike Miller, Community Organizing: A Brief Introduction (Cleveland: Euclid Avenue Press, 2012).

19. Olaudah Equiano<u>, The Interesting Narrative of the Life of Olaudah Equiano</u> (Radford, VA: Wilder Publications, 2012).

20. Cheikh Anta Diop<u>, Civilization or Barbarism</u> (Chicago: Lawrence Hill Books),132.

21. Kofi Agorah<u>, Maroon Heritage</u>: Archaeological, Ethnographic, and Historical Perspectives (Kingston: Canoe Press, 1994).

22. <u>David Walker, Walker's Appeal</u>, in Four Articles, Together with a Preamble to the Colored Citizens of the World, But in Particular and Very Expressly to Those of the United States of America. Written in Boston, in the State of Massachusetts, Sept. 28th, 1829(Charleston, SC: Nabu Press, 2011)..http://docsouth.unc.edu/nc/walker/bio.html (accessed April 16, 2013).

23. Garnet's "Call to Rebellion," http://www.pbs.org/wgbh/aia/part4/4h2937t.html (accessed April 16, 2013).

24. W. E. B. Du Bois, The Souls of Black Folk (New York: Fine Creative Media, 2003 [19031], 878.

25. Nathan Irvin Huggins, Harlem Renaissance (Oxford: Oxford University Press, 1972).

26. Colin Grant, Negro with a Hat: The Rise and Fall of Marcus Garvey (Oxford: Oxford University Press, 2010).

27. Bobby Seale, Seize the Time: The Story of the Black Panther Party and Huey P. Newton (Baltimore: Black Classic Press, 1968).

28. Curtis J. Austin, Up Against the Wall: Violence in the Making and Unmaking of the Black Panther Party (Fayetteville: University of Arkansas Press, 2006), 353-55.

29. G. Louis Heath, Off the Pigs! The History and Literature of the Black Panther Party (Lanham, MD: ScarecrowPress, 1976).

30. Ward Churchill, To Disrupt, Discredit and Destroy: The FBI's Secret War against the Black Panther Party (Routledge, 2005).

31. George Jackson, Soledad Brother: The Prison Letters of George Jackson (Chicago: Lawrence Hill Press, 1970), 249.

32. Huey P. Newton, Essays from the Minister of Defense (Michigan State University Libraries' Black Panthers Digital Collection; orig. pub. 1968), http://archive.lib.msu.edu/DMC/AmRad/essaysministerdefense.pdf (accessed April 16, 2013).

33. Jones, Charles E. The Black Panther Party., Black Classic Press,10/22/2005

34. Churchill, Ward: To Disrupt, Discredit and Destroy, 37.

35. Kenneth T. Walsh, "Barack Obama on the Streets of Chicago" U.S. News &World Report (August 26, 2016

36. Roediger, R. David, Black and White, 1999, Random House

37. Carr, James: Bad, 1995, Peligian Press

38. history.com/news/voter suppression-Opelousas Massacre, Farrell Evans

39. St Louis Post Dispatch-The East St. Louis Race Riots

40. encyclopediaofarkansas.net/elaine massacre 1919

41. Marking a Tragedy; Arkansas Democrat-Gazette, September, 24th,2019

42. The Elaine Race Riot of 1919 Race. V Class and Labor. Anthony Steven.

43. Ben Okri...Starbook...Rider Publising,2007

CPSIA information can be obtained
at www.ICGtesting.com
Printed in the USA
LVHW112140220222
711715LV00008B/390